7.95

Passed On

A John Hope Franklin Center book

Passed On

AFRICAN AMERICAN MOURNING STORIES

a memorial by Karla FC Holloway

DUKE UNIVERSITY PRESS   *Durham & London* 2002

© 2002 Duke University Press

All rights reserved

Printed in the United States of America

on acid-free paper ∞

Designed by C. H. Westmoreland

Typeset in Adobe Garamond with Weiss italic

by Tseng Information Systems, Inc.

Library of Congress Cataloging-in-Publication

Data appear on the last printed pages of this book.

Substantially different versions of chapter 2 appeared

as "The Death of Culture" in *Massachusetts Review* 40.1

and in *College English* 59.1 (January 1997).

for

Bem Kayin Holloway

1977–1999

See! I will not forget you.
I have carved you in the palm
of my hand.
—Isaiah 49.15–16

Because look.
Look where your hands are.
Now.
—Toni Morrison, *Jazz*

Peace be still.
—Mark 4.39

Contents

Illustrations

Acknowledgments

The writing of this book has had a long generation, and each stage has been a process that has benefited and been enabled by many thoughtful intercessors. I owe many thanks to my faculty and staff colleagues at Duke University in the African and African-American Studies Program and in the English Department. I also want to thank a very, very special group of graduate students, colleagues, and friends who listened throughout and who cared about this project and about me: Houston A. Baker Jr., William Darity Jr., Cathy Davidson, Paula Giddings, Kevin Haynes, Candice Jenkins, Wahneema Lubiano, Erik Ludwig, Debbie McDowell, Leslie Mitchner, Ifeoma Nwankwo, Jill Petty, Charlotte Pierce-Baker, Reynolds Price, Nicole Waligora, Ken Wissoker, Wilford Samuels, and Evie Shockley. Colleagues and auditors from the United States, Paris, Germany, and England have been audiences at various points in this process, giving wonderful feedback and encouragement as this writing went on and on, and invariably sharing their own stories and memories with me, a gift that never failed to energize.

I owe thanks to Riche Richardson who assisted at the earliest stages of the book. As I finally moved toward completing this work, I could not have brought it to conclusion without the incredibly fine and persistent research skills and critical insights of my research assistant Stephane Robolin, and the organizational magic effected by Allison Puckett. I am especially appreciative of the skilled insights of Lauren Osborne, who helped enormously in making this a better book. The thoughtful and meticulous work of my readers and editors at Duke University Press significantly strengthened the manuscript. My colleagues and friends in the Dean's office have made this new dimension of my life satisfying, and I thank them for their making room for me at the table. I am deeply appreciative of the example of Bill Chafe's scholarship, and the friendship and support that he has extended to me, and I will be forever in the debt of Maurice Wallace, whose generosity and constancy have been both necessary and kind. I continue to benefit from the warm embrace and love of the Friday Night Women, the sisterhood that masks as a book club.

I am deeply grateful to have a family whose loving support is constant and sure: my father, Claude D. Clapp, and my sister, Leslie Ellen Clapp Ezie. The spirits of my mother, Ouida Eleanor, who died just as this book neared publication, and my sister, Karen Andrea, constantly and lovingly hover. As with my precious son Bem K., I feel their spirits ever and always with me. Finally, the counsel, faith, and love that my husband, Russell, and my wise and wonderful daughter, Ayana Tamu, share with me every day sustains, heals, and allows me to persevere.

I am fortunate to be within such communities.

Introduction

As the twentieth century came to a close, matters of death and dying were the subject of vital public discussion, invading radio and newspaper stories, launching best-selling books about the funeral industry, producing documentaries about the ethics of death and dying, and sustaining debates about how to die well, whether to die at all, and who should assist. Readers and discussants came from all walks of life—from the professions (physicians, sociologists, psychologists, and theologians), as well as from our families (a parent's dying wish, a brother or sister passed on and painfully remembered, our own fears of dying, and our own memories of the first funerals we attended).

Passed On engages the energy and spirit of those interests, experiences, and perhaps most important, of our persistent curiosities about this subject, focusing them into a study of death and dying in twentieth-century African America. Although the text of this book spans the twentieth century, it certainly could not "cover" the century, since there were, of course, more stories of death and dying in African America during that era than could be recovered here. For that reason, the critical process of this book has been to make certain that the stories I do tell sufficiently echo others already familiar to the reader or shadow those that might not get fully recalled to voice or text but that nevertheless continue to haunt our cultural imaginary. This book gives a particular context to these stories, a perspective that my computer program does not like at all. Whenever I write the phrase that identifies my argument—"black death"—a squiggly green line underscores it on my computer screen, suggesting there is something wrong with its phrasing or spelling. There is indeed something very wrong with it—and this is my point. *Passed On* explores a century's worth of experience with black death and dying to argue that African Americans' particular vulnerability to an untimely death in the United States intimately affects how black culture both represents itself and is represented.

My travels have traced the story this book tells. I have wandered through exhibits in a museum of the funeral industry and congratulated soon-to-be graduates as they waited for final reports from their mortuary-school examinations. I have visited funeral directors and morticians in the business places where they practice and the meeting spaces where they plan. I have searched early-century graveyards and late-century cemeteries for headstones and in-ground plaques, stopped at roadside memorials, and lingered in museums and art galleries. I have consulted archives and manuscripts, ordinarily a historian's rather than an English professor's labor. I have talked with physicians, casket manufacturers, hospice administrators, makers of funeral "garments," reporters, palliative care teams, embalming-chemical businessmen, hospital chaplains, neighborhood ministers, and neighborhood residents. From a scholarly perspective, many of these were certainly interviews, but they might more appropriately be called conversations. Each has helped educate me. Each has nurtured my developing understanding that the funeral industry's evolution, character (and characters), and culturally inflected business practices form a necessary introduction to notions and experiences of black death.

My discussion in chapter 1 is absolutely indebted to these conversations. In that chapter, I carve out the landscape of black death and burial practices as experienced during the twentieth century, paying attention to both urban and rural histories—including specific narratives of southern undertakers who took up the business despite being subjected to white rage and violence—as well as data and census records gleaned from historical surveys that counted urban "Negro" undertakers in demographic surveys of professionals and laborers. Each facet of my research was itself a journey, bringing composition and form to my emerging understanding of the industry and its practitioners, and how their professional services were increasingly attentive to and specifically formulated for the black population they served.

African America's shared experiences with dying structured my exploration of black death. I was especially attentive to patterns of black death resulting from white rage targeted at this nation's communities of black folk. The trends I explore in chapter 2 emerged in the collective cultural memory and framed its certain understanding of how *we* die a color-coded death—the residue of riots, executions, suicides, and targeted medical neglect. As I looked at the way in which these categories of dying contained culturally specific populations, the thesis and argument of this book assumed its ghostly shape. Black death is a cultural haunting, a "re-memory" along the lines of that found in Toni Morrison's novel *Beloved,* which insists that "not a house in the country ain't packed to the rafters with some dead Negro's grief."

I wanted to both find the expression of that grief and follow it to its conclusion. Black folk—whose indomitable and full presence articulates the best of this country's spirit, intelligence, and politics—bridge this cultural haunting with hope, grace, and resilience. How is this paradox of memory and presence expressed as we reach the ends of our days? I attempted to answer this question in chapter 3, coming there as close as I could to these final moments as represented in biography, performed in literature and the visual arts, and experienced in the records of both history and memory. In that chapter, the collective "*we*" follows the direction it began to take at the end of the second chapter: shifting to the individual. This seemed to me the most straightforward way to indicate how singular stories and memories drift toward, are shared, and are finally echoed within community narratives. And, because a community's identity is fully and expressively engaged in its youth, I had to acknowledge the ways in which African America's children are, in this particular respect, forlorn legatees of the cultural experience with black death.

With such a subject as death and dying, it seemed the book had not made its journey until it too had come to a ceremonial end, fully engaged with the expressive ritual energy of the cultural vernacularism *funeralized.* Early in the process and planning of this book, I started keeping fragments of the cultural story that I came to call "ephemera": funeral home fans and programs, obituaries, pamphlets, product advertisements. As I approached what seemed to be this book's conclusion, and as I rummaged through what had become boxes full of such memorabilia, I came across a small pamphlet that had been published in 1915. It was a church publication that reported the death and funeralizing of one of its elders,

Reverend Luke Mason. His narrative became the experiential touchstone for my thinking about the intimate role of the black church in the business of burial—the "urge to adorn," in Zora Neale Hurston's words, that was as important to the sermon in the sanctuary as it was to the burial in the graveyard. Reverend Mason's funeralizing centers my final chapter. And, to the degree that this book memorializes "mine own," a funeral sermon, "The Promise of Hope in a Season of Despair," returns the reader to the story revealed in the prologue. That sermon, the exquisite composition of Professor Maurice O. Wallace, has its generation in a particular story, but it additionally claims and underscores the hope that allows—and indeed encourages—us to move beyond the situations and issues of this book to claim the incredible fortitude and strength of a black community whose spirit mightily and finally endures.

My epilogue is a narrative essay that recalls my visits to graveyards and cemeteries, and it is bordered with a necrology of sorts—a memorial to those African Americans of renown who died in the twentieth century. In an important way, this admittedly incomplete list of the passed-on framed my conception of this project. It was the ways and means of their dying—and those of their cultural kin—that formed the substance of this book. Those grave spaces are, quite literally, what remains. In an early decision about the process and plan of this book and my research, I felt that if I could share with the reader the texture of feeling and memory that lay in these burial grounds, it would both complete and make visceral this project. However, as the reader will discover, and as I explain below, I was to have a far more intimate experience with my book's thesis.

Of the passing . . .

Just three years into the twentieth century, William Edward Burghardt Du Bois wrote *The Souls of Black Folk,* a book that would come to be regarded as one of the most significant publications of the era. It told a particular story of African America; Du Bois's careful association of culture, history, and ethnicity gave shape and contour to African American life. His resounding chapters made explicit the ways in which black folk shaped and were shaped by their cultural and social space. In addition to its critical documentation of American cultural and political history, *Souls* gave to that century perhaps its most famous and accurate prophecy: "the problem of the twentieth century is the problem of the color line."

One chapter, "Of the Passing of the First Born," compelled a different kind of attention than the others. It appeared to be a curious diversion—almost an embarrassment in its personal and elegiac excess. This chapter seemed a father's sorrowful and too-individual story of the loss of his infant son, markedly different from the rest of his book's accounting of a collective African American experience. Du Bois wrote:

> He died at eventide, when the sun lay like a brooding sorrow above the western hills, veiling its face; when the winds spoke not, and the trees, the great green trees he loved, stood motionless. I saw his breath beat quicker and quicker, pause, and then his little soul leapt like a star . . . and left a world of darkness in its train. The day changed not; the same tall trees peeped in at the windows, the same green grass glinted in the setting sun. Only in the chamber of death writhed the world's most piteous thing—a childless mother.
>
> . . . [H]earken, O Death! Is not this my life hard enough,—is not that dull land that stretches its sneering web about me cold enough,— is not all the world beyond these four little walls pitiless enough, but that thou must needs enter here,—thou, O Death? (172)

Despite the anguished and deeply personal tone here, the issue in that chapter was as much a *public* black story as were the powerfully provocative discursions on religion, music, freedom, and progress that framed other chapters in *Souls*. Indeed, Du Bois may have been the first to characterize an "African American mourning story," selecting as he did a vocabulary to describe his son's death and dying that had its generation and was fully vested in the symbolic and racialized language of this nation's history of slavery and liberation: "in the Land of the Color-line I saw . . . the shadow of the Veil. Within the Veil he was born . . . a Negro and a Negro's son." When Du Bois wrote of his son's passing as "liberation" and that his child was "Not dead, not dead, but escaped; not bond, but free," he made a critical and essential association between his individual, familial loss and the experience of a collective community of blacks in the Americas. In creating this nexus between a black family's grief and African America's national experience, he revealed the cultural dimension of black America's experience with death and dying. From this perspective, then, his accounting of his child's burial procession had the character of a public incident report: "The busy city dinned about us, they did not say much, those pale-faced hurrying men and women; they did not say much, — they only glanced and said, 'Niggers.'" Although Du Bois mourned the death of his son, he cherished the thought that death had liberated him from living within the veil of race.

The anticipation of death and dying figured into the experiences of black folk so persistently, given how much more omnipresent death was for them than for other Americans, that lamentation and mortification both found their way into public and private representations of African America to an astonishing degree. The twentieth century's literature and film, its visual arts and music (from early era spirituals to latter-day rap), and its contemporary street-corner memorials consistently called up a passed-on narrative. Black culture's stories of death and dying were inextricably linked to the ways in which the nation experienced, perceived, and represented African America. Sometimes it was a subtext, but even then the ghostly presence of those narratives reminded us that something about America was, for black folk, disjointed. Instead of death and dying being unusual, untoward events, or despite being inevitable end-of-lifespan events, the cycles of our daily lives were so persistently interrupted by specters of death that we worked this experience into the culture's iconography and included it as an aspect of black cultural sensibility. For black parents and their youngsters, elders and their adult children, the formative years, the waning years, and each day between were haunted by one spiritual's refrain: "soon one morning, death will come a-calling." In this macabre revision of CPT (colored people's time), death was an untimely accompaniment to the life of black folk — a sensibility that was, unfortunately, based on hard facts. Several measures of mortality (childhood morbidity, maternal death in childbearing, cardiac-related deaths of elders, suicide, death at the hands of police, and other violent deaths of youth) documented rates that were statistically significant and comparatively higher for African Americans than for other racial or ethnic groups in the United States, even when differences in economic class and sex were taken into account. Black folk thus found a cultural code about mortality to be both usable and familiar.

One spring, late in the 1990s, a roadside in Atlanta, Georgia, was packed with flowers and toys left for a black child murdered on her way to school. Certainly these roadside memorials and memories are shared across cultures and with increasing frequency, having become morbid and familiar streetscapes throughout this country; still, no culture bases so much of its identity on the persistent rehearsal of commemorative conduct as does African America. Springtime speculation about the then-unknown assailant in that child's brutal death recalled the dramatically publicized serial killing of black children in Atlanta during the late 1970s and early 1980s. In a move that related rather than isolated either of those late-century tragedies, black citizens quickly constructed a link to another southern story through their painful, angry, and outraged remembrances of Emmett Till, a fifteen-year-old boy from Chicago who was lynched while visiting relatives in Mississippi in 1954. Emmett is remembered by still-aggrieved generations of black folk, grandparents, parents, and their children, each of whom recalls the personally felt terror of that loss. The decades-long passages of time that separated the schoolgirl memorialized with flowers and toys one Atlanta spring, the serially murdered children, and Till seemed irrelevant — the story of Till's lynching lingered like melancholy in the memory of black folk.

The twentieth century rehearsed, nearly to perfection, a relentless cycle of cultural memory and black mourning. Black deaths and black dying have cut across and through decades and centuries as if neither one matters more than the incoherent, associative presence of the other. Even if the story is grief-stricken, the act of memorializing retains a particular aspect of a culture's narrative, and for blacks in the Americas, some notion of racial memory and racial realization is mediated through the veil of death. Ironically, at the beginning of the new century, we find no lack of familiarity with that Du Boisian narrative of loss and sons and souls of black folk. As we recall the insight about the color line that was destined to haunt the twentieth century, we may recall as well and rightly Du Bois's mournful narrative of parental loss. It harbingers a passing of children, elders and infants, young and middle-aged black folk — each of whom is folded into a national narrative as African American legacy. This century-long look at dying and dead black folk is a means of ritual, a gathering of lonely and seemingly isolated occurrences, and a laying-on of hands. Author John Wideman mournfully acknowledged that one way of understanding African America is to articulate the way that it has meant that "black lives are expendable, can disappear, click, just like that" (Wideman 126). It is as well a way of memorial—a testimonial to the fact that the dead and the ways of our dying have been as much a part of black identity as have been the ways of our living.

"Ideas come to us as the successors of grief."
—Marcel Proust

When I started working on this book, I assumed it would find itself most at ease within a documentary and narrative format, rather than in a more scholarly form. But I had not anticipated that it would serve as a Du Boisian-like commemoration for me. I had not imagined how this manuscript would be connected to me in such a visceral and personal way, how it would inscribe a certain and specific melancholy.

As in Du Bois's *Souls,* there is a particular story here, a story of my family that is related to the collective, cultural narrative. I have included it as a prologue to the book "proper," titling (with knowing acknowledgment to Richard Wright) its narrative fragments "Fear," "Flight," "Fate," and "Benediction." These sections are sequenced as the episodes structured themselves for me and form a framework within which the narratives of my community, my culture, and my country find a particular and significant shape. In this way, the prologue locates one intimate story within the book's longer exploration of the social and cultural history of death and dying. And it tells a story of my son.

I could not have imagined that the series of insistent ideas for *Passed On,* which invaded my serenity many years ago (well before my son's life took its tragic, final turn), would find its articulation in this manner. I do not tell his story for judgment or absolution. I tell it instead because it too has the characteristics of an "incident report" that is, finally, community property. Although I neither sensed nor expected that the book I imagined while standing at the edge of an island facing a too-blue sea would eventually find its space so intimately and so tragically mediated through the lives of those I love the most, I have found that I have had no recourse but to give my son's story and the one I imagined in that expanse of sea and sky their earned, shared space.

It is curious how sometimes the memory

of a death lingers so much longer

than the life it has purloined.

—Arundhati Roy,

The God of Small Things

Prologue

Fear

My husband and I were too traumatized to make what is known in the industry as the "first call"—the call to a mortician, notifying him of a death in the family. Hearing the news of the death of our only son, we were frantic only to discover what had happened. And, although the local news station and even CNN were broadcasting the story of the attempted prison escape of three inmates and the fatal shooting of one of them, all we wanted to know was whether or not our child's final moments were as anguished as his life—whether or not his was a lingering and knowing death. Understandably, this was not the interest of the television newscasters or print journalists, for whom the "rest of the story" was the details of his horrific criminal history and the circumstances of his death. But the story we wanted could come only from the coroner (eventually), or perhaps from the prison superintendent, or the chaplain—whose call to me, alerting me to the news that my son had been shot and was dead, was followed in seconds by a call from a local television news station. My husband and I spent the first hours desperately seeking some accounting, some detail of his death. I put the television on "mute" while we were on the phone, alternately waiting for and listening to various personnel in the state prison bureaucracy. But I could see the "breaking-news" television footage, and I know I will be haunted the rest of my life by the still and eerily quiet aerial image focused on the ground below the hovering helicopter from our local ABC affiliate station. A small green outcropping—a spare southern oasis of brush and bush—interrupted the dismal expanse of cotton fields near Odom Prison. A white sheet lay in the middle of the scene, and under it, I knew, was the body of our son.

It was one of our friends who made the "first call" to a funeral home for us, using her cellular phone because ours was occupied. There were the demanding, self-righteous telephone calls from the media needing a "comment" from his mother or father; our own phone calls to friends and family; and, of course, that dreadful call we had to make to our daughter, his sister, whose screams tore apart the rest of my heart.

Even given the trauma and the notoriety of the moment, it was not very long before we fell into the familiar business of a family who is bereaved: calling a pastor, speaking ourselves to the funeral director, arranging for our son's body to come home. Both like and unlike Du Bois, I felt ambivalence about my son's death. Finally free, I thought. After all these years of terror, we finally have our child back. It was not long before we started getting calls from those who would grieve this loss with us—family and friends, colleagues and neighbors. Having heard the news, they called with the inevitable question culturally conditioned for that moment. "Who's got the body?"

Flight

He died immediately, we learned. Weeks later, the autopsy report confirmed the bullet to his heart, a bullet that entered his body through his back, was an immediate cause of death.

I have considered that moment again and again—how he took off running through the midsummer growth of the expanse of cotton fields. Although the scratchy saplings may have tugged at his pants legs, as if pleading for him to stop, all he could feel, I suspect, was something like the rhythmic heartbeat of "took off running." I imagine how he might have been surprised by the threatening combination of fear and exhilaration that his running provoked. Fear because somewhere, even in the midst of the confusion and delusions that were the hourly manifestations of his illness, there were spaces of his childhood sanity that must have let him know, and may even have prompted him toward the decision to run from the prison farm at Odom, that there could be no escape. In all the history of the maximum security institution in northeastern North Carolina, no one had ever successfully fled. Exhilaration because, when he had considered escape, somewhere beneath the delusions and voices of his illness lay the reason that he had buried so deeply and that may have finally and at last been within his grasp. He was closer to freedom than he had ever been in his short, unhappy life. Freer than in the abusive series of foster homes. Freer even than in the desperate clutch of his adoptive family, whose unconditional love confused and tormented him. Certainly freer than in the series of mental institutions, jails, and prisons of the last five years. And absolutely freed from the angst of the ninety-five-year sentence for rape and attempted murder that he was serving, the likely convictions for murder that were pending, and the nearly certain consequence of a death penalty that lay ahead in the fall, when the fields would be ready for harvest.

I suspect he never heard the beat of horses' hooves behind him as the prison overseer assigned to that cotton-field work unit galloped after him, nor the seventeen shots fired. There was no warning yell to hear. Their orders were to shoot first, and say nothing. So they did shoot and they didn't speak and our child fell—mortally wounded, face down in that small outcropping of bushes and trees, that oasis of green surrounded by miles of cotton fields from which there would be, could be, no escape.

When, following the autopsy that is mandatory in cases of homicide (including legislatively endorsed homicide), they returned our child to us, we went to see him at Lea Funeral Home. Only his small brown head was visible. He was still in a body bag, covered insufficiently with a clean, pressed sheet, its folds still crisp. Since we had asked that he not be embalmed, that arrangements be made for his cremation, his body—although chilled by the refrigeration unit—was still his. He was brown in his familiar summer chocolate-chip-cookie color. His sweet, poochy lips were still soft, and his hair, grown wild and unkempt, was soft as well, and spongy. I thought that he looked like he had the day he came to us from the foster home. Without recalling then that the first thing I had done those many years ago with my new four-year-old son was to braid his hair, I found myself doing a last thing like the first. I asked for scissors and then cut locks of his hair to give us something, some little, small, touchable thing left of our child to come home with. We kissed him goodbye, his father, sister, and I. We prayed for his spirit, knowing the loving heart that had been buried under so much pain and whose absence had let loose such terror was finally safe, and unconditionally free. And then we went home to prepare for the funeral of our child.

Fate

Ours was a death watch. We knew North Carolina judicial history and practice, we knew the national tendency to impose the ultimate punishment for crimes committed against white victims by black men, we knew the vicious circumstances of the events, and we knew we loved our child. It was bearing the sustained ambivalence of our days, and his, that was the most difficult.

I had already imagined the end. Imagined the glass wall in Central Prison as they wheeled my son in and prepared to give him the lethal injection. As his adoptive mother, I had not been at his birth, and as a consequence I felt a kind of inescapable irony and even, perhaps, a perverse satisfaction that I could be present at his death. I had already anticipated how, in the intervening years, I would struggle to prepare both of us for this moment, to help him focus on solace and redemption, to guide him toward some contemplative dimension of spiritual peace that his given name, Bem, signified.

As an adolescent, he had given himself a new name almost monthly. These name changes should have alerted us to the deeply troubling mental illness that destroyed our child and that led to what was nothing less than a reign of terror. Because his had been a court-ordered separation from his birth mother—in whose adolescent hands and home had occurred the neglect and physical abuse that led him through the social service maze of too many foster families—we were required to change his name in order to complete the adoption process. I think now what confusion it must have meant for a four-year-old to lose the name he had been called all his life and to adjust to a new one. The wonder is that we never knew his full history until after his imprisonment for charges of breaking and entering. Discovering the terribly wrong turn our child had taken was a shock to us. We knew only the endlessly polite and considerate, thoughtful and compassionate son we had raised. There was no history of fighting, anger, or violence that would have predicted this dire outcome. In fact, as we know now, his best talent was to bury the horror that was building in him from his memories of the sexual abuse he experienced in the foster homes and the racial and sexual taunting that greeted him as a black child in white foster families. We saw only a gentle spirit and, until the day he was arrested, had detected none of his potential for terror. The judicial decision to send a child with what emerged in court as a documented narrative of mental illness to prison for first offense, nonviolent crimes may have had an undesired (but not unpredictable effect). He emerged from prison with whatever anger and delusion he had successfully stifled, fully formed and terrible. And, he had a new name.

The week after the funeral, we received a packet of cards from the inmates at Odom prison, carefully and thoughtfully inscribed with poetry, condolences, and prayer. Each personal message began by referring to our son with a name we had never heard before. They may never have known his given name, and I think now that he may never have owned it.

There was as much violence in the death he did have as there would have been in the death he might have faced. And there was an old, rehearsed cultural familiarity in each phase of his final day. After all, the pitiful traverse from plantation landscape to prison cotton fields was only the short matter of a century and a few score years. The mostly brown and black faces who were bent to tend the fields where he labored were the same. And the violence attached to their presence, real or imagined, was still a violence linked to their color.

Benediction

These days, what I imagine about my child has stronger presence than what I know. "You were born, you had body, you died. . . ." I am suspended between the loss and the memory . . . the intrusive mind's eye of scraggly patches of cut-over and a white shroud; the mindless and meager analysis of newsprint; a vague but lingering sensory imprint of the last time I held him close, and how he was warm and whole and hugged me back.

There is some irony in the fact that he came to us through a state's authority—an adoption process that made his ritual and repetitive fosterings a coming and going of black plastic garbage bags. When he first came to us, four years old and precious, he dragged one of those bags along with him. It held his clothes and a Yogi Bear pillow stitched by some relative he would never remember. I still have the bear.

Some days after his death, we opened another dark plastic garbage bag sent along with him once again by order or process of the state. This one ostensibly held his final "effects." Except they weren't his. Not one single item in the jumbled mix of papers and clothing belonged to him. One final bureaucratic carelessness had made certain that whatever was left was lost and, as they were to tell us later, "irretrievable." Not one of the letters that had constructed our long-distance relationship; not a single book selected to urge him toward a life of the mind; no cards with verses chosen with lingering precision; no pictures mailed with deliberative embrace to remind him as carefully as we could that he was held whole and lovingly fixed within our family—"See? Remember when?" Just someone else's toothbrush, sneakers that were tellingly too large to have been his, an empty soap dish, and pages and pages of writing that was neither his words nor in his hand. We stuffed it all back into the bag and sent it back. Left fully alone at the end of his days, as he had been at the early edge of his short life, there seemed to be no remains.

This, then, in part in defiance of memories that depend on our vitality, is my postmortem and our memorial. It makes certain the deliberate embrace of those last words of Reverend Brown, who, each Sunday of my children's youth, reminded us all in benediction that neither death, nor life, nor things past, nor things to come could separate us from a greater grace and the promise of love everlasting. I measure my days folded into the solace of that assurance.

"Soon one morning,

when this life is over . . .

I'll fly away."

—Traditional

"Who's Got the Body?"

THE BUSINESS OF BURIAL

Quiet as it's kept, if the question "Who's got the body?" had been asked very early in the twentieth century, the answer could have been white folk. Given the decided weight of that century's experience with a clear separation between blacks and whites, including funeral home professionals and their clientele, the brief anomaly of these early-century shared mortuarial spaces were nearly as remarkable as the fact that at the end of almost a century of separation, black folk began to return to white businesses for the burial of their dead. While African American funereal practices—from rituals surrounding death and dying to the business of burial itself—have always depended on a long history of allegiances, this is a specifically twentieth-century narrative of color and class, mortuarial and ministerial alliances, and ceremony and performance. The specific and certain cultural identity of these stories may be the last of their kind. All indications are that the twenty-first century will form a different narrative.

We can give you better service

When the century began, many communities in the United States had no black funeral homes. Even though, for example, there had been a black funeral business in Louisville, Kentucky, owned and operated since the 1920s by S. Leroy Mason, just across the Ohio River in Jeffersonville,

Manigault, Gaten, and Williams, Undertakers and Embalmers.
Photo by Richard Samuel Roberts.

Indiana, a white mortician would have "had" black bodies, at least for
the preliminaries of embalming. There was no local black funeral home
in Jeffersonville until Henry Mason, Leroy's son, opened one on Watt
Street in 1948. Prior to its opening, black families who wanted their deceased relatives embalmed were forced to use back doors and basement
entrances of white mortuaries. Even in death, the color line was a persistent—albeit sometimes ambiguous—line of demarcation.

Although the involvement of a white undertaker in Jeffersonville
was a necessity, it created an additional psychological burden for African
Americans when death occurred in their community. White violence,
including the vicious practice of lynching, was complicit in too many
black deaths, and whites were often as disrespectful to black bodies in
death as they were in life. The biased social codes of the day were very
much in play. So, when black men embraced the burial business, they
were responding not only to a business opportunity but also to a sense
of cultural responsibility and community necessity. Black families *knew*
black morticians—they were our kin, our neighbors, our fellow congre-
gants in Sunday worship services. However, despite the ease of intimacy

African Americans had with these businesses, or whether our familiarity with them came from their relationships to family or community, the burial business was not the unproblematic enterprise that is legend. Instead and predictably, the laws of segregation, Jim Crow practices, and discriminatory conduct made it certain that a black undertaker would endure aggressive challenges of racism in arranging for the burial of black folk.

In some communities, black undertakers were vulnerable to violent reprisals for threatening a secure income source for white undertakers. Writer LeRoi Jones (Amiri Baraka) described this as the experience of his grandfather, an entrepreneur who owned two grocery stores as well as a funeral parlor in his home in Alabama, but whose business acumen was compromised by his cultural kinship. Each of his enterprises was "burned out from under him," and he eventually had to escape the county, fleeing north in search of sanctuary from the white terrorists whose ideas about race did not include black men as managers or owners of commercial ventures (Leroi Jones 96). Jones's grandfather's undertaking business *could* have emerged as a particular kind of racialized opportunity for black folk in a country that had consistently denied entrepreneurship to its black citizenry. It was, after all, a business that involved the most intimate kind of contact with the black body—and even the potential for interracial contact such as this shaped the angst that motivated white racism. However, like other racialized responses in America, the reactive anger of whites toward blacks who practiced undertaking belied reason or expectation. And, as a consequence, black men who moved into these professional roles found themselves forced to take courageous advantage of the era.

Just before World War I, in Hattiesburg, Mississippi's, black township, Piney Woods, Malachi Collins and E. W. Hall opened the county's first black funeral home. The event so aggravated Hattiesburg's white undertaker, who had had the embalming business of Piney Woods blacks, that he passed out handbills in the black community with the warning "Don't patronize these niggers, we can give you better service" (McMillen 92). It was not difficult to intuit that his warning was contained in the directive ("don't patronize"), rather than the declaration ("we can give you better"), and Collins and Hall had to take the threat seriously. When their business first opened, the tense atmosphere actually forced the partners to take turns with an armed patrolling of the premises each night. Although this challenged inauguration prefigured many years of intimidation and threats, Hall and Collins Funeral Home weathered the hostility and survived for many years (McMillen 193).

In other communities, if competition did not itself motivate the violence, the Ku Klux Klan stepped into the vacuum. When William Ragsdale Sr. of Muskogee, Oklahoma, opened the Home Undertaking Company in the last decade of the 1800s, he hoped it would be a successful transition from his business as a horse-and-carriage supplier for funeral services and other community events. But he also anticipated that Klan violence could be provoked by this new enterprise. He knew their bloody ritual — they had already murdered one of his sons in a confrontation that had at its root their anger at his entrepreneurship. Although it was traditional for a family business to display a surname as a means of claiming the family's concerns, Ragsdale did not. Instead, he selected something to mask his ownership ("People's," and later "Home," Undertaking), hoping that this less-public declaration might forestall attack and protect his family (and his business) from the Klan's violent attention.

There were already habits of tradition in the 1900s that would follow the funeral business in America, which already had nearly a century of practice, into the next hundred years. The term *undertaker,* in reference to a skilled occupation, had appeared in popular usage sometime during the first half of the 1600s. At that time, undertaking was not much more involved than arranging for removal of a body, securing a casket (even though families often made their own), and burying the dead. This labor was not nearly as evolved as it was to become when, at the turn of the century, critical innovations transformed the labor into a skilled profession. These innovations included the manufacturing of coffins, the development of a widely accepted process of embalming, and the professionalizing of the practitioners. Of this new generation of American undertakers, Prince Greer was among the first blacks to practice embalming. Greer was the "colored assistant" to Nashville businessman W. R. Cornelius, who had been contracted to embalm civil war soldiers. Cornelius explained that he "undertook the embalming myself with a colored assistant named Prince Greer who appeared to enjoy embalming so much that he became himself an expert." Greer continued to work successfully with Cornelius during the remainder of the war (Habenstein and Lamers [1955] 210).

The skills, techniques, and formulas that developed during and immediately after the Civil War years led to the institutionalization of the trade, which included the building of specific establishments with the requisite equipment to do on-site embalming. And, although business practices steadily evolved, generational memory haunted many in the profession. Thus, although black mortuary businesses followed a line of development somewhat parallel to their white counterparts, they diverged significantly in cultural matters and economic stability. One elderly member of the profession told me how, during the early years of his Louisiana practice, although he had the "facilities" in an office, he would also embalm bodies in the houses where they died, "right up there on their beds." At the beginning of the twentieth century, undertakers doing this work in homes would place a decorative funeral emblem—a badge or ribbon—on front doors as a signal to the neighborhood not just that someone had died but also that certain rites were being performed in the house. The funeral wreaths that still appear on the homes of deceased Southerners—black and white alike—echo this history. I heard an almost wistful tone in the voices of two Louisiana morticians who told me about their profession. The elder explained his early-century practices in exquisite detail: "First, we'd use a hand pump to get the blood out. [Rubber tubing] led from the body to the jar and after it would get full, we'd just open a window and just pass the whole bottle outside." He also explained how he and his assistant would run a tube through a keyhole to fumigate the formaldehyde smell of the room after an embalming. As for the body fluids that had been replaced with the embalming mixture, "One of my assistants would dig a hole in the ground outside, and that's where we put the blood. We just poured it in and covered it back up right where it was." He doesn't have much respect for modern, manufactured embalming chemicals. "Back then," he explained, "we'd just mix our own [solution of formaldehyde, alcohol, glycerin, borax, and water]. And it was better than this stuff they give us now."

As a mortician, the undertaker became a skilled technician, a transition that led to the occupation's professionalization and its incorporation of trade organizations and institutes, training and educational requirements, regulatory systems, licensure, and schools into its environment. Despite segregation, black professionals were able to take advantage of some of the schooling that emerged, especially in the North. For those who remained in the South, the practices of Nashville's Gupton-Jones

Fan and diploma from the Worsham College of Mortuary Science. *Photo by Les Todd. Courtesy of Duke University Photography.*

school were the norm. When it opened in the 1920s, its calendar echoed the racial separatism of the era: black students attended the professional courses that began in February and July, while white students attended classes that began in November and May (Wilson 24).

During that same decade, one of the better known northern professional schools—the Worsham College of Mortuary Science in Chicago, Illinois—was critical to the development of the black funeral businesses due to its African American graduates. In my conversations with some of those graduates, they noted that it was one of the few accredited schools and it was "*the*" place for the elite of the African American community to get their credentials. A 1930s graduate spoke to me with a clear sense of pride and accomplishment about that degree, noting that, when you went to Worsham, "you were really somebody special. We had real cadavers to work on—because all the poor, you know the unclaimed bodies at the Cook County Morgue, we went and did all the autopsies on them.

And we only had a year to learn our anatomy—but we used the same textbooks as the medical students, and they had two years to memorize theirs. A Worsham graduate knew everything about anatomy that they did."

Given the rampant segregationist impulse of early-twentieth-century America, there was very little shared commerce between black and white funeral parlors. A "colored undertaker" explained that "'Twenty-five years ago we had competition from the white undertakers [but] they bury few Negroes now'" (Drake 456). Although most blacks in Houston, Texas, historically patronized white businesses, those that "offered services *specifically oriented toward black needs*—barber shops, beauty salons, photographers, and *funeral homes*—encountered little outside competition" (Beeth 93; emphasis mine). Nevertheless there were those renegade few who, like Decatur, Illinois's, "leading white undertaker," who, when a "Negro mortician opened his business" there, reportedly declared, "I will bury Negroes for nothing before I let a Negro bury them!" ("Death is Big Business" 18). Whether it emerged through racist violence or competition, maltreatment or segregation, the specific, racially defined sociocultural environment of the century's early years supported the development of black-owned and -operated businesses.

Those white undertaking establishments that did provide the service of embalming for the black community frequently subjected their black consumers to disparaging and demeaning treatment. Back doors, basement entries, casual and careless night-time and after-hours services characterized what commerce there was between the black community and the white undertakers. Memories of the disrespect for black bodies in those early days ran deep among professionals of both the nineteenth and twentieth centuries, and was generationally passed on. John Scarborough Sr.'s father opened a funeral home in North Carolina in 1888, partially prompted by his experience with white morticians who "would keep the bodies of whites upstairs in his establishment as they awaited burial, while dead blacks were hidden in the basement" (Chen 1E). Historian Cheryl Greenberg explained that African American "beauticians, undertakers, and a few others offered services the white community was unwilling to provide" (27), as well as services that they did grudgingly provide. And cultural ethnographers St. Clair Drake and Horace Cayton, writing midcentury, recalled the early years in the black South Side of Chicago, Illinois, when "Negro undertakers [had] a virtual monopoly on burying the colored dead," because most of the white undertakers never "catered to the Negro business [or] conducted a Negro funeral."

When white morticians did have access to black bodies, it was generally not to bring a body to burial but merely to do the embalming. One can easily appreciate, given the biological factors at play, how an adequate embalming could assure the potential of a burial with which one could exercise some flexibility. In other words, no matter who had the body, it was important that somebody have at it rather quickly. Blacks had no investment in skipping embalming for reasons of racial politics or pride, especially because the embalmed body could assure the potential of a funeral and burial service where a black minister, congregation, friends, and family could officiate, gather, mourn, and be comforted within the community's norms. Whites, on the other hand, had little interest or place at the services commemorating the black dead. So, when white undertakers performed the first step, they then returned the bodies to the family or to a black preacher for burial and funeral services.

The ministerial association with the business of burial would emerge as a strong presence in black communities. Morticians were "very careful to maintain wide connections with lodges, churches, and civic and social clubs," even to the extent of negotiating with ministers to "have funerals thrown their way. Some pastors advertise a special undertaker for their church and use various forms of subtle pressure to force their members to use him. In fact, the undertaker's name appears on many church bulletin boards beside that of the pastor" (Drake 457).

As black mortuary and funeral directors' businesses were formed, they emerged into communities that already had well-established church histories and practices. In addition to the consistent role of the preacher in the black church as arranger of funerals and burial services, the especially traumatic and frequent situations of African American death and dying and the vigorous presence of the black church community in offering solace on those occasions paved the way for an intimate association between the church and these black businessmen. Indeed, the fact that many black funeral homes were themselves owned and operated by preachers indicated the degree of intimacy the institutions shared.

Preston Taylor, a nineteenth-century black undertaker in Nashville, Tennessee, was also the pastor of a church. Taylor opened his Taylor and

Company Undertakers on Cherry Street in 1888, taking over the business of Thomas Winston who had operated an "undertaker shop" from the end of the Civil War until he died in 1888. Five years later, Taylor had the "largest and most prestigious" funeral home in the city. His city-wide renown was assured when, in 1892, he conducted the funeral for three black firemen who died fighting a downtown fire. Taylor constructed "an ingenious carriage" to carry the three firemen's bodies "side by side during the public funeral procession" (Lovett 109). The pathos of the moment and the dramatic history of expression and performance of the black church were perfectly paired within the context of black death and dying. The close association of pastor and mortician represented a consummate merger of cradle-to-grave services as two institutions that were both consistently defined through their racial exclusivity shared clientele for the most critical ceremonies in life. The preacherly connection articulated a necessary relationship between that profession and the consistent needs of the black community, and it prospered because of the way in which, in the black community, ceremony and event—whether political or social—had a historic center in the black church.

An additional dimension of the early-twentieth-century evolution of the black funeral home was the way in which the role and perception of the mortician in the black community were closely associated with issues of class and social status. As the twentieth century began, the black undertaker emerged as a businessman in a community of few independent black-owned businesses. Sometimes, he was the only one, other than the preacher, who wore a suit during the week, and the fact that it may have been his only suit mattered less than the fact that his business gave him license to wear it on some day other than Sunday. Indeed, the "24/7" suit and the authority it brought were not insignificant considerations in the decisions of some young men to go into "the business." It was an important and visible sign of status, and although the income may have sometimes been paltry, the look was always prosperous. Nashville's Preston Taylor was reportedly a "leading member" of the city's black elite and, as in many communities, the burial business in Nashville was a significant dimension of a newly emerging black middle class. One new businessman, Andrew Johnson, moved to Nashville from Alabama in 1907 and, in an effort to establish himself as successfully as possible, brought with him credentials that would signify his status—a letter of introduction from Booker T. Washington. Johnson subsequently did very well. At the "height of the local Negro business progressive move-ment," he not only served as an undertaker but also built and operated the Majestic, Nashville's first black theater (Lovett 109).

The accomplishments and status of the black mortician are espe-cially notable in the comparative. His stature was earned in part through his appearance and his acquisitions: his dress, accumulation of cars (even though they were a part of his business), and ownership of property (whether storefront or an entire building). Such things distinguished him in a community for whom these highly visible acquisitions were rare. In a caustic analysis of the black bourgeoisie, sociologist E. Franklin Frazier wrote of "Negro 'society' [as] constituted largely of professional and business men and women with large incomes that enable them to engage in conspicuous consumption" (200). It is not surprising that Frazier would include undertakers among his culprits of the new black bourgeoisie and their "conspicuous" displays of wealth, for the black undertaker's business required some appreciation of dramatic display. In 1953, *Ebony Magazine* ran a multipage pictorial feature, "Death is Big Business," declaring undertakers as among "the most influential men in Negro society." This popular African American monthly noted the "pub-lic demand for extravagant funerals" and defended this demand as cul-tural legacy, quoting one mortician who even believed that "some Afri-cans went so far as to sell themselves and their children into slavery to give a relative a proper funeral." The unnamed mortician concluded his analysis saying: "Some of the modern day families are almost as bad" (27). Understanding the cultural expectation and catering to it, perhaps in the extreme, Preston Taylor's Nashville funerals had horses adorned to match the colors of his funeral wagons and drivers who were clothed in identically colored uniforms. But the image-making of this business was more complex than ensuring a spectacular final appearance of the dead. Undertakers were also significantly invested in matching their own image to the culture's expectations of the business. Historian Lovett wrote that the "Negro masses were impressed by these elite men with their fine horses, carriages, and business houses" (109). Black funeral par-lors melded into this environment, with morticians and funeral directors advertising their businesses in ways that dramatized the "mortician." The opening of a new funeral parlor was usually "news," and sometimes in-cluded a "bevy of charming ladies . . . on hand to serve all in attendance to a sumptuous tea and refreshments" (Drake 457).

"Our people"

Despite the changes of class and culture that have made a significant impact in the ways and means of African America, the response to the postmortem inquiry "Who's got the body?" was not, at the end of the century, insignificant. The answer was telling, not only in immediate terms of knowing where to send the traditional floral tribute but in understanding something of class and community—the social place, the cultural milieu and moment of the deceased and the family. When a black family was bereaved, matters involving church affairs, culturally colored politics, social class, and profession all came into play. These kinds of issues and considerations affected a family's choices as much as the selection of the black funeral homes that "had" black bodies throughout the twentieth century. Privy to the most intimate family affairs and poised to arrange the final public presentation, the morticians' undertaking entered a once-in-a-lifetime arrangement, sharing the specific privacy and intimacy of this moment, and yet being responsible for orchestrating a public performance often not matched in the entire lifetime of the deceased. Among many other considerations, appearance counted.

In the 1900s, it was traditional in African American communities to leave the casket open for viewing sometime during the wake and church services. A laying-on of hands, touching, kissing, and expressing one's grief by viewing the remains have traditionally mattered deeply. African American morticians certainly encouraged these practices because they made more money when families decided to embalm a body and make it available for viewing. Theirs was, however, an encouragement that resided easily within African American traditions that respected the emotional power of the presence of the deceased. It was a practice that additionally recalled west African funeral traditions in which the family and the deceased were honored with visitations that indicated respect and esteem. In the United States, however, the tradition also represented a different kind of memorializing, as it recognized specific evidence of the racialized violence done to black bodies. For example, when Emmett Till was lynched in Mississippi in 1955, hundreds of thousands lined South Side Chicago streets to view his remains. After Till's mother received the lynched, mutilated remains of her son and had arranged for the funeralizing and burial, she insisted on an open casket "so that the world could see what they had done to my child" (Powledge 44).

A huge crowd at the funeral of Emmett Till. *Bettman/CORBIS.*

The cultural importance attached to an open-casket viewing required of morticians a particular skill with and attention to the appearance of the deceased. At a 1996 professional convention, an African
American mortician who had practiced since the middle of the century
explained to me one consideration that always mediated his preparation
of the body for the wake and "visiting hour"—that final social encounter
between the body of the deceased and his or her family and friends, and
the time when public respect and sympathy were extended to the bereaved. In order to be prepared for the demise of certain elderly members
of prominent families, the mortician in question always made certain
that he had some of the lighter shades of cosmetics on hand. It is a culturally shared truism that age darkens the skin tones of some black folk,
and a professionally shared one that death accomplishes the same cos-
metic effect. So, if skin tone mattered at all to the family—and skin tone
has, of course, had major implications in the culturally colored sociopoli-
tics of America's history, and it had even weightier implications for some

of the very light-skinned families this mortician serviced for decades—death was no time to acknowledge or suggest a darker-hued past. "Our families have always depended on me," he explained, "to lighten up their loved one. The last thing they would want is for somebody to pass by the casket and say, 'Your mama looks a little dark, doesn't she?'" If this happened, "it would be the last time we would have any body from that family—and they've got several left to go."

The last rites of color-coded lifestyles were both this superficial and this significant. The embalmer's artistry constructed his own narrative of a death, a skill in postmortem cosmetology honed within a cultural history of ironic extremes. Preferences for and prejudices toward skin tone demanded the same attention from these decorative and restorative arts as did violence and horrific death. Members of the National Funeral Directors and Morticians Association (NFDMA), the African American professional society founded in 1937, assert that the African American embalmer is not only generally more skilled than his white peers because of the challenges of the varieties of skin tone among black folk but also because embalming of black bodies often requires a repair job that masks the residue of violent death. James McCarty, chief embalmer at Angelus Funeral Home in Los Angeles, "increasingly spends his days using special putty to rebuild the faces and bodies of young people torn apart by gunfire" (Wilkinson A15). His is an experience as old as the particularities involved in professional attention to the ways and means of black death in the United States. The generational circumstance may change, but the violence done to black bodies has had a consistent history. That fact, paired with the cultural expectations of an open casket, presented a particular challenge to the black mortician's skill.

The story of children's deaths early in the century was not, however, only a northern tale. Black children were as vulnerable in the American South, where they were, as in the North, victims of malnutrition, poor maternal health, and infectious disease. Perhaps as a testament to the familiarity of the experience, African Americans upheld the tradition of formal portraiture of the dead in final sleep, a tradition Euro-Americans did not continue into the twentieth century (Ruby 75). James Van Der Zee and Southerner Richard Samuel Roberts were two noted photographers of this era. Van Der Zee noted a rationale for the tender portraiture in one particular case. "The mother was sick in the hospital and couldn't get out," he explained. "The child died in the meantime. If it

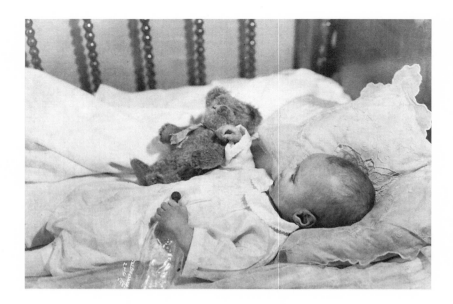

This infant's funeral portrait was constructed to contradict the tragedy of her death. Its calm scene, suggestive of a baby just dropping off to sleep in the midst of play, was characteristic of memorial artistry. *Photo by James Van Der Zee.*

wasn't for the picture, the mother wouldn't have seen the child for the last time" (Van Der Zee 83). Richard Samuel Roberts's South Carolina photographs of infants indicate the shared cultural aesthetic between his work and Van Der Zee's Northern memorials. For both, there was a deliberate attempt to construct a memorial of the dead child that contradicted the fact of the event.

Everywhere, but in the South especially, weather and temperature conditions put constraints on the amount of time that could reasonably be devoted to a display of the deceased, especially during the summer months. Another factor in the timing of black funerals in the early part of the century was the then-recent citizenship of a great majority of African American northerners, who still had close ties to family who had remained down South. Early in the century—the time when massive numbers of African Americans, singly or in family groups, made the "great migration" north—not all embalmers had the skill and where-

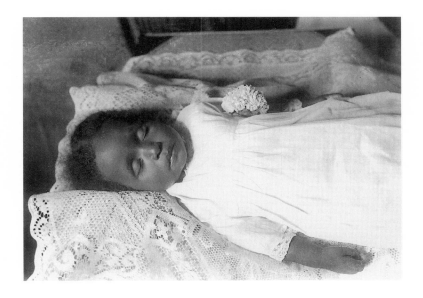

Like Van Der Zee's photographs of the dead, this pacific and gentle reconstruction of the moment serves to sustain the memory of this southern child. *Photo by Richard Samuel Roberts.*

withal to effect a final presentation of the deceased that could hold intact long enough for all the family to assemble. But in African America, the cultural tradition of going home for a funeral was strong and seriously attended to. Warren Harrison left Detroit in the 1930s as a young man to return to his birthplace in Alabama, where he worked for a time as an embalmer for Welch Funeral Home in Bessemer. In reflecting on the cultural expectations surrounding death and funeralizing, Mr. Harrison was quite explicit about the expectations surrounding a death in a black family. "We went *home* for a funeral. No questions. Nobody worried about what it cost or what we were doing with jobs or whatever. When somebody died—and I don't care *how* you were related—if you were family you went back home where you were supposed to be. With your family." To compensate for displaced relatives, in the South especially, funeral sermons were sometimes preached nearly a week after the burial, the ceremony having waited for the family to gather, but the burial having been unable, because of decomposition, to wait for the same. Van Der Zee's and Roberts's "domestic" artistry of photographic composition, with their deliberate framing of the effects of home and hearth within the image, argued the cultural familiarity of black death. Photographs of infants and children assured bereaved parents of their child's storied place in the family history.

As the century progressed, common experiences between black funeral parlors and their communities sustained their close association. This relationship was reinforced by shared economic history, neighborhoods, and churches with networks of community families known from one generation to the next, as well as by a critical understanding of the social codes, community mores, and cultural specificities of living as a black person that came into play during death and burial. Members of the profession say, for example, that it takes a black mortician's practiced skill to know how to handle black hair textures and treatments. Discussing some of the culturally contextualized issues of the profession with a group of new African American graduates from the Commonwealth Institute of Funeral Service in Houston, Texas, I was assured by the newly licensed morticians that whites do not have enough cultural acumen to do a good job. When I asked for specifics, one graduate told me—quite seriously and either unaware of or intentional in her irony— "Well, they don't know how to do our hair. And then, they put all that pancake make-up on us and it makes us look dead."

Journalist and memoirist Jill Nelson revealed one dimension of the necessary cultural sensitivity of the profession in writing about her life in the "district" and a date with a local mortician:

> I follow him downstairs to the embalming room, a large, cold-feeling space with corpse-size metal tables along two walls and an array of nozzles and hoses mounted above them. In the middle of the room is a long, rectangular table with a motor underneath it. In the ceiling above is a trap door that opens into the floor of the viewing room, a kind of dumbwaiter for bodies. Once they are all dressed up, they have someplace to go; the table rises and zaps them upstairs to wait for their bereaved relatives. . . . The mortician looks down into the coffin. . . .
>
> "What are you doing?" I ask. . . .
>
> "Trying to fix this guy's hair," he says, pointing to the coffin on the elevator table. . . .

"Come here, I need you to help me. . . . You're a woman. Just look at his hair for me. . . . You don't have to touch anything."

. . . I'm looking. . . . I . . . notice the tendrils of hair creeping out from under the man's hat brim. The hair is brittle, dry, a strange grayish-green color. Instead of flowing down to the man's shoulders, it sticks out from his cheeks as though he'd died by electrocution. I snigger.

"It looks horrible. What happened to him?"

"That's what a dead Jheri Kurl looks like," he snaps. "I can't get it to curl up and lie flat. You think this business is easy?"

Nelson had apparently met one of the less-skilled members of the profession. As they pondered what to do about the decedent's hair, she asked, "Have you tried hair spray?"

"Of course I have. I've tried spray, gel, mousse, I even got a can of Sterno and tried to use a hot comb on it, but his hair started to burn and when I yanked the comb away I burnt his cheek and had to re-do the make-up on that side. . . ."

I notice the caked pancake on the man's left cheek, but don't mention it. Instead I say, "Have you tried Vaseline? It used to do wonders keeping my bangs flat when I was in fifth grade. . . ."

Whether because of some mystic property of Vaseline or simply because of the weight of the oil, the hair begins to lie flat. . . .

"Twist it around your finger while you're greasing it so it curls. . . ."

Finished, he stands back to survey his handiwork. The guy looks like Ron O'Neill in Superfly. (26)

A dead Jheri-Kurl is about as culturally specific as one can get.

Although the funeral director's skill and status were historically a matter of public pride and notice, the intricacies of the profession encompassed extremely private matters, and somewhere betwixt and between the private matters and public concerns lay the messy issues of cost. Some funeral directors and morticians expressed frustration with the public perception of these money matters. A Florida mortician complained to me that "our people have always believed that you just want to take their money." But, at the same time, he unwittingly provided some context for the troubled image. "Now, I've got to admit that twenty or so years ago, some directors would do stuff like price a funeral at something like $4000 when they knew Mrs. Jones or whoever was coming in with a $3,000 insurance policy. Then they'd say, 'Here's what I'm going to do for you.' And they'd give her that funeral, which really only cost about $1–2,000 for the price of her $3,000 policy." The practice he described was unfortunately too common (although his memory of the costs "twenty or so years ago" were likely inflated). Drake reported a similar swindle, with figures that were (except for the price of the Lincoln hearse) somewhat more credible for the 1940s.

> Doug and his brother had a funeral parlor. I think he is now the owner of the Eureka Funeral Association. You pay him so much a year to get a high-class funeral—something like ten cents a week. These Negroes will do a lot to be sure of a classy funeral. You see, Doug is in the insurance end of this just as much as the funeral business. He has a $15,000 Lincoln hearse and a whole string of Lincoln limousines. He offers an "All-Lincoln" funeral. He tells them they are getting a thousand dollar funeral; what he really does costs him probably a hundred dollars. He uses cheap coffins with a lot of paint. The way the thing is worked, they sign over their insurance policy for maybe a thousand dollars and are promised a big funeral. . . . You should see his funeral parlors; they are elegant. (459)

Once black funeral homes were established in African American communities, they could depend on a neighborly familiarity and loyalty that made their customers particularly vulnerable to a variety of unregulated financial practices such as these. Because the customer base in black urban areas was consistently made up of folk who had to struggle each day with economic self-sufficiency and with the too-frequent need for use of the morticians' businesses, the funeral homes' culturally reinforced dependence on such historically poor and underclass markets could not guarantee their stability. Some black morticians went north anticipating and hoping for relief from impoverished southern clients. A midcentury Chicago undertaker who took up his business in that city because he had had his fill of southern "relief funerals" explained his move this way: "I think I had three; then I refused to accept any more. They only paid $75. There was no kind of decent funeral you can get for that amount. With the case workers and clients demanding so much more than they can pay for, I got fed up. On one occasion, I had to cuss out a case worker. Then, too, I did not like going into some of the dirty, filthy homes. I realized that by locating here, I would be among the better class" (Drake 458).

Some morticians who were seeking a higher socioeconomic class increased their income by supplementing their mortuary businesses with the selling of burial insurance policies—especially to new urban migrants. This practice was the legacy of southern community organizations, fraternal lodges, and clubs, which had also provided this service but whose benefits did not follow their members north. By the 1920s, southern church "burying leagues" and lodges had been replaced with associations that the undertakers organized. Northern undertakers in this business also assumed the insurance policies of those migrants who did not have the resources to keep up their payments. The founder of Chicago's first black burial association, a mortician, explained it that he saw his clientele coming from those who "didn't have any protection left" (Drake 458).

Burial associations emerged as a way for African American communities to handle the recurrent financial and social obligations of death. These enterprises—the earliest date to the 1700s—provided death benefits to the community, specifically burial insurance. Although the main function of these societies was to cover the costs of burial, they also guaranteed their deceased members the pomp and ceremony critical to the occasion. Badges, gloves, special collars, and aprons—often at the wake and again at the gravesite were necessary displays. The Bury League, for example, was

a cooperative society that grew out of the Negro's sincere desire for an elaborate and respectful funeral. Every neighborhood has a local chapter headed by a "Nobel [sic] Shepherd," and the members pay a small sum each week to a common fund which provides for the next funeral. The Nobel Shepherd keeps the "treasury," and once a month . . . empties it into the hands of the Leader of the Flock, who owns and drives the automobile hearse and provides fine store-bought coffins and white stones to stand at the head of the graves. Bury League members are required to attend every burial unless hindered by providence. They all wear white gloves, the women carry white paper flowers, and officers who carry the banners of the organization wear large badges.

> The reward for complying with [the League's obligations] is a fine coffin, a journey to the grave in the automobile hearse, and a tombstone. (Hughes 105)

Thus, a black community would anticipate the financial burden that would greet its members, given the frequency of unforeseen illness, death, and associated costs of burial. In response, these benevolent secret societies, with their contributions to a common till, provided a consistent source of financial relief for their community's persistent experiences with death and dying. The Brown Fellowship Society of South Carolina, founded in Charleston in 1790, was another example. As clubs are wont to do, there were membership restrictions associated with these groups. Black clubs were no different, except that their restrictions emerged around color and (therefore) class. The Brown Society's early membership of light-skinned, free Negroes would have been known as the "sedity" among the various social clubs in that era. Herbert DeCosta, one of the society's contemporary members, spoke of its roots: "[T]he . . . founders of this group organized as a sick and death benefit society . . . to help themselves in times of sickness, misfortune, and death. Although they were considered free persons of color, we know that they lived in a world of shadow, constantly fighting to retain the degree of freedom they enjoyed" (Roberta Wright 271). The society's records attest to the seriousness of their purpose.

> In case of sickness afflicts any member . . . and if he dies, the Stewards shall attend . . . after which he shall report the case to the President, or presiding officer, who shall order a meeting immediately, and consult on the management of the funeral; and in case the circumstances of such deceased member be low and indigent, that a decent funeral cannot be afforded out of their own estate or effects, the President or presiding officer shall have power and authority to appoint a committee, to regulate things . . . for the funeral, which charges shall be paid off of the Society's funds. Every member in Charleston shall attend the funeral, with a Black crepe around the left arm, by invitation from the secretary; and on neglect (if able) to attend, he shall be fined in a sum not exceeding twenty-five cents, payable at the next meeting, unless a good and sufficient excuse be then made. (Roberta Wright 273–74)

Burial associations and black funeral home policies met the specific cultural need of a "proper" funeral. Robert Harris, a scholar of African American history, explained this cultural particularity and focus. "Without a doubt their major concern was the death benefit; making sure their members received not only a decent but a *special* burial." The authors of *Lay Down Body,* a graveyard ethnography, suggested that the sentiment came from a belief that "the soul of an African American would eventually return to the mother continent—but only if the body was given a proper and respectful send-off. Hence a great deal of attention was given to burials. Elaborate funeral ceremonies . . . were the order of the day. . . . [A]s the black church began to grow, they slowly took over many of the functions of the societies and lodges, including burials. Some societies and lodges themselves evolved into local churches" (Roberta Wright 268).

In Chicago in 1922, the largest burial association was founded by an undertaker with "an eye for increased business" (Drake 459). Unfortunately, undertakers' own pressing financial needs (and objectives) sometimes encouraged the kinds of practices that novelist Richard Wright experienced when he worked for a "Negro" burial society that operated on Chicago's South Side in the 1930s. It was, for Wright, a "new kind of education" when he "found that the burial societies, with some exceptions, were mostly 'rackets.' Some of them conducted their business legitimately, but there were many that exploited the ignorance of their black customers. . . . Most of the policyholders were illiterate and did not know that their policies carried clauses severely restricting their benefit payments, and, as an insurance agent, it was not my duty to tell them." With some sense of chagrin, Wright recalls that "it was necessary for me to take part in one swindle. It appears that the burial society had originally issued a policy that was—from their point of view—too liberal in its provisions, and the officials decided to exchange the policies then in the hands of their clients for other policies carrying stricter clauses" (Richard Wright, *Eight Men* 187). He and his "superintendent" would visit the policyholder, and while one was engaging her in conversation, the other one would ask to review their policy and then exchange it for one with the newly restrictive conditions The problems of equity and fairness that emerged with such underhanded insurance business practices contributed to the regulatory environment that now oversees these industries. Although by 1937 undertakers were able to "secure the passage of a law requiring the burial associations to pay the value of the policy in cash, rather than in the form of a burial," the law was not particularly successful in keeping the unethical practice from seeping into the negotiations between businesses and their clients (Drake 459).

Regulations still did not keep some of "our people," as the black morticians and funeral directors fondly call their black customer base, from expecting that the funeral director could enter into a personal rather than businessman's relationship when it came to tallying up costs. Morticians told me some version of this story enough times for me to suspect it as a professional legend: a despondent "church lady" comes into the establishment and asks to see the funeral home director alone. Deep in grief, and passionately expressive over the death of her spouse, she explains through tears and sobbing about how she has been "in prayer" over the matter before coming to the director. Her plea takes some form of: "Now you know, Brother [fill in the name of the undertaker], I been praying over this and—have mercy!—the Lord done told me you going to take care of my husband for free." The response was equally performative: After a respectful pause and handing over a strategically placed box of Kleenex to the grieving widow, he says, "Well Sister, when the Lord comes in here to make these arrangements, I'll be glad to talk to Him about it. But until then, why don't you and me just set down right here and figure out to how you're going to pay me for this funeral."

The black mortuary business nurtured close and amicable relations with members of the community, with minor but important activities like making its folding chairs and limousines available for parties and weddings, and its hearses—especially during the days of segregation in the rural South—available as standby ambulances at black high school sporting events. Perhaps more important was the way the funeral home found its cultural membership unequivocally tied to the racial business of the community. When there were deaths from lynchings or riots, executions or neglect by hospitals or doctors, black undertakers commonly found these bodies and the families of the victims in their establishments, contracting for services that had as much to do with color as with circumstance. Consequently, they have a history of an intimate involvement in the most serious issues of the black communities. In the South, for example, undertakers' "combinations" (hearses manufactured to also serve as ambulances) were often held on standby to answer accident calls for African Americans, because, due to segregated emergency services, physician care, and hospitals, such vehicles were sometimes the only transportation option for injured black folk. During the sixties, Dr. Martin Luther King Jr. and other civil rights leaders sometimes used hearses driven by funeral home personnel to leave rallies and church appearances discreetly. In these ways, the relationships between the community's needs—both political needs and needs that framed the residue of black death—and the morticians' occupation led to the development of special associations between the mortician, funeral director, and preacher. This collusion and community between the church and the burial business increased the intimacy of these professionals with private family matters.

"Show is going to cost you. . . ."
—J. C. Bennett

Many black folk alive at midcentury remember how firm the color line once held. They can recall the nudges and whispers when a white person even showed up at a black funeral, which thus bestowed a certain crossover status on the family ("Humph—even some *white* folk come to the church"). As the twentieth century ended, that mark of distinction had been done one better, as increasing numbers of black families elected to voluntarily give the bodies of their deceased relatives to white-owned and -operated establishments to prepare and put away. This growing end-of-century phenomenon of black people mingling and mixing in white funeral homes and making final arrangements there for the "putting away" would cause some early-century black folk to turn over in their graves. One of my friends gently suggested to me, after my husband and I had specified the black funeral home that we wanted to handle the arrangements for our son, that there were options—we could use the white business somewhat nearer to our suburban home. For us, this simply was not even a momentary desire. Despite our disarray and despair, we felt that the familiarity and nearness of shared, remembered cultural spaces would contribute to the little solace we could find. But black morticians cannot count any more on a decision like ours. Things came full circle in the twentieth century. What began as an integrated market that was segregated through force and circumstance ironically returned to some dimension of that early-century integration. The color lines that evolved and solidified as black businesses took over the task of caring for and preparing the black dead for burial and that managed to stay intact in the black community for most of the century were, at the century's end, again being transgressed. This time, however, it was not the force of necessity, nor was it a reaction to threats of hostility or intimidation. It was a matter of choice.

As the century came to a close, the competition for black bodies heightened as whites began to contest the historically and culturally enforced claim of the African American mortician. Social class and personal preference intervened in new ways in what had been the culturally dictated selection of the black mortuary. For some black folk, white funeral homes became the new option and a visible mark of a certain status. During most of the century the only question had been whether to use the upscale parlor with a chapel on-site or the older, less up-to-date establishment that had been burying members of the family for decades. Attending this change of preference within the African American community, the ever-present lure of market economies and a changing social climate compelled whites to pursue the newly available black remains. The matters and *materia* of black death became cultural capital, less a matter of family history and culturally dictated practice than fodder for the entrepreneurial.

J. C. Bennett, corporate development manager for the black-owned Wilson Financial Group has adopted the contemporary parlance for his profession: "the death care industry." In an interview, he told me that "this new generation of upper-middle-class black folk is being buried out of white homes. There is no neighborhood loyalty." In his home base of Houston, Texas, Bennett argued that they "ain't coming into the city to the Fifth Ward to bury their wife, child, mother, or anybody else." If black folk do not live in the inner city, it's not likely, "that they are going to drive past four or five white funeral homes just to get back to the neighborhood." Instead, they are "going to stop at the one most convenient to them—and it ain't going to be one of us." Bennett's experience was neither unique nor local. By the 1990s, this was a nationwide, crossover phenomenon, with black funeral homes in urban areas throughout the United States experiencing decline as their traditionally black clientele shifted to white funeral homes. According to Bennett, unless black businesses expanded in ways that allowed them to reach out from their traditional, inner-city locales, white-owned funeral homes were going to become the nearest "neighborhood" dealer for an increasing number of black folk.

When asked if whites were also beginning to patronize black-owned funeral parlors, a chorus of emphatic "No's!" was the response from a group of professionals attending an NFDMA annual convention in the late 1990s. Although this was absolutely the case—whites do not return the crossover business that some black folk engage in—there were ironic exceptions. NFDMA members pointed to the inequity that bothers them the most, noting that "they'll bury our elite, we bury their poor." If black morticians did prepare white bodies, it was often a matter of doing so under city contracts negotiated and awarded for burying the indigent. One longtime member of the profession put it bluntly, telling me that black businesses were often awarded these contracts, because "frankly, we're the cheapest." It was usual for these pauper or welfare burials to involve cremation—a practice that avoided incurring the significant costs of embalming, caskets, burial vaults, and cemetery expenditures.

A study of black businesses in the early years of the twentieth century in Houston, Texas, called race a "limitation" that "led black entrepreneurs to rely heavily, if not completely upon the African-American community," and although some black morticians in Houston "occasionally" buried whites, most of the time "they handled all black corpses due to the requirements of Jim Crow" (SoRelle 104). For welfare cases, some black morticians attempted to save as much as they could of the allotments given for the "pauper" burials—even to the extent that, as one told me, "back in the 1930s, we would take the body out to the garage, place him on a couple of straight boards, and wrap him in muslin. Then, we packed newspapers into the pine coffins that we put together and buried him without any further ado—it only cost us about fifty dollars." Cost-conscious city governments were quick to award these contracts to the lowest bidders without, regrettably, much follow-through to see how the remains were handled. Black-owned businesses anxious to increase the numbers of bodies they handled annually, no matter the source, were often the repository for these forgotten citizens.

The funeral color line was not directly challenged until 1973, when Wilbert Jean Oliver won a federal lawsuit that had the practical effect of forcing funeral homes to provide equal service for black and white customers. Oliver sued because two funeral homes in Louisiana—Escude

Funeral Home and Hixson Brothers Funeral Home—"either refused to deal with blacks, or provided distinctly inferior services" at the same prices they charged whites. In the Oliver case, the funeral homes would not provide visitation for his deceased mother. The grandson of the Escude patriarch who had run the funeral home at the time of the incident explained that his grandfather "provided all services, including embalming, but stopped at offering visitation to blacks because if he did, he'd lose business from whites." None of his competitors at the time offered any service at all to black clients. When Escude's refused the wake for Mrs. Oliver, her body had to be set up for visitation and viewing at a "run-down storage building" on the grounds of a nearby church (Honan).

But the point is that, at the century's end, the competitive environment for getting black bodies dramatically upped the ante, and for black businessmen, the traditionally dependable customer base of African Americans became both more selective and less loyal. The tradition of family-owned funeral homes that thrived on competition within but not outside the black community had some difficulty in being appropriately responsive. One family business that made a particular and comparatively early effort to address the issue of securing crossover clientele was the Ragsdale family, descendants of that original 1880s Oklahoman undertaker, William Ragsdale.

Ragsdale's grandchildren opened homes in California and Arizona, following the lead of their fathers who had opened family business sites across Oklahoma. Ragsdale Mortuary Chapel in the Valley was opened in 1948. As the first black owner of a funeral home in Arizona, Lincoln Ragsdale Sr. felt secure and proud of the name he was able to publicly identify with his enterprise, no longer haunted by his father's experience with the Klan. But twenty years later, in an ironic twist, he decided that his family name was still a liability—albeit of a different sort. The predominately white market of Phoenix would not support his business in its traditional, family-named form. Whites did not choose black funeral homes to bury their dead and in midcentury Phoenix, there simply were not enough black bodies to be profitable. Lincoln Sr. decided to reorganize, and acknowledging that color was a factor in his market share, he attempted to erase race by making the fact of black ownership nearly invisible. He eliminated the family name from his marquee, changed his office personnel so that there were whites in the front offices (specifically at the reception area), and as a final gesture, commissioned a sculpture that would visually represent his multicultural effort: in the parking lot, the golden figures of three women now rise from a concrete base. From a distance, the figures seem nearly indistinguishable. However, on closer inspection, it is clear that their respective facial features have been designed to represent a black, a white, and an Asian woman.

Lincoln Sr. explained his motive: "I was almost bankrupt. . . . There just wasn't enough business to support me, so I decided to go after the white business." He argued the rationale of his choice, noting that "we talk about integration but too often continue to work in all-black situations." So in the late 1960s, he made "a business decision. I took down my pictures of Martin Luther King Jr. and Booker T. Washington and put up some white folk. I hired white personnel and my business increased over 300 percent. For every black body I get, I have three white ones" ("The Business Side of Bereavement" 57). By the late 1990s, neither of the two Phoenix funeral homes owned by the Ragsdales bore the family name. And on the wall of the Home in the Valley was the painting that Lincoln Sr. chose to replace the portrait of Reverend Dr. King. Its large frame nearly covered the back wall behind a sofa in the reception area. The painting's subject is a fifties-era white woman—a dead ringer for a "Breck girl"—surrounded by a multicultural assemblage of children. In a 1997 conversation, Lincoln Ragsdale Jr. purported that the business decision his father made proved to be a successful strategy, although the contemporary market for his integrated clientele still had "to be tweaked." "Tweaked" was the operative word. Toward the end of the century, it seemed that the Ragsdale business found its multiculturalism primarily in Hispanic bodies, not in white. The flaking, chipped statue of the three women in the parking lot told the story. Although the market indications for his father seemed to bode well for developing an integrated clientele, for Lincoln Jr. the palette was black and brown, and his market share had no guarantee and little promise of white folk.

Lincoln Jr.'s sister, Emily—who joined her brother in the business after graduating in 1997 from the Gupton-Jones Mortuary School in Atlanta, Georgia—seemed wistful but resigned about the difficulty of the "tweaks." She told me that Ragsdale bodies are only "infrequently white." In explaining the family's failure to realize their father's dream of a business that successfully competed for black as well as white bodies, Emily shifted from a quiet resentment to calm resolution and even a dramatic, personal reconciliation that called up her sense of the cultural history of service, at whatever cost, within their business situation. She explained that those whom she "celebrates" in the professional post-mortems of the business "are the unsung heroes . . . the truest angels, the greatest souls, *the ones who went without.*" Emily seemed to have found some culturally inclined spiritual solace for the business absence of white bodies. She claimed that "to celebrate their [black] lives is the honor." In mixing professional and entrepreneurial objectives with cultural sensibility, Emily articulated an aesthetic of black death and the quandaries of the black businesses involved.

There was passionate resentment among many African American professionals about how white businesses were successful in ways that they themselves were not, especially with crossover clientele. In 1996, Gerome Primm, the immediate past president of the NFDMA, charged that, although white funeral establishments were overpriced, some blacks turned to them because the "mentality" of "our people" had changed. In a telephone conversation, Primm noted with dismay that black people thought of themselves as "celebrities" in need of an "exotic" (i.e., "white") funeral home as evidence of their difference. Primm implied that such choices are often made without regard to the (to him) requisite "quality" service in which "artistry" matters. He felt that white funeral establishments were in it for the money and that they did not have a genuine concern about people. His attitude—his resentment—was widely shared by black-owned representatives of the industry.

One funeral director from Tennessee explained to me how one of the largest white funeral homes in his city targeted the black community. "They are going to different churches, talking with the pastors, and writing up an entire congregation 'pre-need.'" This practice led to some suspicion, raising concerns about whether pastors were getting financial returns for granting white funeral directors access to their congregations. As a consequence, toward the end of the century, African Americans in the business learned to anticipate some degree of desertion by their traditional color-coded customer base. Ironically, according to black funeral industry insiders, African Americans' choice of funeral home was still color-coded, because both the rejection and the selection were being made for reasons other than quality and price. "Here's the way I see it," one Ohio funeral director explained. "If you've got ten black folk and ten white folk, there's always going to be two of us going over there and not none of them coming over here." Part of his resentment came from his assurance, shared by many others, that "we give better service." But service was not the only attraction. As with the use of cosmetics that still governed some people's choices of black funeral homes, appearance counted once again. Many white funeral homes had a long history of successful fiduciary arrangements with banks and investment firms and were thus able to build facilities that were significantly more upscale than some of the long-standing, family-owned black businesses, many of which still operated out of older, less modern, and less well appointed facilities, although those same facilities had for decades been sufficient for their clientele, carrying them in good "neighborhood" stead.

The mix of church, family, and community service was the "cradle-to-grave" network of membership in the African American community that some in the business felt justified their right to expect loyalty. "I look at it this way—I contribute to my community's Little League groups. I contribute to the NAACP. I belong to our church and tithe there. They don't give anything to our community, and they do all they can to stay away from us while we're living, and then they got the nerve to come in here when we die and get the body."

Suggesting that both race and skin tone motivated some crossover decisions, one Louisiana mortician explained to me that the bodies that go to white homes these days are likely to be Creole, or "e-lights," according to some midwestern members of the black association. One forty-something, upper-class professional, who counts himself among a growing number of black Republicans, buried his mother in a New England community in the mid-1990s and used a white funeral home. When asked about his choice, he said that there were probably some black-owned funeral homes used by families related to the "older" and "underclass" communities, but that he "felt no compelling reason" to consider them when it came to making arrangements for his mother. And herein lay the rub of the generational difference. The least-stable market for black morticians was African Americans who were young, suburban, and disconnected from the church and neighborhood bonds that their parents nurtured. This younger generation was now making family decisions about burial.

The effort to gain entry into the black market share was fierce at the century's end, and it wasn't just spearheaded by independent white funeral homes. White conglomerates, whose financial marketing groups targeted historic neighborhood and family-run businesses, saw vulnerable points of entry into the black market within selective populations of the black church. In 1996, the black Empire State Funeral Directors in New York protested an association that the National Baptist Convention (NBC/USA) — an African American ministerial association — had formalized with the Loewen Group — a white-owned, multinational funeral home chain. NBC/USA had, in fact, formed a marketing firm in an arrangement with Loewen. The new group was charged with directing a percentage of the profit from funeral expenses back to the preachers and to congregational members who were to be trained, compensated, and appointed as "grief counselors." NBC/USA-affiliated local congregations were to be tapped for local talent whom the corporation would train to sell headstones, graves, crypts, vaults, and urns in Loewen cemeteries. Not surprisingly, the local pastors and their state and national denominational affiliates were due a commission on each sale.

As a result, black church sanctuaries evolved into new business networks. In Pleasant Lane Baptist Church, one of the oldest black churches in the nation's capital, built by freed slaves in 1863, "the latest class of cemetery sales recruits practiced its pitches. . . . They press the wisdom of making cemetery arrangements now with the 10% discount for buying through the National Council of African-American Churches, the marketing firm established by the National Baptist Convention, USA to sell for Loewen" (Tilove 3E).

Reverend Henry Lyons, the 1996 president of the NBC/USA who engineered the Loewen deal, faced public approbation not only because of the many questions regarding how the deal was orchestrated but because of how it undercut the black funeral-home owner. Black businessmen who had counted on the loyal relationship of the pastors with whom they had had years of business and community association were afraid that pastors who catered to Loewen would no longer cater to them. For Lyons, the employment opportunities and financial rewards available through association with Loewen weighed more heavily than tradition. Nevertheless, with attention to the public relations postures of good cultural citizenship and a significant nod to the traditions that he knew his business deal flaunted, Reverend Lyons spoke directly to the topic of most concern when he promised that his body would "go to a black funeral home before it comes to rest in a Loewen cemetery" (Tilove 3E).

He did not specify whether the owners of the funeral home would be cultural kin to the folk who operated the business.

Loewen's interests did not stop at the cemeteries. They extended to "lucrative" (in the sellers' eyes) buy-outs and consolidations of neighborhood funeral homes, so that Loewen might fully control the urban markets that African American businessmen had served. Although the personnel in these funeral homes continued to be black, the off-site owners would be Loewen or another conglomerate.

At the century's end, the threat of conglomerates to black-owned funeral businesses was fueled in part by the financial precariousness of those businesses. Not only did diminishing loyalty compromise their markets, but technological changes challenged their old organizational strategies. And, for some of these black businesses, the appeal of a tradition of black ownership became much less interesting than the appeal of financial security. Unlike the relative security in which black morticians and funeral directors had previously conducted their undertakings, the late-century moves of the conglomerates and the fact that the new upper class did not provide a dependable customer base created a deeply uncertain market for black-owned funeral homes. That whites had successfully co-opted the traditional allegiances of the business was an irony not lost on some. According to Reverend Al Sharpton of the Harlem-based National Action Network, "It's not enough that white folks exploit us while we are living, now they want to exploit us when we're dead" (Salaam 36). Unfortunately, the passivity engendered by the long-secure black customer base resulted in inconsistent formal and structural attention to competitive and futures-oriented market and management strategies. There had been a misleading comfort for some in operating out of the same establishment and/or in the same manner as their fathers. These were the business owners most vulnerable to being left behind by the late-century emergence of plush, well-appointed, technologically current, and meticulously managed businesses that thrived on competition.

The 1995 agreement between the NBC/USA and the Canadian conglomerate Loewen created considerable tension between black funeral homes and the churches who had a relationship with Loewen. Critics of the Loewen association argued with biblical fervor against its intrusion into black social/business networks. The same critics targeted the National Baptist Convention in particular, saying "The prophet Jesus advised his followers to give unto Caesar what is Caesar's and give unto God what is God's. But some Harlem funeral directors charge that the National Baptist Convention is giving almost all to Caesar, and pocketing the rest" (Salaam 1). In the summer of the agreement, Loewen made a donation of $100,000 to the Christian Education Fund of that Baptist Convention, a move some considered an outright purchase of their services, especially after the convention assigned Loewen the rights as its "death care provider of choice." According to Earl Banks, a fourth-generation owner of the People's Funeral Home in Jackson, Mississippi, "It's almost like Judas and the 30 pieces of silver. . . . Are black churches for sale? At this point I'd have to say if they are affiliated with [Loewen] the answer may be 'yes'" (Tilove 3E).

Most agree that the NFDMA responded late to the need to help its members develop competitive business practices that could assist them with developing trends. Its own history had not been without the kinds of conflict perhaps best illustrated by its series of name changes, mergers, pull-outs, and reorganizations. At the end of the century, the NFDMA found itself challenged with its own failure to anticipate and appreciate a changing marketplace. Lincoln Ragsdale Jr. told me that his father faced ridicule from some members of the NFDMA for his crossover attempt to secure white bodies for his funeral home. The collegial consequence of his father's business decision was that "he isolated himself" from that African American professional organization, which "could not do anything to help him." As the century came to a close, the concerns of the network of state organizations that gathered each year for the annual NFDMA convention had shifted from the "how" of mortuary practices and ways of meeting licensing requirements to the survivability of a black business in integrated and "conglomerated" times.

The financial aspects of death and dying certainly provided significant drama. Costs varied widely, and (or but), as was widely noted among members of the professional organization, "our people like to put on a good show." Negotiations were always delicate, and families—especially during times of grief and distress—could be particularly vulnerable to the cultural traditions of "show." But "show is going to cost you," as one Tennessee funeral director explained. NFDMA members had not-so-well disguised impatience with the way that "our people" had little appreciation for the costs of the business, and they had a shared appreciation and even dependence on the assumption that, among black folk,

Like the cars that were parked in front of the Manigault business in the early twentieth century, the automobiles from Detroit's House of Diggs illustrated the intended impact of "show."

the performance—its drama, elegance, and extravagance—was critical to the occasion.

Many families were concerned not only about the overall spectacle of funeral but also about its details. The Tennessee funeral director I spoke with told me, "Cars are important for our people. We want to have four or five cars in the procession. It's something our folk are looking for." Another interrupted, saying, "But at the same time, we do strange stuff like—with my business, we have white cars. Everybody in the city knows we have white cars. And then folk come to me, make arrangements for the service: pick out the casket, select the flowers, get the obituary ready, all of this, and then they say, 'Just one thing: I want black cars.' Now you tell me—Why'd they come to me in the first place? Everybody knows we've got white cars. If they wanted somebody's black limousines, they should've gone across town. Sometimes we just don't make sense!" The color and car issues were not casual concerns. For years, McFalls Brothers Funeral Home in Detroit has been known for its blue Cadillacs. They became a visible announcement of the family's choice of funeral home. When the company sent its fleet of upscale blue limos from its offices on Livernois to pick up the family for the first viewing, everyone in the neighborhood knew that McFalls had the body. This issue of cars as an indication of family preference and as an essential element of show followed the funeral business throughout the century. Midcentury, a Chicago mortician reported that "People nowadays don't want to ride in anything but fishtail Cadillacs. Recently a family refused to ride in a funeral I was conducting in a 1950 Cadillac. They insisted they would ride in nothing older than a 1952. And they didn't" ("Death is Big Business" 17). In another lavish funeral, this time in Texas, a wealthy Masonic potentate who was born the son of a slave and who "lived to amass one of the greatest fortunes in Negro history" made certain that his last rites did not miss the car connection. His procession was "resplendent evidence of his tremendous wealth. Nearly 2,000 people streamed past his bier as he lay in state in a $5,000 satin-finished bronze casket. More than $2,000 in wreaths and floral designs were sent by friends and associates. Cadillac followed Cadillac in his two-and-one-half mile long funeral procession. Two funeral homes were engaged to handle burial arrangements, one of them providing complete Cadillac limousine service even to the two specially-built Cadillac flower wagons" ("Death Comes to the World's Richest Negro" 68). Not unexpectedly, for folks who did not have the resources of the potentate above, grave issues emerged when show confronted costs.

Caskets—the most expensive item on the list of costs—were always a bottom-line issue. Some funeral directors complained that "our people" still believed that caskets were reused from burial to burial. Even though America was not the home of "slip coffins" with hinged bottoms that could be lowered halfway into the grave and then opened, dropping the bodies into the earth (Iserson 472), stories of reused coffins were recycled in black communities. One Louisiana funeral director told me about a time when he drove one of the limousines in a funeral procession. He left the cemetery, following the hearse after the graveside service had ended. Both he and the hearsedriver looked back and noticed that one of their staff had been inadvertently left at the gravesite. The hearsedriver turned around to go back and get him. To a person, the mournful occupants of the funeral director's car emerged from their grief just long enough to comment sarcastically: "See, I told you they go back to get the cas-

Example of Batesville Casket Company's Kente Line.

kets!" In upstate New York, one black family habitually remained at the graveyard after the funeral service. After the other mourners left, family members brought out hammers and axe handles to bang and dent the casket before it was lowered into the grave. The mortician who told me this story said, "We keep telling them we don't reuse these caskets, begging them not to destroy their purchase, but they want to make certain that after they are through with it, that there is nothing but damaged goods left behind. So now we all know what's going to happen. I just sit in the car and wait while they just go on hammering and banging away until they make that beautiful casket look like it came out of a war zone." He shook his head with a solemnly. "It's just pitiful to see." Still, rental and reusable caskets were not unheard of in the modern funeral industry, and some suggested that African American clergy, concerned with decreasing the financial burden on their parishioners while honoring the century's tradition of a "special" funeral, supported this practice, although to a lesser degree than whites (Iserson 473).

By midcentury, suppliers to the funeral home industry were fully appreciative of the money available from its culturally concerned clientele. As black consumer culture started to make its own "dent" in advertising and product strategies, one of the largest casket companies in the business, Batesville, designed a line of caskets that catered to black families, complete with "African"-inspired fabric selections that could be made into funeral garments for the deceased. The pity is that a best-seller of this line, the Kente Casket, was used mostly by baby boomer parents to bury their teenaged or adolescent children — a decision that pointed not only to the funeral industry's economic strategy but to the available market and cultural experience of black death that guaranteed the viability of the product line.

The coffin — or "casket," as it came to be known in the United States — often caused a good deal of drama, and as middleman between supplier and customer, the funeral director was not immune. Although this story has been denied by some, several in the state association told me that at least one leading casket manufacturer had been known to lock caskets that were on display in some black-owned businesses. Caskets accounted for tens of thousands of dollars of funeral-home merchandise. Generally, after a family selected a particular casket, it was removed to the viewing room and readied to receive the body. At this point the funeral director would expect to receive a check. Business owners viewed with suspicion requests from financially strapped customers who wrote checks at 5:00 P.M. on Friday for a bank account that would not be available until Monday and who tried to "rush" a weekend funeral. Some casket companies having found that merchandise could be "occupied and in the ground" before they received payment from the funeral home, starting sending keys via next-day and overnight mailings or revealing combinations on the telephone only after the bill had been settled.

At midcentury, and even through the sixties, one to two thousand dollars could easily have covered the cost of a funeral. Jessica Mitford wrote: "The average undertaker's bill in 1961 was $708 for a casket and 'services' exclusive of cemetery or crematorium charges. As the century ended, however, the average was $4,700" (115). When elderly citizens got their insurance "back in the day," it promised to cover the burial for what it cost at that time. But when "they come in here wanting me to put somebody away for the same price I did twenty-five years ago, I can't do that. And when I explain it to them, they look at me like it's my fault. And then, after sitting there and telling me that they can't pay me what I am worth, they tell me they want three brand new limousines to pick them up at their house! Well, that's just not going to happen!"

Although insurance policies went a long way toward minimizing friction, these legal documents also gave funeral directors an opportunity to take the upper hand in determining the family's cost and the funeral home's financial recuperation from a burial. "Whenever somebody asks me for the death certificate," one funeral director explained, "especially when that somebody tells me they don't have any money for the funeral and need to get some help from the family, I know there's an insurance policy somewheres. That's why they be asking for that certificate. They can't get to the insurance without it. But—if there is one, what they don't know is my hands are going to be on it first."

Some funeral directors were aggressive about courting their business. In the 1950s, *Ebony* reported that "many have contacts with hospital orderlies, policemen and doctors to get tips on possible business. In Los Angeles a Negro doctor was threatened with a suit by a minister, who came home to find his wife dead with a mortuary's card pinned to her clothes. The card had been left by the doctor who attended her" ("Death is Big Business" 20).

The association decided that some of the financial issues could be resolved by a better or even simply more consistent fiscal education of its membership. We go after the "cash money," one young entrepreneur explained, but consistent use of insurance opportunities in the African American community—especially among the elderly population—was still not the norm in 1999. Criticism by some of the younger members of the profession about dependence on "cash money" or "money in the pocket" revolved around the traditional and conservative ways the elders in (and out of) the business handled some financial affairs. Corporate concerns especially wanted to see organizations like the NFDMA become less vulnerable to "conducting business out of their pockets" or to "how many folk attending the business meeting at the convention have paid their membership dues," and to pay more attention to issues of investment, African American corporate alliances, and new technologies. One corporate development manager told me about a funeral director who had, in the mid-1990s, proudly bought an electric typewriter for the office—finally replacing the old manual Underwood that he had used since starting his business back in the 1940s. That funeral director's pride at his nod to technology was obviously disproportionate to the occasion, and his misunderstanding of the times—when most forward-looking companies were developing websites and business-specific software for office personnel—was worrisome to someone like that executive, whose business and professional orientation are a better match for the computer age. Shaking his head with both distress and understanding, he commented: "It's hard to get our people to change."

Before the century ended, change was in the wind, however, and most agreed that funeral-home directors were extremely vulnerable. When the Loewen group made its NBC/U.S.A. deal public, it also revealed a $50 million association with a west coast black funeral business to begin buying and consolidating black funeral homes. Although the arrangement with the National Baptist Convention eventually floundered, the west coast association did not. Despite the need for the black industry's change, and in the face of the negative critique of black churches' involvement in this business, it was the survival of the African American funeral home itself that caused much concern. This was where the charges of loyalty and the memory and challenge of tradition were the most fragile.

"Do the baby well"

Ironically, black businesses were losing their traditional customer base in part because of an association between the increasing number of black children's deaths and the greater financial flexibility of their white counterparts. Because children's funerals were nearly always unexpected, "we encourage our funeral directors to absorb the costs for a child's funeral," a North Carolina funeral director and officer in the state NFDMA explained to me. "The average person does not expect to lose a child, and there's no generally no insurance to cover the cost of their burial." Nevertheless, it was a business decision that some African American funeral directors were hesitant to make. Although every funeral had the potential of adding to their income by building loyalties, some were reluctant to carry this temporary loss of income "If you do the baby well, when the mother or daddy dies, we'll get them on down the road. Some of them don't see it, but children's funerals give directors exposure to a particular customer base." Certainly, the unexpected association we entered into with Lea Funeral Home will carry a certain weight with our family in future years. Another African American funeral home in North Carolina forfeited that potential customer base with at least one black family whose five-year-old daughter had been tragically killed in an automobile

Scarborough and Son. Durham, N.C. *The News and Observer*

accident in the spring of 1997. Ironically, family members had recently
discussed the question of whether they would ever use a white funeral
home and agreed that they would not. After the child's death, however,
when the black establishment in question would not extend them the
credit to bury the little girl, and when a white funeral home did exactly
that, their sentiments changed. It is likely, as well, that as other deaths
occur within that family, the white business has the benefit of loyalty
that the black business sacrificed to their "business" decision.

The adult, professional children of the elder morticians, having entered the business themselves, were included among the members who
attended the national and state conventions. Many of this younger generation grew up in homes that housed both the family and the family's
business. One young man explained how he grew up to "stand next to
his father," working right alongside him in the funeral home. He saw
his first dead body at thirteen, while looking for his father in the back
rooms of the funeral home, ducking his head into hallways, calling out
for "Pops," opening and closing doors, until he picked the door to the
embalming rooms and saw "gentlemen back there embalming." He recalled, "I used to really dislike coming down here, and I was quite frightened about death and dying and bodies." He apparently got over these

fears and, although he dabbled in other careers, finally went to mortuary school because he didn't want to be the son who would "turn over the business to strangers." His circuitous route back to the family's (funeral) home was not unusual. There were third- and fourth-generation morticians who worked as flight attendants, office workers, school counselors, and even ministers before, later in life, coming "home" (Chen 1E).

Children whose parents were in the business harbored many strange understandings of what happened in the back rooms of their homes. Some of the smallest children marched into the annual business meeting of the NFDMA, wearing T-shirts printed with the association logo and the phrase "Future Mortician." In my conversations with them about their parents' occupation, one explained, "they hang [the deceased] up to dry, and then they dress them up and put them in those boxes." "I get to push around the baskets [caskets]," another youngster told me, "but I can't go in there where he gets the dead peoples from."

"Where do they come from?" I asked.

"From the hospital."

Another youngster interrupted. "No! No he don't! He gets them out of the freezer and has to wait thirty minutes, and then he can come in to eat dinner. After that, then they unfreeze, and he puts clothes on them, and then we put them in the car, and I help."

"He gets them out from under the ground," I was told by an assertive eight-year-old girl. "And then, he puts those fancy dresses on them [the industry's name for these is 'garments'], and then he puts them back. After that we can eat."

Some morticians claimed that adults were not much better informed. One was told by a grieving sister who had lingered by the casket of her brother, "Well, I better go, so you can put him back in the freezer."

"Excuse me?" he inquired.

"Well, I know that he's going to melt if you don't take him out the casket soon."

For the record, the deceased do not melt. Nor do legs have to be cut off for half-couch displays. One young professional explained that when he was a child, he always tried to look into and past the half-closed lid to see what was covered up. The full-couch display (a fully open casket lid) may rid some of the half-a-body and missing-legs perception — but there are other understandings that are as astonishing to the professionals.

Embalming, for instance, does not require refrigeration, nor do undertakers have to remove the body's organs in order to begin the embalming process, pharaonic stories of ancient Egypt notwithstanding. Although bodies that have been autopsied may arrive at the undertaker's without bowels (the hospital may dispose of them after pathology), or with the organs placed inside the body cavity in a plastic bag (undertakers will inject embalming solution into such bags), neither disemboweling nor "ice caskets" are among current practices of the professionals. Ice caskets and trays with ice placed on the trunks of the dead did not work particularly well. They leaked, actually causing bodies to decompose more rapidly. Both methodologies gave way, early in the century, to embalming. This practice of replacing the body's fluids with chemicals can also include the use of a hollow needle—a trocar—to replace fluids in the chest and abdomen with "cavity fluids." After an arterial incision (usually in the carotid artery) drains the blood from the deceased, the blood is replaced by embalming fluid.

Many children (and some adults) believe stories of dead people suddenly sitting up on the embalming table—it doesn't happen. However, as rigor mortis advances through a body, it can cause a limb to move. C.C. told me about an attempt he once made to get a corpse into a basket to remove it from the house and how, when he bent it (rigor had not yet fully set in), there was a sudden belch from the dead body. From that point on, he made sure he handled the other end. He also remembered going out to a mental institution to retrieve a body one night that was especially dark and dreary.

> When we got there we could never go through the front door—bodies were always kept around back, and there was never any light back there. I remember walking through the pathway, certain I could hear somebody else's footsteps echoing my own. When we finally got the body loaded in the car, we looked back and one of his arms had fallen outside the basket. It was probably an effect of rigor, but we just knew he wasn't dead at all, and if he hadn't been in that insane asylum for a good reason before that, he would be when we told him where he was.

At the end of the twentieth century, these narratives of business and exchange and their embedded texts of absence and loss found themselves woven into a cultural fabric. Black death—that is, the dying of

African Americans that was in some way related to cultural identity—
continued to be specific and identifiable, as did cultural familiarity with
and acknowledgment of the consequences of loss. The violent absence of
our children especially, whether buried in urban cemeteries or interred
in rural prisons, forced a consistent reckoning. Author John Wideman
underscored the culturally pervasive black experience with this unfath-
omable absence. "In the rituals of mourning for our lost children, there
seems to be no sense of communal, general loss, no comprehension of
larger forces. . . . Funerals for our young are daily, lonely occurrences. In
some urban ghetto or another somewhere in America, at least once a day
a small Black congregation will gather together to try to repair the hole in
a brother or mother's soul with the balm of singing, prayer, the laying on
of dark hands on darkened spirits" (126). Especially bitter was the way in
which absence and loss, politics, business, and industry found a partner-
ship. The booming economy of state investments in a prison industrial
complex, legislation that assured a consistent prison population, and the
changing nature of the funeral business revealed a certain experience of
African America. And these issues and events each became a particular
story because of and through the matrix of a specifically racialized era in
the history of the United States—surely, a generational consequence of
an earlier "peculiar" institution. The dense weave locking the threads of
black death framed a century as well as a people.

If we must die,

then let us nobly die.

—Claude McKay,

"If We Must Die"

Mortifications

HOW *WE* DIE

Black folk died in mournful collectives and in disconcerting circumstances. We died in riots and rebellions, as victims of lynching, from executions, murders, police violence, suicides, and untreated or undertreated diseases. In such deaths, being black selected the victim into a macabre fraternity. Certainly, there were innumerable personal stories and discrete situations, both noble and ignoble. But, collectively, the story of how *we* died shaped a tragic community narrative.

Many years ago, on a bus trip in upstate New York with the Roosevelt Field Club, my sister and I sat with our group of hikers, just before disembarking on our annual expedition to Niagara Glen at the edge of the rocky slopes of the Canadian side of Niagara Falls gorge and the river's tumultuous rapids. It was the habit of our group to sing, and I don't recall who suggested a certain spiritual, it might have been my sister Karen, or me. But I remember distinctly the sharp voice and even the aggrieved tone of one of the members of our group—Juanita Zbrezyny—who loudly declared that she hated those songs because they "all sound like a funeral." I felt hushed and guiltily marked by her comment, ashamed and sorry to have been associated with something that would not appropriately elevate the mood of our happy occasion. I've remembered her comment these many years, always with chagrin that I had not delivered a proper and stinging retort and with regret that I felt so vulnerable. Today I think of my reaction as evidence of how, even as a youngster, I had developed some sensitivity related to the idea of my color and my association of my color to the experiences (as well as the songs) of black folk. In the last chapter of *Souls,* Du Bois wrote of spirituals as "The Sorrow Songs" and claimed them as "the music of an unhappy people, of the children of disappointment; they tell of death and suffering and unvoiced longing toward a truer world, of misty wanderings and hidden ways." Juanita's sense was perceptive and right. And my response was a chilled acknowledgment of their haunting potential and my vulnerability.

"The only thing I have to do is stay black and die"

This aphorism is an old and familiar retort in the black community. Judged purely by its grammar, it is an odd phrase, for it identifies two "only things" that the speaker has to do. Yet, this tellingly simple and straightforward statement says exactly what it means. Over time, as the fact of a color line became absolutely distinguishable, and even predictable, staying black and being dead formed a singular relationship. What contributed to the persistence of that association between color and death? And what did it mean to the culture's collective sense of itself that mortality was associated with appearance?

After the Civil War, America's troubling response to its newly freed black citizenry was a constructed pattern of violence that confirmed the aphorism's saliency. The lynchings that laced this country made it perfectly clear that color was a danger in postbellum America. Many understood that law enforcement officials' benign neglect toward, and often even participation in, lynchings placed the human rights of black folk out of bounds of the protection of the law. The extent to which lynching became associated with black presence, rather than black conduct, inculcated this sense of vulnerability. As the nineteenth century turned, the violence directed toward blacks did not dissipate. In fact, it increased. More than four thousand African Americans were lynched between 1882 and 1942 (J. Mitchell 31). Documents record hundreds upon hundreds of African Americans who were twentieth-century victims to this vicious manner of death (see Table 1). One report noted that "lynching focused the hostilities of a mob, often of riot proportions, on a single human object, who became a symbol, an actor in a violent racial

TABLE I. Black Victims of White Lynch Mobs
by State, 1882–1930

STATE	NO. OF VICTIMS
Deep South	
Mississippi	462
Georgia	423
Louisiana	283
Alabama	262
South Carolina	143
Border South	
Florida	212
Tennessee	174
Arkansas	162
Kentucky	118
North Carolina	75

Reproduced from Tolnay and Beck, *A Festival of Violence* (37).

drama" (J. Mitchell 32). It was the singular, colored vulnerabilities of these "single human objects" that made the crime so wicked and vicious. And it was the common understanding of that vulnerability, whether one was directly affected by this violence or just afraid of it, that forged a cultural association between color and death.

Some painful version of this history of lynching, either as literature or as factual record, constructs the stories of black deaths. In the first third of the century, in the South especially, where the majority of lynchings occurred, America's experience with the crime was familiar and complicit. Lynching is a pitiful example of how *we* die—a phenomenon complicated by its appearance in our literary records and in aesthetic expression, as well as by its longevity. It found victims, in mass numbers or tragically alone, throughout the century. In one of the earliest records of the twentieth century, the *Denver Republican* described the aftermath of Fred Alexander's death. He was lynched in Leavenworth, Kansas, in the first month of 1901.

The U.S. Postal Service was complicit in the commodification of this lynching. This postcard could be purchased, endorsed with the message of choice, and sent through the U.S. mail to friends and family.

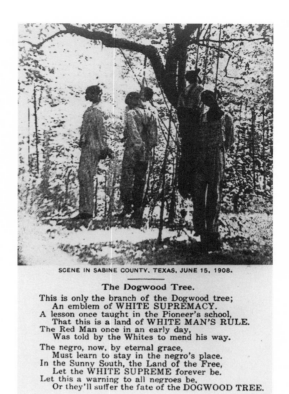

SCENE IN SABINE COUNTY, TEXAS, JUNE 15, 1908.

The Dogwood Tree.

This is only the branch of the Dogwood tree;
    An emblem of WHITE SUPREMACY.
A lesson once taught in the Pioneer's school,
    That this is a land of WHITE MAN'S RULE.
The Red Man once in an early day,
    Was told by the Whites to mend his way.
The negro, now, by eternal grace,
    Must learn to stay in the negro's place.
In the Sunny South, the Land of the Free,
    Let the WHITE SUPREME forever be.
Let this a warning to all negroes be,
    Or they'll suffer the fate of the DOGWOOD TREE.

As soon as the crowd saw that life was extinct, it began to slowly disperse. There were hundreds of the more morbid, however, who stayed to the last. . . . There was a continuous stream of people going to the scene of the burning. These were persons who had been unable to get away from their work in the afternoon, but were determined not to miss the awful spectacle. When the fire had died down sufficiently to allow the crowd to approach what remained of Alexander, there was a wild scramble to obtain relics. Bits of charred flesh, pieces of chain, scraps of wood — everything that could possibly serve as a souvenir, was seized on with morbid avidity by the eager people. (J. Paul Mitchell 34–35)

The evidence of our history continued to argue for some association between color and death, much as one might have wished it to be otherwise. As if in response, African American cultural practices — music, literature, and visual arts—all used the facts of black death and dying as their subject. There was an overlap of fiction and fact, artistic subject and streetscape, lyric and conversation. The spirituals, those "sorrow songs," also, of course, captured black melancholy. But that spirit was as pervasive and evident when Billie Holiday first sang Lewis Allen's lyrics, "Strange Fruit." An elegy to black bodies as the hanging fruit of southern trees, this song debuted at the end of a decade in which—although the twenty black men who had been lynched during the decade "amounted to nowhere near the numbers at the turn of the century," according to historian Paula Giddings—"the news reports of the horrible crimes were made more vivid by the technological advances in communication and photography" (206). Angela Davis wrote, "'Strange Fruit' publicly bore witness to the corporeal devastation occasioned by lynching . . . [and] compellingly stated the fact of lynching and contested its cultural permanency" (194). Lynching crossed cultures in the powerful threat of its imagery; blacks and whites both were too familiar with its potential.

The twentieth century's most consistently damning literary record of violent deaths like lynching are found in the writing of "protest" writer Richard Wright. Literary scholar Trudier Harris wrote that his "preoccupation with the ritual violence [and] one of the prevailing dangers of black life . . . paralleled in part the increased concern in the 1920s and 1930s over the lynching of Blacks and the brutality with which they were killed. . . . [O]ther black writers [experienced] a heightened attention in their literary productions" (95). By midcentury, Wright's powerful collection of short stories and his novels created a grim literary record that spared no reader the horror of the black lives lost.

Wright, though the most prominent, was not the first writer to tackle lynchings head-on. Sutton Griggs's 1905 novel, *The Hindered Hand*, graphically detailed an episode that Harris labeled "a shockingly stomach-turning" lynching. Griggs's scene foreshadowed the role lynching would play in both black literature and black life:

> The mob decided to torture their victims before killing them and began on Foresta first. . . . One by one her fingers were cut off and tossed into the crowd to be scrambled for. A man with a cork screw came forward, ripped Foresta's clothing to her waist, bored into her breast with the corkscrew and pulled forth the live quivering flesh. Poor Bud her helpless husband closed his eyes . . . [but] . . . Men gathered about him and

forced his eyelids open so that he could see all. When it was thought that Foresta had been tortured sufficiently, attention was turned to Bud. His fingers were cut off one by one and the corkscrew was bored into his legs and arms. A man with a club struck him over the head, crushing his skull and forcing an eyeball to hang down from the socket by a thread. . . . After three full hours had been spent in torturing the two . . . the photographer present [took] a picture of the scene. This being over, the match was applied and the flames leaped up eagerly and encircled the writhing forms of Bud and Foresta. (Griggs 133–35)

This episode was horrific enough as fiction, yet Griggs constructed the appalling text from an actual event, which was reported in the *Vicksburg (Mississippi) Evening Post.* The news account was chillingly parallel to the fictive rendition:

When the two Negroes were captured, they were . . . forced to hold out their hands while one finger at a time was chopped off. The fingers were distributed as souvenirs. The ears of the murderers were cut off. Holbert was beaten severely, his skull was fractured, and one of his eyes, knocked out with a stick, hung by a shred from the socket. . . . A large corkscrew . . . was bored into the flesh of the man and woman, in the arms, legs and body, and then pulled out, the spirals tearing out big pieces of raw, quivering flesh every time it was withdrawn. (Harris 1, 2)

In 1906, following the black-man-accused/white-woman-accuser trend of these lynchings, a black man accused of raping a white woman was sentenced to die in Tennessee. U.S. Supreme Court Justice Oliver Wendell Holmes issued a stay of execution so that the court might decide the weight of the evidence. Justice Holmes's and the Supreme Court's intervention notwithstanding (or perhaps even serving as a contributing factor), the prisoner was summarily taken out of his jail cell and lynched by a mob of whites focused on their own particular brand of justice. The Supreme Court was so outraged by this defiance of its authority that it immediately charged the sheriff and deputies with contempt of court and found them guilty in the only criminal trial in Supreme Court history.

Lynch mobs had both a macabre and sick sense of occasion and space, and one that fully compromised any possibility that judicial au-

Aftermath of the violence in Rosewood, Florida.
Florida State Archives.

thorities were not complicit. William Fitzhugh Brundage wrote that "public mobs chose the site of their executions for explicitly symbolic reasons." And he noted the way in which their tutelage of their control of public order extended to the ways in which they would predetermine the sites for this violence. In Griggs's novel, Bud and Foresta were lynched at the scene of the white man's murder of which they were accused. "The mob that lynched Albert Aiken near Lincolnton, Georgia, on May 24, 1909, stormed the county jail, carried their victim three miles away to the scene of his alleged crime, and hanged him . . . 'in view to let the many negroes in the neighborhood see that it is time that they quieted down and stopped their efforts to ride over the farmers in that section'" (141).

These mobs additionally had the assurance of a history of judicial "benign" neglect toward their activity. Sometimes, mobs hanged their victims in the black community itself—at sites near the victims' family homes, next to cemeteries, or at the scenes of the alleged crimes. At other times, these rituals of violence occurred in public squares or right outside the courthouse or jailhouse in which the victim had been incarcerated. Sociologists Stewart Tolnay and E. M. Beck explained, "Through their actions, white mobs demonstrated the ability to run roughshod over the rights, lives, and property of the black community. Mob action etched clearly in the minds of blacks their relative standing in the southern social hierarchy. The message was given additional emphasis by the notorious reluctance of legal authorities to arrest, prosecute, and punish members of lynch mobs despite the fact that such people were often easily identifiable" (113).

These were not just crimes of a raging mob in pursuit of one or two persons. Sometimes an entire community was targeted. In Rosewood, Florida, the precipitating event was a familiar one—the accusations of a white woman against a black man. The concluding event was just as familiar. On New Year's Day, 1923, all of Rosewood—its homes and gathering places, the lodge and the churches, as well as its residents were marked for destruction and death. Seventy years after the New Year's day tragedy, journalist Lori Rozsa wrote that Rosewood survivors were

> still tortured with the lingering image of a parent or grandparent being lynched or shot, of the family home being burned to the ground, of crawling through the woods in the dead of night . . . hiding from an armed and crazy mob . . . hunted and attacked for nothing more than their color. A black man whose left arm was paralyzed was forced to dig his own grave, then was shot and shoved into it. Another black man was hung from a tree in his front yard when he told the posse he couldn't lead them to the alleged rapist. A pregnant woman was shot as she tried to crawl under her porch for protection when the mob rode in. (Rozsa M4)

When Billie Holiday first sang "Strange Fruit" in the 1930s, it was, according to Angela Davis, "one of the most influential and profound examples—and continuing sites—of the intersection of music and social consciousness" (196). This kind of aesthetic intersection crisscrossed African American artistry. Acknowledging the potential significance of black artists' commentary about this social reality, but also recognizing the silence that they had been forced into by their government and foundation fellowships during the Harlem Renaissance years, the NAACP sponsored an exhibition in New York City that made it clear that the arts too spoke out about the crime of lynching. Their 1935 exhibition, "Art Commentary on Lynching," was finally hosted at the Arthur Newton

Galleries after the original exhibitor reneged. The Seligmann Galleries had canceled their agreement to host the show of multicultural artists — African American, white, and Asian — telling the *New York Times* that the show had been taken "merely on its artistic merits" and that the "outburst of opposition" ran counter to Seligmann's wish to "keep the galleries free of political thought or racial manifestations" ("Macabre Exhibition Canceled" 12 February 1935). One might easily read this cancellation as a historical repetition of the very issues of censorship and silencing that made lynching a pathetically vital and viable story in much of the twentieth century. Certainly lynching itself was a macabre production of white silence — and the artists who focused our gaze on this event in New York City vigorously and creatively disengaged the silence and the censorship.

One of the most disturbing pieces in the show that eventually opened at the Newton Gallery was the "sensational work of Reginald Marsh, a black and white titled 'This Is Her First Lynching.'" Its subject was a young girl being held above the heads of the crowd by her mother so that she could get a good view of the scene. Titles of other pieces in the show also dramatically understate the macabre content of the photos, which included George Bellows's "The Law is too Slow," William Mosby's "Dixie Holiday," and Harry Steinberg's "Southern Holiday." Although the efforts to secure a national tour for the New York City show failed, lynching stayed on the African American mind and within African America's experience throughout the century.

It is difficult to calculate the degree and complicity of white rage, fear, and distrust of black folk in these episodes. What is evident, though, is that a particularly powerful triggering mechanism for white rage was the black soldier's uniform.

Just prior to the return of World War I's black veterans, there had been a few years of decline in the number of lynchings in the United States. Just after the war, however, in 1919, lynchings increased. According to military historians Arthur Barbeau and Florette Henry, at least ten of the lynchings in that year were committed against black veterans. Pitifully characteristic was Daniel Mack who was lynched in Sylvester, Georgia, after returning home from France and making it clear that he had already fought abroad for human dignity and freedom and had no intentions of experiencing any mistreatment at home. For this indiscreet remark, he was sentenced to jail for thirty days. Before that month

Reginald Marsh depicts the way in which lynching's ritual was generational. In "This Is Her *First* Lynching" (my emphasis), the implication is clearly that there will be others in this child's life and that her attendance is anticipated.

was concluded, Mack was taken from his cell and, still wearing his military uniform, beaten to death. His fate was shared by an Arkansas veteran who dared to speak back to a white woman who told him to move from the sidewalk so that she could pass. He retorted that it was a free country and refused to do what was expected from all black folk at the time—move off the sidewalks so that whites would not even have to move around them to continue passage. His assertiveness led to a mob response. He was taken out of town, lashed to a tree with tire chains, and shot between forty and fifty times. Barbeau, whose book on black soldiers in World War I recalled these incidents, commented that "although the underlying causes of the riots were profoundly economic, social, and psychological, it was the return of black veterans that seemed to trigger riots everywhere in the country" (77–78). In Beaumont, Texas, a white southern population obsessed with the imagined menace of black men initiated a vicious confrontation with black soldiers who were readying themselves for duty in Europe's World War I battlefields. The black men who faced these mobs and had "a new black self-respect, conceived in battle and inured to violence," fought back, and seventeen whites were killed. As a result of the hastily arranged "trial" following this event, thirteen black soldiers were hanged for murder and mutiny. Given the developing patterns of violence as the nation's most consistent response to black servicemen and veterans, some of these events were almost predictable.

The war years saw urban areas in the United States form a macabre fraternity. From 1915 to 1919, more than twenty cities erupted in violence and mayhem, their tragic link being race. These trends forged an ironic cultural relationship between ethnic identity, military service, heroism, and death. Today, cultural historians refer to the worst of these years— 1919—as the "Red Summer." During that summer, there were riots in Elaine, Arkansas; Washington, D. C.; Chicago; Norfolk, Virginia; Knoxville, Tennessee; New York City; and Longview, Texas. But two years earlier, in July of 1917, a riot in East St. Louis proved a tragic precursor of the summer to come.

It is no coincidence that the *St. Louis Globe-Democrat* chose to headline this episode "Race War." It unambiguously connected urban riot with foreign soldiering and the communities that were empowered and authorized by the example of these newly emboldened citizens. One editorial cartoon pictured a black woman, kneeling in front of the president

This headline captures the language of the World War I era, as well as the panic specific to this event. "War" is the operative term.
St. Louis Globe-Democrat.

with two children clinging to her skirts. Smoke rises ominously from the skyline of East St. Louis behind her. While he clutches a newspaper with his famous wartime proclamation—"The World Must Be Made Safe for Democracy"—as its banner, the black mother pleads, "Mr. President, why not make America safe for Democracy?" (Rudwick 58).

A carload of white men drove through the black community and shot indiscriminately and without provocation into black homes, sparking the riot in East St. Louis, Illinois. Black residents responded to the crisis in kind, arming themselves to protect their homes. A police car investigating the incident, perhaps mistaken for the original car of shooters, was attacked, and its occupants were killed. Almost immediately, white citizens of St. Louis took indiscriminate revenge on any black they saw. Crowds drove into black neighborhoods and beat, burned, and killed their residents. Some newspapers reported mobs of "10,000 blood-crazed whites" roaming the cities. Although these numbers were certainly exaggerated, "there was no doubt that they had the encouragement of thousands of spectators watching from the sidewalks" (Rudwick 44). These roving mobs of white men and boys left their victims bloodied and beaten, lying helplessly in the streets where they were shot and killed by mob leaders. Some African Americans—women and children included—attempted to find refuge in their homes but were forced to escape when their homes were torched. "Residents faced a terrible decision—to remain inside and await incineration or to risk slaughter by gunfire outside" (Rudwick 46). A report from the event in the *St. Louis Republic* described the unimaginable scene: "A crazed Negro would dash from his burning home, sometimes with a revolver in his hand. Immediately revolvers by the score would be fired. He would zig-zag through the spaces between buildings. Then a well-directed shot would strike him. He would leap into the air. There were deep shouts, intermingled with shrill feminine ones. The flames would creep to the body. The Negro would writhe, attempt to get up, more shots would be fired. The flames would eat their way to him, past him, and further east along Railroad Avenue" (46).

Final body counts for these horrors were difficult to make accurate. Mutilated bodies were found days later—on Independence Day, ironically—floating in the Cahokia Creek, verifying rumors that the marauding whites had indiscriminately tossed some of their victims in a creek. Many corpses, bloated from their watery graves, would re-emerge; but some reports claimed that "ashes and burned bones of victims consumed by the fires" and other charred remains, which would leave no evidence of atrocities, were thrown into the creek. Following is testimony of the local coroner to the investigating congressional committee regarding the torched victims he examined:

> *Congressman Johnson:* Doctor, to what extent were they burned . . . ?
> *Dr. Renner:* They were just burned to a crisp; as much as a human body can burn without being in ashes; enough to be agglutinated together, showing the form of the human body.
> *Johnson:* The bones were of course left.
> *Renner:* The bones were left and the skulls were left.
> *Johnson:* And the cooked flesh?
> *Renner:* The cooked flesh was in a crisp. (Rudwick 51)

Numbers in the press ranged from 100 to more than 400 "Negro" dead. However, the investigating congressional committee used local undertakers' reports to make their "understated" estimates of about forty deceased. In a pattern that became morbidly consistent for post–World War I riots, including those in Rosewood and Tulsa, black mortuaries could only bury those they found. Throughout the century, survivors continued to lament the family and folk who just disappeared and could not even be funeralized.

The 1917 parade in New York City was silent, punctuated only by the beat of drums accompanying the grim participants. *Bettman/CORBIS*

Across the country, African Americans marched in protest of the events in East St. Louis. The parades in black communities were deliberately and dramatically silent, except for the accompanying beat of marchers' drums. In the New York City march, the silence of 15,000 marchers and those who watched on the sidelines marked the gravity of the loss in Illinois. In *Jazz,* Toni Morrison adds imaginative context and character to the drama of the actual event:

> That day in July . . . the beautiful men were cold. In typical summer weather, sticky and bright, Alice Manfred stood for three hours on Fifth Avenue marveling at the cold black faces and listening to drums saying what the graceful women and the marching men could not. What was possible to say was already in print on a banner that repeated a couple of promises from the Declaration of Independence and waved over the head of its bearer. But what was meant came from the drums. It was July in 1917 and the beautiful faces were cold and quiet; moving slowly into the space the drums were building for them. (53)

The explanation in Morrison's story of the event is close enough to the social historian's interpretations to argue the cooperative venture of black fiction and black life. "Some said the rioters were disgruntled veterans who had fought in all-colored units, were refused the services of the YMCA, over there and over here, and came home to white violence more intense than when they enlisted and, unlike the battles they fought in Europe, stateside fighting was pitiless and totally without honor. Others said they were whites terrified by the wave of southern Negroes flooding the towns, searching for work and places to live" (57).

The battles America fought abroad for democracy were consistently shadowed by the battles African Americans fought at home for the same. And, as the nation moved its mostly white armed forces to Europe, blacks in the United States moved north. The historic moment known as the Great Migration saw its most significant shifts in population during the war years. During World War I, blacks migrating to the urban areas in the north caused significant employment displacement as they took the jobs that had been vacated by whites who were in the armed services. After the war, the competition between returning white veterans and black laborers was deliberately manipulated by employers, and it contributed to some of the discontent. Additionally and critically inflammatory were the attitude and demeanor of what Alain Locke labeled the "New Negro." These soldiers returned from abroad, where they had earned a measure of respect and gratitude for their contributions to democracy, to a United States that perceived them as a threat. Blacks wearing uniforms (which included government-issued weaponry) and commanding a newly authoritative self-respect threatened an America that had cultivated a different psyche and rewarded a different demeanor in its black folk.

In 1919, Alexander Jackson was director of the "Negro" branch of the Chicago YMCA on Wabash Avenue. Speaking to the City Club of Chicago, Jackson explained that "the pressures of migration and housing, combined with a new mind among colored soldiers," could lead to trouble. Jackson warned that the Negro soldiers were returning with a "consciousness of power hitherto unrealized" (Waskow 39). Military historian Bernard C. Nalty also noted the association between the military service of blacks and the summer's tragedies. In one specific incident, Nalty writes of a "returning veteran, still in uniform, [who] was beaten to death in Georgia, not because he had been accused of rape or murder, but because he had vowed, while in jail for ignoring a 'whites only' sign, never to yield to Jim Crow" (Nalty 126).

Soldiers' stories of the Second World War were distressingly similar to those of the First. Black soldiers were murdered in South Carolina, Texas, and Alabama. In Little Rock, Arkansas, white military police killed a black soldier whom they had arrested for public intoxication. While Sgt. Thomas Foster lay dazed on the ground, they fired five fatal shots into his body. When the Justice Department refused to prosecute because "there was no prospect of conviction," Adam Clayton Powell castigated their decision in an editorial titled "Mr. President, Just What Is It We Are Fighting For?" and argued that "more Negro men have been killed and beaten, so far this year, than in any similar period of this century." Powell predicted that that "great tide of racial hatred" would move the nation "rapidly toward a national race riot" (Brandt 130). The Harlem uprising of 1943 was one dimension of that troubled forecast.

With its involvement of a black serviceman, the Harlem riot was classic for the age. A police encounter with Private Robert Bandy, a member of the 730th Military Police Battalion in Jersey City, precipitated the event. On the evening of 1 August 1943, Bandy and his mother were in the lobby of the Braddock Hotel on the corner of 126th Street and Eighth Avenue. Bandy came to the assistance of a young woman who was arguing with a police officer — a rookie patrolman named James Collins — in the lobby of the hotel. The officer physically restrained the woman — Marjorie Polite — and in her panic she called to hotel guests to "protect me from this white man!" According to historian Nat Brandt, "Bandy started to grapple with Collins, to loosen his grip on Polite. His mother joined him. In the scuffle, Bandy grabbed the policeman's nightstick and struck Collins on the head, knocking him to the ground. Bandy started to bolt, but Collins . . . pull[ed] his service revolver from its holster and fired at the retreating soldier" (185). The story spread with the crowd that gathered around the hotel and in the street. Although Bandy had not been wounded so seriously as to prevent his walking to Sydenham Hospital, a block away, an alternative but, given the history, credible story developed that a black soldier was dying and that he had been shot by a white policeman — right in front of his mother. By nightfall, the rumor was that the soldier was dead. Columnist Walter White commented that the rumor "fell like a torch into dry summer grass." Brandt reflects, "No one doubted that a white policeman had killed him. Hadn't cops shot black GIs in Louisiana, Arkansas, Texas? Was New York another Detroit? Another Beaumont?" (186).

Harlem joined a tragic litany of cities across the United States that shared the repeated trauma of twentieth-century riots. The racialist rage and indignation that fueled these episodes had a specific relationship to the experiences of black veterans. These violent encounters framed an essential passed-on narrative as they revealed how black soldiers consistently died as a result of extraterritorial constructions of America's politics. Black veterans' war stories were engaged at home and abroad, and did not dissipate after the end of the war. Nor were these narratives disabled after the soldiers died. Instead, they lingered, haunting the national subject of democracy and dislocation. Consider the letter that photographer Gordon Parks received, a culturally coded postmortem of a black veteran:

> Dear Gordon,
>
> Sorry to miss you but I'm on my way to Steubenville with Judy Edwards' body. As you probably heard, poor Judy spun in and I had to take his body all the way to Detroit because "there are no facilities" for handling Negro dead up there at Oscoda. It's about three hundred miles from Oscoda to Detroit, and in a goddamn Army ambulance you can imagine how long it took us to get there. Even as I write this to you, my feelings keep swinging from a murderous rage to frustration. How could anybody do anything like this? His body was lying wrapped in a tarpaulin in the back of the ambulance. . . . We have all suffered some brutal indignities from the whites in this country but this was the final indignity of all. . . . I felt shame and revulsion for having to wear the uniform I had on. The driver seemed to be caught up in the same mood. We were two of the loneliest soldiers in the world. . . . (David and Crane 153–54)

Parks's friend was tragically not alone. Throughout the century, African American soldiers continued to earn the antipathy of their nation, even though they died fighting for the country.

The riotous response—often no different from a lynch mob's—to a militarized black America would emerge again in the era of activist civil rights. But prior to that moment, during the 1940s and 1950s, a "social and political activism" became apparent in a cadre of African American visual artists. Elizabeth Catlett's linocut print "I Have a Special Fear for My Loved Ones" (1946), from her *Negro Woman Series,* was among the most riveting of the era. Art historian Richard Powell writes that Catlett's print "revisited a grisly theme that so many American artists had explored a decade earlier, and took on a new urgency from Catlett's inclusion of three, cropped-off pairs of feet, so placed as to suggest either spectators, standing in perspective, or more lynch mob victims, hanging above the body that had already been cut down" (Powell 116). There were both audience and company.

In Mississippi, in 1964, the lynching of three civil-rights workers—James Chaney, Andrew Goodwin, and Michael Schwerner—forged a bitter link between the first half of the century's history of lynch mobs and the second half's civil-rights violence. One significant difference was the defiant response of black communities to the violence directed toward them during the civil-rights era. Indeed, riots and rebellions became hallmark responses to injustice. Reporters covering the trial of the white police officers who brutalized Los Angeles black motorist Rodney King in 1993 repeatedly asked their interviewees whether they thought there would be a riot in response to the not-guilty verdict. There was. But the reporters did not ask their question in a vacuum—they remembered the connection between "no justice-no peace" from the Watts uprising of 1965.

The western states, especially California, had been strongly affected by the Great Migration, as their black communities grew substantially. The congestion of Harlem in the 1920s, for instance, compared in kind but not in degree to that in Los Angeles, where the black population had increased eightfold in the 1950s (Horne 36). Conflicts of race, color, and ethnicity were especially frequent in this city, due to demographics that were among the most radically stratified—economically as well as ethnically—of any city in the United States. By midcentury, blacks in Los Angeles "were greeted by a compounded racism and caught in a crisis of rapid change. They were coming to the city while jobs, which historically had been disproportionately in the suburbs, continued to flow into outlying regions" (Horne 36). Racial and class prejudice joined color and ethnic prejudice, clashed with religious biases, and fought regional biases. The turbulent uprising of violence and death in the Watts neighborhood seemed almost inevitable. Social scientist Gerald Horne

Elizabeth Catlett's linocut acknowledges both company and crowd in this ambiguous lynching scene. Do the three pairs of feet suggest other victims or a gathered crowd?

described it as a "riot by the LAPD against Black LA" and underscored how the response of black Los Angeles to the violence of their condition was a significant dimension of a documented history of struggle and revolt against racism in America. On the evening of 13 August 1965,

> the first official death by gunshot wound was recorded. Leon Posey was a slightly built twenty-one-year-old African-American. This native of Texas . . . lived at 126 West 93rd. . . . He died . . . at the hands of the LAPD at 6:30 P.M. at 89th and Broadway in a death ruled "accidental" by the coroner. According to Emerson Lashley, a witness to the shooting, Posey was "standing outside the barber shop." They had gone there together, and serendipity dictated that Lashley was in a chair and not standing where his friend met death. "People had started gathering, you know, further down, north of Broadway. So, he would go outside, to see, you know, just what was going on. . . . [T]he next thing I knew, then I heard some shots. Then, I just saw him fall." Police were apparently firing wildly, and "people were running." . . . [A] black community weighted down with years of oppression and with encoded memories of resistance was striking back and accumulating the merit badges and necessities of consumer society—couches, food, fans. Leon Posey, the young black Texan, was the first victim of this historic departure. (70–71)

Others who joined the grim parade of victims hailed from Atlanta, Georgia; Elaine, Arkansas; and Tulsa, Oklahoma. The gathered dead from the Rosewood, Florida, massacre of 1923 bore a tragic similarity to those who lost their lives in riots of the civil rights era in New York, Detroit, and Chicago.

The involvement of law enforcement officials of course recalled the lynchings and other crimes of the early part of the century. But their complicity reached new levels as the century progressed. Historian Gail O'Brien documented the rise in police abuse in urban locales in the postwar era and explained its association with "politics and the distribution of power": "The very anonymity of urban blacks often led police to typecast all with whom they came in contact as 'bad niggers' . . . and to confront them aggressively. When officers were exceptionally abusive, African Americans frequently responded in kind, so that killings by police and killings of police tended to be high in the same locales" (141). The

Aftermath of police action in Philadelphia's MOVE massacre.
Bettman/CORBIS.

nightmare of Philadelphia's official response to MOVE, John Africa's organization, was one horrific example. Another was the 1999 murder of Amadou Diallo, who stood harmlessly in the vestibule of his New York City apartment building and, judged suspicious by policemen, was shot forty-one times. One black parent who gathered with the crowds of protesters following the Diallo shooting raised his infant son in the air and shouted, "Shoot him now!" in an enraged and mournful acknowledgment of his child's color-coded potential (Chua-Eoan 24).

In May 1985 in Philadelphia, the city mistrusted and feared an "alternative" family who had taken up residence on Osage Avenue and whose dress, manners, and music openly flaunted the community's norm. Each family member had taken the surname "Africa." While neighbors worried over the safety of their own children and complained of noise and disruption, the city focused on a cache of weapons thought to be on the property. This anxiety turned into a murderous carelessness with the lives and property of all on Osage Avenue and its surrounding community: after Wilson Goode, then mayor of the city, issued warrants designed to force the family off the premises, and after those warrants failed to have the desired effect, Goode ordered the police to bomb the house.

The bombing plan had been thoroughly planned beforehand and certainly was not, as some claimed, a frustrated act of last resort. A series published in the *Philadelphia Inquirer* detailed the weeks and months of secret police testing of "various explosives," which were used in the attack.

Seven adults and six children—all immediate and extended members of the Africa family—were inside their home on 13 May 1985. Only the child Michael, known as "Birdie" Africa, and an adult, Ramona Africa, managed to escape. Reporters recall the scene:

> Suddenly a naked child dashed from the flaming wreckage. . . . A team
> of policemen charged in pursuit. They grabbed him by the shoulders
> and just carried him off. . . . His feet kept paddling, like he was walking on air. "It shook the whole house up," said Michael in his videotaped testimony to an investigative commission. . . . He and the other
> children were huddled under wet blankets in the basement during the
> siege. The MOVE adults told the children to run after the bomb was
> dropped, but they were too terrified to go. Michael described how one
> of the adults . . . tried to carry a 9-year old boy, Tomasa, . . . to safety,
> but was driven back by gunfire. "It was do-do-do-do-do-do like that,
> like going off, like bullets were going after each other." As the smoke
> thickened in the house, Michael saw Tomasa lying silent and still on
> the lap of Michael's own mother, Rhonda. . . . The charred remains of
> Conrad, Rhonda and Tomasa were found in the rubble the next day.
> (Kunen 68)

The century's consistency seemed to be that black folk, especially and specifically black males, were likely to die before their time in America. The fear of white rage, especially when white women were victims and or accusers, gave the death penalty—whether an extrajudicial terror or a juridical consequence—a particularly intimate history with African America.

A look at just one southern state provides startling evidence of the vulnerability of black men to execution, that state-sanctioned murder. Between 1923, "when the state began carrying out executions for the various circuits throughout Georgia," and 1991, "81 percent of those persons legally executed [this excludes lynchings] by the state have been black" (Winn). Georgia, like other southern states, had a peculiar legal tradition—"only black men died for the crime of rape" or the allegation of rape, "and nearly always it was for the rape of a white woman" (Robertson 5). Late-century activists against the death penalty constructed their argument in part by making clear the ways in which the race (and gender) of the victim was statistically relevant to the execution of the death penalty, with black males accounting for a disproportionate number of those convicted and sentenced to death.

The literary record took advantage of the drama inherent in such confrontations. As the twentieth century approached its midpoint, Richard Wright's *Native Son* placed his character Bigger in a strategically dangerous situation—in the home of white folk. When Bigger accidentally kills the white family's daughter, all readers can predict that his death is to be the novel's denouement. The execution of Bigger—who before being led to the death chamber pitifully asks his mother and friends for forgiveness, pleading that "what I killed for, I am"—is one of the most tragic and sensational literary stories, especially of its decade. Few recall, however, that the actual experiences of Robert Nixon, who was executed in Chicago in 1937, formed the fact of Wright's fiction. In its drama and pathos, and for its impact on family and community, Nixon's story challenges that of Wright's Bigger. Chicago newspapers relentlessly followed Nixon's case, headlining the pursuit and capture "Hunt Sex Moron." On 3 June, the *Tribune* headline ran "Science Traps Negro Moron"; on 4 June, it reproduced the map he drew for police under the banner "Moron Maps Crime Expedition"; and on the next day, it gathered its by that time loyal followers of the story with the header "Brick Slayer Is Likened to Jungle Beast: Ferocity Is Reflected in Nixon's Features," detailing impressions of "a giant ape . . . baring his teeth . . . in a snarling attitude" who "demonstrated his jungle strength and agility" for the police (Leavelle 6).

One of the most persistently offensive dimensions of these tragedies-turned-media events was the demeaning representation of black folk, as such occasions seemed to unleash the biases that challenged black humanity. Criminal activity, or the presumption thereof, allowed this invective to emerge uncritically and with seeming justification—but black folk in the twentieth century understood its signal and its malicious capability. In *Native Son,* a black preacher mournfully confronts Bigger, knowing Bigger had read the characterizations of himself in the *Tribune.* Understanding the racial dynamic encouraged in the news reports and the loss Bigger faces, in part because of that dynamic, the minister pleads with him to "fergit ever' thing but yo soul, son. Take yo mind off ever'thing but eternal life. Fergit whut the newspapers say. Fergit yuh's black" (279–80).

As if to revisit the mournful narrative of *Native Son* and the experience of a century of Bigger Thomases, Ernest Gaines published *A Lesson Before Dying* in 1993. Unlike Bigger Thomas or Robert Nixon, the character who faced execution in Gaines's novel was innocent. But this was not Gaines's emphasis; instead, he wrote a novel that forced his readers to confront the tremendous power of language on a society's consciousness about race, showing how police, the courts, and the media engage and affirm racially destructive language. And, to indicate its pervasiveness, Gaines gave the following text not to a prosecutor but to the defense attorney's appeal for his client Jefferson:

> Gentlemen of the jury, look at him—look at him—look at *this*. Do you see a man sitting here? Look at the shape of this skull, this face as flat as the palm of my hand—look deeply into those eyes. . . . A cornered animal . . . a trait inherited from his ancestors in the deepest jungle of blackest Africa. . . . What you see here is a thing that acts. . . . [How could] this man plan a robbery? O pardon me, pardon me, I surely did not mean to insult your intelligence by saying "man"— would you forgive me for committing such an error? . . . I would just as soon put a hog in the electric chair as this. (8)

Early in *A Lesson,* Gaines made clear its task to reclaim the human spirit that the courts had erased. The novel's task was not to save Jefferson from the execution imposed by a racist justice system but to save his personhood. As Jefferson faced electrocution, he wrote to his teacher: "good by mr wigin tell them im strong *tell them im a man*" (234; my emphasis).

A midcentury case in Virginia was characteristic. The *Richmond Afro-American* reported that the young men accused of raping a white girl were "forced by police to sign confessions of guilt" as they were "seated in a chair, ringed by police, one of whom held a night stick over their heads and told them that if they did not admit their guilt they would be beaten to death" ("One of Doomed" 1). Despite their pleas of innocence and evidence supporting that claim, evidence that the NAACP accused the governor of suppressing; despite the fact that no white man in the same state had been sentenced to death for the crime of rape, seven young men were led to the electric chair. Two of them—Booker Millner and Frank Hairston Jr., who was just twenty—shook hands with each other as they were being led to the chamber. And, "while waiting his turn in the chair," Millner prayed, "Lord . . . bless these ministers who have been so good to us, who have done all they could to help us, bless and forgive the men who are doing this to us. I thank you that the next time Frank and I shake hands, we won't have to do so through bars." They died in two groups. The first four were executed on Friday, 2 February 1951: Joe Henry Hampton was "seated" (strapped into the chair) at 8:05 A.M. and pronounced dead at 8:12; Howard Lee Hairston died at 8:32; Booker T. Millner at 8:49; and Frank Hairston at 9:05. The remaining three were executed the following Monday: John C. Taylor, 23, seated at 7:35, pronounced dead at 7:41; James L. Hairston, 22, seated at 7:51, dead at 8, and Francis DeS. Grayson, 38, seated at 8:10 dead at 8:15" ("Last 3").

Following their deaths, a front page editorial in the *Richmond Afro-American* noted "a consistent pattern covering a period of more than 40 years under which not one of 808 white men convicted of rape has been sentenced to die for his crime, and during the same period a total of 45 colored men have, is proof positive that white men have been immune to the death penalty for the crime." The newspaper then pointed directly to the issue that haunted the entire judicial system's dynamic: "we will continue to have cases like the infamous Martinsville Seven so long as we have juries . . . packed with white people who are called upon to mete out *justice to beings which they consider less than human*" ("There's No Justice Here"; my emphasis). That day's headlines (19 February 1951) condemned Virginia's "lynch executions." But Virginia was not unique. Tolnay and Beck revealed that in the era of lynching, "southern blacks visited the executioner in truly *prodigious* numbers. . . . Between 1882 and 1930, 1,977 African-Americans were executed in . . . ten southern states . . . an average of forty executions a year" (100; my emphasis). During this same period, only 451 whites faced a similar fate. When these sociologists combined their statistics for lynching and executions, they found that "an African-American was put to death somewhere in the South on the average of every four days" (100).

"If you mess up that body,
you won't get another"

Early in the century, Harlemites distrusted Harlem Hospital. A record number of African Americans died from what should have been curable diseases—tuberculosis and pneumonia—at this hospital, which was understandably referred to as "the morgue." Midcentury, this time in the South, a similar distrust developed for Tuskegee Hospital at Tuskegee Institute, Alabama, a hospital that became the site of literally murderous maltreatment.

It was not until 1972 that the full story would emerge. For nearly *forty years* prior to that, white physicians participated in a project funded by the National Public Health Service to study the effects of syphilis on black men. The study was the brainchild of white physician R. A. Vonderlehr, who was certain that the effects of the disease—especially in terms of syphilitic heart disease—were racially distinct. His only way of proving his hypothesis, as he explained in a letter to a colleague, was "the continuance of the observation of the Negro men used in the study with the idea of eventually bringing them to autopsy" (James H. Jones 132). In other words, the physician watched syphilis progress and made no attempt to treat it with the curative drugs available at that time. Further communications between Vonderlehr and his colleagues emphasize the terminal treatment plan. "As I see it," one of the doctors observed, "we have no further interest in these patients until they die" (134). Macabre communications among medical personnel and between them and their patients documented the researchers' efforts to track patients until they died and then to convince the deceased patients' families to allow the physicians to perform autopsies.

Patients told they were being examined for "bad blood" were encouraged to be loyal to the study because their local doctors would administer a palliative drug—which was actually aspirin that had been dyed pink to look like a specialized pharmaceutical. The aspirin was, of course, effective for relieving daily aches and pains, and because patients saw some palliative effect, it assured their continued participation. Of course, and of necessity, aspirin did nothing to abate the progress of the syphilis. Local physicians were encouraged to keep close watch on the patients. Vonderlehr received one report stating, "I have my eye on several who could qualify for a place on the [autopsy] table" (149). Eunice Rivers, the

'NOW can we give him penicillin?'

Editorial cartoon. *Universal Press Syndicate.*

African American nurse who was hired as an on-site coordinator for the study and especially for convincing black families to submit their loved ones to the indignities of the medically valuable autopsy warned doctors that "if you mess up that body, you won't get another" (153). Rivers was highly motivated. She knew that her job was on the line, but she believed as well in the worth and significance of the study's objectives. In trying to convince bereaved families to submit the bodies of their loved ones to autopsy, she told the families that the procedure was "just like an operation, except the person is dead" (152). In the first twenty years of the study she garnered 144 autopsies out of 145 families. Eventually, at her urging, the Public Health Service offered burial stipends in exchange for permission to perform the autopsy.

For forty years, black men in the Tuskegee study died, went blind, or experienced insanity in an egregious violation of medical ethics and in a prejudicially distorted hypothesis of medical science. Trust in hospitals and in the government, never strong in the black community, was further eroded by this pathetic episode. This legacy was to re-emerge during the AIDS crisis that began in the 1980s. A 1992 *New York Times* editorial claimed to be shocked at the skepticism some members of the black community had for the health industry's efforts to organize a com-

Editorial cartoon. *The Atlanta Journal* and *The Atlanta Constitution*.

munity response to AIDS. "Bizarre as it may seem to most people," the editorial reported, "many black Americans believe that AIDS . . . [is] a part of a conspiracy to wipe out the black race" (*New York Times* 56.92).

Some believed that AIDS was a man-made disease, formed in a laboratory and directed toward a vulnerable black population. Others insisted that condom campaigns were a mask for genocide—an attempt to thin the numbers of black babies. Of course, as in other issues in African American history, the funeral industry was not long in responding to the crisis. And, like the black public, the black funeral industry suffered from misinformation and panic. More than one black mortician at a 1990s convention of the professional association explained to me how undertakers were "especially susceptible" to "the" AIDS. One black-owned chemical company responded to the fear in the black mortuary community by manufacturing a special fluid, Aids-O-Dyne, for victims of AIDS. Of course, even with its stronger concentrations of embalming chemicals, it could not protect the morticians in the way implied

by its subtle advertising. But it was a commercial response that represented the fear that swept the community of black funeral professionals.
Furthermore, rubberized body suits—generally reserved for those embalming jobs that required the body to be sealed in such a way that bodily
fluids would not leak (out of skin that had decomposed, been burned, or
was otherwise broken-down)—were put to use for embalming of AIDS
victims, in a precautionary effort to protect morticians.

Families whose loved ones succumbed to AIDS were often shamed
into silence because of the public attitude toward the disease, and "cancer," once a hushed word itself in black communities, became the de-
fault public pathology for black folk (and others) who actually died
of AIDS. Literary theorist Sharon Holland thoughtfully explores this
silence, noting that "decades of political activism and academic theo-
rizing" notwithstanding, there is "a plethora of silences in the national
discourse on sexuality." Holland notes that the slogan "silence = death,"
used as it was by 1980s AIDS activists, is appropriate for the conversation about the "contentious" spaces between death, race, and sexuality
(Holland 103–4).

The turbulent and noisy silence about the relationship between black
death and black and "queer" sexuality was most evident in the shocked
response of the medical communities and the media. Holland reminds
her readers of an "infamous *New Yorker* harangue" about dancer-chore-
ographer Bill T. Jones's premiere of "Still/Here" in Lyons, France—a
dance composed from Jones's workshop experience with the dying. Holland's insights here are invaluable as she explains that the *New Yorker*
author Arlene Croce "indicates [a] fear that borders on a seething hatred
. . . a kind of recognition and unmasking [where] the face of death has
been unmasked, and the black face staring back . . . is almost too much
to bear" (Holland 176–77).

Throughout the twentieth century, the media's representations of
and responses to black artistry's performances of black death focused on
censoring either its ethic or its intent—or even maligned its very interest
in the subject. The media's cultural panic failed to consider, to respect,
or to understand the historical construction of African American distrust of the medical community. It remains critical, as these histories of
dangerous (dis)regard collapse onto each other, to understand the implications of the Tuskegee Study. The intentionally murderous neglect of
black syphilis victims in Tuskegee, Alabama, was revealed merely a de-

cade before the AIDS crisis began garnering wide attention in the popular press. For African Americans, inevitably, there was an entirely plausible parallel between the AIDS epidemic and the social policies that led to the black community's mistrust. As late as 1997, a prominent young African American entertainer, actor Will Smith, spoke publicly about his belief that AIDS was a deliberately man-made disease. It was the same year that basketball superstar Magic Johnson's wife proclaimed him "cured" of the incurable disease on the cover of Ebony, one of the "Negro National Magazines." Such misinformation, prominently and forcefully entered into our national conversation, combined with the accurate history of benign neglect, murderous maltreatment, and segregated medical attention, directly contributed to the folk stories or urban legends that gained cultural capital in the black community. And such stories seemed all the more plausible at the end of the twentieth century, when—although blacks made up only 14 percent of the U.S. population—they represented a devastating 45 percent of new AIDS cases ("AIDS Infects Blacks" 31).

Again and again statistics from agencies like the National Institutes of Health and the Centers for Disease Control clarified that, when it came to death rates, race was a consistently predictable factor in patient mortality. This was true in every decade of the century, for urban as well as rural areas, and for northern as well as southern regions. (Table 2 illustrates the degree of black death and dying.) Maternal death rates from childbirth, for example, formed one of the most distinctive gaps in public health. Black women in the United States were four times as likely to die during childbirth, or in the period immediately following childbirth, than white women. Whether the numbers cited infant mortality, adult death from heart disease, young adult death from violence, or children's deaths from diseases about which medical knowledge had made tremendous strides (asthma, for instance), the death rates for black folk were dramatically higher from the beginning to the end of the twentieth century. In cities with populations of more than one million between 1939 and 1941, the difference in death rates for black and white patients with tuberculosis was striking (see Table 3). Medical sociologist Anthony Polednak indicated that the comparative data from these indices in the first third of the century only grew more dramatic by the century's end and explained that "black-white disparities in health status persist. . . . U.S.

86

TABLE 2. Mortality from Certain Causes: Central Harlem and Manhattan, 1925, 1937

CAUSE	HARLEM (1925)	MANHATTAN (1925)	HARLEM (1937)	MANHATTAN (1937)
Tuberculosis (deaths per 100,00)	247.0	111.8	243.3	90.3
Pneumonia	244.0	164.0	109.0	97.0
Infant Mortality (deaths of children under one year per 1,000 live births)	114.4	72.9	75.0	54.0
Maternal Mortality (deaths per 1,000 women giving birth)	8.2	4.8	7.9	4.6
Stillbirths (per 1,000 births)	71.8	55.0	76.0	53.0
Homicide	18.7	11.0	24.1	3.6

Reproduced from Greenberg, *Or Does It Explode* (187).

black-white mortality differences involve mainly 'preventable' deaths" (61). He further explained that

> Preventable causes of death (including hypertension) were common among blacks in the District of Columbia, where the highest black-white disparities in death rates in 1980–86 were from tuberculosis, certain other lung diseases, and hypertensive heart disease. . . . *[R]acial inequities in access to and quality of health care . . . were important.* In Chicago, asthma mortality rates increased continuously from 1968 to 1991 (by a total of 337% over the entire period) among African Americans 5–34 years old but remained constant among whites after 1976. (Polednak 112; my emphasis)

In a 1989 review of childhood mortality indices, medical anthropologist Margaret Boone wrote, "Blacks have the highest infant mortality

TABLE 3. Tuberculosis Death Rates, 1939–41

CITY	FOR WHITES	FOR NEGROES
Chicago, Illinois	45.4	250.1
New York, New York	40.4	213.0
Philadelphia, Pennsylvania	44.3	203.5
Detroit, Michigan	36.5	189.0
Los Angeles, California	49.7	137.3

Reproduced from Drake and Cayton, *Black Metropolis* (204)

rate of any racial or ethnic group in the United States," noting especially the "stubborn and substantial rate difference between the two racial groups. Black infants are at twice the risk of White infants" (Boone 15, 75). The late-century indices were not different enough from those of the early century and midcentury. An analysis of the treatment and survival patterns for black and white cancer patients was characteristic. Medical researchers Lillian Axtell and Max Meyers found that, for all cancers, "Among males, survival for blacks was lower and continued to diverge from the curve for whites throughout the ten year period" and black females suffered "excess mortality" relative to their white peers (3). Neighborhood, education, economic class, access to medical care, and contributing illnesses other than cancer were certainly significant factors in these rates.

But relatively little public attention was devoted to other well-documented problems in black health care—the attention, respect, and intervention given by medical personnel to their black patients. When research shifted from looking at medical causes for the disparities in black and white mortality rates to ethnography and psychology, doctors' approaches and attitudes toward their black patients began to come under appropriate and revealing scrutiny. The Tuskegee episode, in which patients were viewed as experimental subjects, characterized the significant bias and dangerous psychological distance that health-care workers often displayed in their care of black patients. As a result of such attitudes, black people in general and black women in particular were less likely to receive aggressive, costly care—whether diagnostic or palliative—than their white counterparts. In a late-1990s report on the state of health care for cardiac crises, the *Journal of the American Medical Association* states that in an examination of treatments including "cardiology and cardiac surgery, kidney transplantation, general internal medicine and obstetrics, data emerge that indicate that when African Americans are in the health care system, they are 'less likely' than whites to receive certain surgical or other therapies." They have a 45 percent higher rate of lung cancer and "10 times the likelihood of dying from hypertension than white men." In a review of racial disparities in the diagnosis of circulatory system disease or chest pain, it reported that "racial disparities in treatment persisted even after differences in income and the severity of disease were taken into account." Whites were one third more likely to undergo coronary angiography and more than twice as likely to be treated with bypass surgery or angioplasty. In terms of general internal medicine, the review reported additional evidence of "racial disparities in treatment," noting, for example, that a patient's race, when hospitalized for pneumonia, correlated with "the intensity of care provided" ("Black-White Disparities" 2344).

"It is a great demonstration for everyone to die"

Perhaps the loneliest of our deaths was suicide. Suicides had the ironic potential of revealing the private and quiet storms of publicly well-managed lives, and they were likely the most underreported. The quiet brutality of suicide paralleled the noisy rage against violence in some African American communities. During the period from 1980 to 1986, the suicide rate for elderly black men grew 42 percent. Like their youngsters, older black men most often chose guns. In the mid-1990s, the figures from the National Center for Health Statistics reported that 64 percent of young black males who committed suicide used guns (Houston 28).

Following homicide and accident, suicide was the third leading cause of death among black youth. A 1997 story in the *Washington Post* reported that "although violent death rates—which include accidents, homicides and suicides—among teenagers had worsened nationally, the rate in the District of Columbia was even more distressing: It increased by 669% from 1985 to 1994" (Houston 28; Brown A1). Suicides among African

American men of all ages rose by 18 percent between 1987 and 1994 according to the Centers for Disease Control and Prevention. And they soared more than 57 percent during the same period for young black boys and men aged fifteen to twenty-four (Houston 28). Even during the period from 1980 to 1992, when suicide rates declined among young white adults, black young men had dramatically increased rates of successful suicide. Although the rate among black teens had generally lagged behind that of white teenagers, the last decades of the century indicated a dramatically narrowing gap. After having experienced the consequences of the trend, Kenya Bello of Atlanta founded the Free Mind Generation, a suicide-awareness organization that distributed a newsletter on black suicides. Bello's twenty-seven-year-old husband, a graduate student, jumped to his death from the thirty-second floor of a hotel just before he was to start graduate studies at the Johns Hopkins University. In a CNN interview in June 1997, one young African American man who had attempted suicide on at least three occasions explained that although he was a student at the prestigious Brown University, he felt the uniquely black burden of serving as a role model — being "a credit to the race" and living up to the reputation of being an outstanding member of the community. He noted ironically that it was "a nice set-up to go high enough to fall." Despite his success, he was a psychological victim of black death.

Chronic sorrow, profound despair, and unresolvable loss are day-to-day realities for some black youngsters. Carl Bell, psychiatrist and director of the Community Mental Health Council in Chicago explained in a National Public Radio report with Jim Lehrer that "many young Black males don't feel they have a place in a society that increasingly shows little value for their lives. Add to that the proliferation of guns throughout the nation and the risk of suicide becomes greater for those who feel trapped, disrespected and hopeless" (Lehrer). He also noted the particular dilemma of "the middle class black child . . . in-between the poor working class black world and in-between the white professional world, and they don't fit in either world to some extent. They're at risk for getting a depression and then being alienated and isolated" (Lehrer). Many reports noted how black men and women tended to avoid the mental health networks that might have helped them work through suicidal depressions. During the CNN interview, Kenya Bello agreed. "We think mental illness is something that White people get and suicide is something crazy people do." Speaking with NPR correspondent Eliza-beth Brackett, Dr. Carl Bell also noted the "reluctance of some African-Americans to talk openly about suicide, and the stigma associated with mental health treatment" and called for greater attention from mental health organizations to the cultural components of black suicide risks (Lehrer).

In addition to suicide itself, suicide-like behaviors rose exponen-tially and in comparison to white youth. In fact, in the young black community, suicide and accidental death were sometimes indistinguish-able. Our children's deaths from gun violence, drugs, and gang warfare shared characteristics with suicide, in the sense that those children re-lentlessly and unerringly pursued self-destructive lifestyles leading some scholars to suggest a relationship between suicide and homicide. And, partly because of the sheer number of such situations, our suicide rates were underrepresented and incompletely reported. An additional site for underreported suicidal behavior was in the steadily rising population of AIDS victims. Reports from the 11th International Conference on AIDS suggested that not only were botched suicide attempts by HIV-positive individuals—so-called coat-hanger euthanasia—increasing, but physi-cians were more likely to have participated in helping patients die by pre-scribing deadly doses of narcotics (*"Assisted AIDS Suicides Increase,"* 11 July 1996).

Aside from these numerical reports and narratives, suicide provided a critical prosaic text for African American mourning stories as it tex-tured the narrative of cultural deaths and recorded the doubly veiled dif-ficulty of being black and living in America. Consider the well-rehearsed story of Dorothy Dandridge. In 1964, when she decided to write her autobiography, she telephoned friends to let them know of her contract for writing the book *Everything and Nothing: The Dorothy Dandridge Tragedy.* Dandridge's life story, if told near to truth in this book, would have lurid and sensational detail. The birth of her tragically brain-injured daughter whom she relinquished to a mental-health hospital would be told, as would her failed marriage to one of the Nicholas brothers, her af-fair with movie mogul Otto Preminger, and her drug and alcohol abuse. Her friends reacted negatively to her plans. "Much to my astonishment they said, 'What, an autobiography? Who are you to do an autobiogra-phy? What have you accomplished? If you tell your story, you'll set Negro womanhood back a hundred years. You make a damned poor image of a Negro woman. You will do us no good. Nothing in your career has any meaning for the Group'" (Dandridge 212).

Dandridge wrote that, as she listened to their response, "I wanted to die. . . . It was about all that I needed to finish off my profound interest in living. I lay as near to death from that Sunday through Wednesday as I can ever be, without dying" (212). Dandridge's life was consistently compromised by her color. Many in her profession experienced the incredible conflicts of public life and private persona, but as an African American woman, Dandridge was conflicted as well by the unrelenting call of the community—to be the ideal of the woman who could be, again, "a credit to the race." She wrote, "there was only one decision I could make: I must either kill myself if I was that unworthy, or die of attrition then and there—simply will myself to death, which I felt like doing—or tell my story." She did tell her story, but she also killed herself with an overdose of drugs on 8 September 1965.

The psychic toll of this responsibility was not unique to Dandridge. Nearly twenty years later, another high-profile African American woman also killed herself with an overdose of drugs. Leanita McClain was the first black woman columnist and editorial board member at the *Chicago Tribune*. She was, in the words of her former husband, journalist Clarence Page, a "ghetto to Gold-coast success story," as well as "a portrait in walking woundedness" (Page 47). Like Dandridge, and like too many other African American women and men, she found that personal success was to bring public and private anguish. Page quotes from a *Newsweek* column, "The Black Middle Class Burden," where McClain wrote, "I am burdened daily with showing whites that blacks are people. I am, in the old vernacular, a credit to my race . . . though many of them have abandoned me because they think that I have abandoned them. . . . Some of my 'liberal' white acquaintances pat me on the head, hinting that I am a freak, that my success is less a matter of talent than of luck and affirmative action. . . . As to the envy of my own people, am I to give up my career, my standard of living, to pacify them and set my conscience at ease?" (Page 68).

Neither success nor failure daunted the criticism leveled by the black and white worlds at individuals prominent in both. Either position was equally problematic, and the cost to those especially vulnerable—to despair or to anguish, or even to feeling deeply—could be suicide. Some

critical and inescapable dimension of suicides like Dandridge's or Mc-
Clain's is cultural, a black event. The physical loss in these circumstances
was accompanied by psychic despair and tied to a tragic acknowledgment of color. Leanita McClain's suicide note's bitter judgment tells the
tale of race. She wrote, "I'll never live to see my people free anyway"
(Page 68). Because blacks exist without the ease of racelessness and because race matters, suicides among African Americans tell the culture's
stories, as well as the soul's.

Singer Phyllis Hyman and poet Terri Jewell were both victims of
suicide and perhaps victims as well of the hazardous interplay of public success and private anguish. Jewell fought the demons of memory, as
flashbacks about incest and her abusive childhood threatened to overwhelm her. Phyllis Hyman, better known in national circles, fought painful depression, finally leaving a suicide note that explained, "I'm tired.
I'm tired." In a conversation with a former lover only days before her
suicide, Hyman lamented that she had no personal life and no energy
(Iverem, 120). The requisite energy of public lives and the pressure of
black success may not be different in kind from the cost exacted by sorrow that predicts an association between loneliness and cultural identity.
Leanita McClain seemed to echo this emotion. Page writes that she "did
feel alone in a lot of ways" (Page 69).

In *Go Tell It on the Mountain,* James Baldwin told the story of a black
death—a suicide complete with the hallmarks of racial trauma, spiritual vulnerability, and an overwhelming and unresolvable sense of loss.
In Baldwin's novel, Richard only barely escapes a prison sentence for a
crime he did not commit. He had been arrested because he was confused with a group of black youth who had robbed a convenience store.
When Richard protested, "Look at me, goddammit—I wasn't there!"
the eyewitness replied, "You black bastards . . . you're all the same" (171).
Ironically, Richard had always tried to be different. But all of his ambi-
tions proved insignificant in the face of his blackness. Faced with this
ultimate and final judgment, Richard knows that no act of his defiance
will matter more than the color of his skin. Elizabeth, his friend and
lover, tries to reach through his despair but

> he would not be held. His body was like iron; she could find no softness
> in it. . . . By and by he called her name. And then he turned, and she
> held him against her breast, while he sighed and shook. He fell asleep

at last, clinging to her as though he were going down into the water for the last time.

And it was the last time. That night he cut his wrists with his razor and he was found in the morning by his landlady, his eyes staring upward with no light, dead among the scarlet sheets. (174)

That fictional suicide told a story not distant enough from the frightened and despairing stories of the many black youths who killed themselves when they found their encounters with the justice system too traumatic for them to survive. Certainly, for instance, there was a dimension of my son's death that fits this "suicide-by-other-means" scenario. Some experts, discounting the official reports of about ten children who kill themselves yearly in juvenile detention centers, argued the numbers were closer to 100.

Because black youth have been disproportionately incarcerated, their deaths implicate the justice system in the high rate of suicide among young black men and boys. In Wisconsin, John Willingham was accused of nothing more than stealing a bicycle. The police arrested him and incarcerated him in the youth section of the adult jail. His mother had warned that "he couldn't handle the confinement," but this did not justify, for the police, his "acting out" in the jailhouse. At one point he was seen "huddled on the floor, leaning against the door, looking out the glass window, crying . . . that he missed his mother and he wanted to go home." That evening, separated from the other juvenile inmates and ignored by prison guards who were charged with checking him at regular intervals, he killed himself. In a wire service story, Christopher Sullivan described a "frantic radio call":

"I have a juvenile male who is hanging himself," a guard shouted after finding John "slouched in front of his bunk . . . a bed sheet tied around his neck," according to a detective's report.

"John, John!" the guard yelled, lifting the boy to relieve the weight on his neck. But John had no pulse.

At a hospital he was placed on life support machines; a family photo shows him swathed in sheets and connected to tubes. He was brain dead, doctors told his mother, but she couldn't believe it when she looked at his eyes.

"I didn't understand why there were tears coming out," she says.

Dorothy Dandridge's suicide note claims the intentionality of her death and accurately describes the condition in which her body was eventually found.

. . . "I was talking to him: 'Wake up, Little John, it's Mommy. Mommy loves you. Wake up.'"

Finally the machines were disconnected. (C. Sullivan A1)

It is not unusual to challenge the doctors, to argue against the reality of death when faced with the body of a loved one. Dandridge's body, for instance, was discovered by her lover, manager, and confidant Earl Mills, who, in his sensational, titillating, and clearly self-serving "tell-all" biography, told the story of finding her: "I tried the doorbell and knocked. I got no answer. . . . I pried the door open with the tire iron. As soon as I entered the apartment I walked toward her bedroom. I could see Dorothy's feet at the doorway of the bathroom. . . . She was lying on the floor. . . . I thought somehow she had fallen asleep. She wore no clothes but a blue scarf was wrapped about her head. She was cuddled with her face resting on her hands. . . . I shook her shoulder to awaken her. She felt cold and it scared me" (195). Mills called an ambulance. When the driver arrived, and examined her, he went straight for the telephone.

Dorothy Dandridge's body being carried away. The fact
that her body was found in the condition her suicide
note had predicted quickly became public record.

I asked him who he was calling. "The Sheriff's office," he replied.

"How is she? . . . Can't you do something for her?"

"She can't be helped by anyone . . . she passed some time ago. Sheriff," he said, "we've got a cold one. Her name is Dorothy Dandridge.
. . . She's that colored singer, isn't she?" (195)

The note some regarded as her suicide note had actually been written
a few months before she died. Mills suggested that its noncontemporary
composition indicated the accidental nature of her death. But this seems
to be his attempt at a self-saving assessment. Dandridge's deep depression, her own autobiographical comments about her suicidal condition,
and the "morbid fascination" Mills indicated she had always had about

death made it naive, at the least, to read it as merely providing directions and instructions for her burial.

Despite her friends' protestations at the suicide judgment, the psychological evidence of exactly that scenario was powerful. Dandridge's note, with its curious attention to the condition of her body at death—she was found naked, curled on the floor in a fetal position with her hands cupped beneath her cheek, and her only adornment a blue scarf on her head—told its own sad tale. Poet Terri Jewell also thought about her adornment. She dressed in purple, reportedly the color she loved most, before driving to a quiet roadway in a Michigan park in 1994 and shooting herself in her head.

Dandridge's death certificate lists acute drug intoxication; the drug was imipramine hydrochloride (Tofranil), an antidepressant. It is unlikely that her overdose was accidental. Tofranil is a common suicide drug. Although it makes you drowsy, it is not possible to poison oneself by taking a couple, getting sleepy, and then taking an extra dose or two. Suicidal dosages require twenty to thirty pills at one time, which will cause heavy sedation, then heart irregularities. Alcohol and other drugs can amplify this effect. According to medical experts, barring poisoning by someone else, there really isn't any way to overdose on Tofranil accidentally. The quantities found in Dandridge's system at autopsy were significantly greater than an accidental overdose could explain.

Ironically, Leanita McClain overdosed on the same antidepressant. She had made previous attempts—with a gun, approaching a window ledge, and with a razor blade. Page's reflections on these attempts and on her death were tortured and tender both, and, finally, they were wise. He wrote:

> A certain awkwardness permeated reaction to Leanita's death. Suicide is disparaged severely in some ethnic communities . . . and the black community is one of the most severe. . . . "We don't kill ourselves, we only kill each other," Leanita joked morbidly during peaks of manic humor. . . .
>
> . . . [T]he suicide rate among blacks tends to increase along with income. The white man's psychic burden seems to accompany the white man's lifestyle. And there very well could be a black suicide undercount, I was told by Dr. Derek Miller, head of psychiatry at Chicago's Northwestern Memorial Hospital, particularly among adolescent black

males. Miller suggests that much of the street violence . . . may be "suicide by other means." (64–65)

One of the most infamous suicides of the twentieth century earned the nation's attention because of the numbers of people involved, the politics, and the drama of the occasion. In 1978, black folk died in the hundreds in Jonestown, Guyana, reportedly victims of a suicide appeal by their charismatic and sadistic cult leader, the Reverend Jim Jones. Although his was a multicultural following, African Americans constituted a significant percentage of the "congregation." Jones's victims drank a noxious mix of Kool-Aid and cyanide. The members of the People's Temple in Jonestown stood in line to await their call to the cauldron. A survivor described the horrific scene this way:

> The babies were the first to die. The cyanide was squirted into their little mouths with syringes. Then came the older children. They lined up in the central pavilion, where Jim Jones had addressed them so many times. This time they did his bidding again. They lined up to accept cups of Kool-Aid laced with poison. Next came their parents and the old folks. They, too, waited their turn to obey the orders to die, while armed guards stood by ready to shoot down any who tried to escape. . . . Jones, "the Father," had called his flock together and told them it was time to depart for heaven. "We're going to meet," he promised, "in another place. . . . There is great dignity in dying. It is a great demonstration for everyone to die." . . . In that awful time in the late afternoon of Saturday, November 18, over nine hundred men, women, and children perished in the settlement of Jonestown, Guyana. The cyanide took about five minutes [to] kill the victims. The strongest and healthiest probably lasted a little longer. (Kilduff and Javers 179)

Although there were whites among the victims, a majority of the victims who lay dead in the dust of Jonestown were African Americans. Acknowledging the cultural mix of the deceased, the black NFDMA arranged for a contingent of its morticians to meet the plane returning bodies to the United States and to aid in the processing of the dead. News reports played the story as the actions of a "suicide cult." Over and over, the suicide at Jonestown became the narrative of the event, despite the stories that reported gunshot victims among the dead, the screams

Corpses from the Jonestown massacre/suicide. *Bettman/CORBIS.*

of children and mothers, and taped recordings that emerged in U.S. Government investigations, one of which eerily replayed a mother's plea for the children—"What have they done?"—and Jones's admonitions, shouted from his pulpit—"Mothers, you must keep your children under control" (Treaster A1). Other victims were found with syringe marks in their arms and thighs, presumably injected with the fatal dose. This was an important counternarrative to the images the headlines suggested of a congregation willing themselves dead. One might wonder how suicide could be an appropriate description of the behavior of the mother who, clutching an infant to her bosom, felt a gun shoved into her ribs. *Newsweek* reported that Rauletter Paul was called "a dumb bitch" and warned that, if she didn't let the attendant "nurses" squirt cyanide down her one year old's throat, "we're going to shoot your ass off" ("The Cult of Death" 40). Another man, who resisted, was tackled to the ground, and the poisoned mixture was poured into the back of his throat while his mouth was held open by the attendants. K. Ogletree perceptively wrote that "no one needs any help to commit suicide" and determined, faced with this evidence and supporting stories, that "our brothers and sisters who died in Jonestown did not commit suicide. The evidence clearly indicates that they were victims of mass murder" (Ogletree 329). Ogletree then posed an even more deeply disturbing query, when she asked whether the media story, which pointed to suicide, assisted our passive response, one that might have been different, with the "fear . . . panic . . . anger . . . and . . . hostility that would have been generated among Black people in this country if the truth had been told from the very beginning. . . . [T]he Jonestown massacre could have possibly become an explosive racial issue here in the United States" (332). Instead, the suicide story lulled us into a different emotional set—shock, disbelief, horror, sadness—all relatively safe and passive responses compared to those the alternative narrative might have produced.

The tragedy at Jonestown became a national obsession, covered thoroughly in the press and reviewed in congressional hearings, books, Hollywood movies, and independent documentaries that followed the episode. The blackened and bloated bodies of these victims—strewn across the boardwalks of the commune—still haunt the margins of our national memories. In one of the final ironies, even the bodies of those white victims of the cult grew darker in death and consequently share the inhabitation of our national memory with their (visual) participation in a black death.

But the Jonestown story, too, found a certain kinship to earlier public "incident" reports in the way that it earned and engaged a national space in the media, that "front-page" media interest linking it with an event that had occurred much earlier in the century.

Ota Benga was an African American only reluctantly. In 1904, the Saint Louis World's Fair had "gathered species of many races of color to exhibit," including Benga, who would never return to the country of his origin. The "missionary" responsible for bringing the "pygmy" exhibit from the Congo returned all but one to their native land after they had served their purposes of display during the World's Fair. Ota was transported not to the Congo but to New York City, where he was first left at the American Museum of Natural History and finally caged in the Bronx Zoo where he was placed on exhibit as the "missing link" for an exhilarated and eager public to view at their discretion. The *New York Times* reported that

the Bushman has been put by the management on exhibition here in the monkey cage. . . . Few expressed audible objection to the sight of a human being in a cage with monkeys. . . . [T]o the majority the joint exhibition was the most interesting sight in Bronx Park. . . . Sometimes the man and the monkey hugged each other. That pleased the children, and they laughed uproariously. . . . Occasionally the pigmy mimicked the laughter of the crowd. In one instance a boy yelled, "Shoot." "Shoot! Shoot!" aped the little bushman. ("Man and Monkey Show" 1)

Black citizens were of course outraged and began a lengthy protest that the mayor "snubbed." Finally, following the threat of a suit by a group of Baptist ministers, including Professor Gregory Hayes, President of the Virginia Seminary, Ota Benga was released from his "habitat" at the zoo. After a stay in an orphanage in Brooklyn, Benga left with Professor Hayes to live at the seminary, where he enrolled in the lower-level courses. But Hayes died soon after Benga moved south. In her memoir, sociologist Carrie Allen McCray reported that her mother Mary Allen "took him in." She remembers the "gentle, smiling man whose room was down the hall from mine, and I remember the gestures he made when he told us stories" (113). Despite the warmth and concern he experienced in those days in Lynchburg, Ota Benga had also experienced overwhelming loss and the agony of derision and exhibition. However he was able to benefit from the good and generous spirit in the Allen home, he doubtless held memories that caused him great anguish, including all of his years in America and the deeply wounding and callous experience of American racism. Benga's very presence in America advanced the racialized "science" that had questioned black humanity ever since America had first begun to use such notions to justify slavery. McCray remembers that "he wanted to go back to his home in Africa, *as the missionary had promised he could,* but there was never enough money for that. It must have been terrible for him" (115; my emphasis). She suspected that he was not happy and that going into the woods by their home with her brothers must have made him homesick. She wrote, "I wonder if our calling him Otto, instead of Ota, bothered him. Did he ever think, 'Nobody knows my name'? When he took [her brothers] spearfishing, didn't those waters remind him of happier days on the banks of his Kasai River?" Ota had left behind a wife and children, allegedly killed in a tribal war, according to the suspiciously convenient report of the missionary who captured him. McCray wrote that eventually Ota Benga changed from "a smiling and patient teacher" to a "silent, solemn man [who] often sat for hours, motionless under a tree, all alone." And then she tells the stunning story of his death—all the more remarkable because of the disgraceful counternarrative that appeared in a *New York Times* obituary in which the arrogant missionary Samuel Vermer, eager to absolve his complicity in this pitiful human drama, prevaricates. Vermer was quoted in the *Times* as having "urged him to go back to Africa, but he would not. . . . The homeless pygmy found no abiding place" ("Ota Benga"). McCray reported the more sorrowfully credible narrative:

> [L]ate in the afternoon, the boys watched Otto as he gathered wood and built a fire in the field between our house and the seminary. When the fire rose to bright blaze, he began dancing around it. [My brothers] watched in awe as Otto danced around the fire, faster, faster, faster, whirling around and around faster, faster, faster, making strange sounds as he danced, chanting, moaning. Sweat on his brow, faster, faster, faster, around and around, chanting, moaning. The boys stood back, confused and afraid. The dance had some meaning they could not comprehend, something mysterious, almost foreboding. They were frightened, but they stayed and watched Otto twirl around, and around, and around, chanting, moaning, moaning the same sounds the slaves made, laying bare their sorrow. (116)

Carrie Allen McCray's story concluded with a sad echo of a day in the Bronx Zoo when "A boy yelled 'Shoot.' 'Shoot! Shoot!' aped the little bushman." McCray continues: "That was the last the boys saw of Otto. That night while they were sleeping, Otto went into the old gray weathered shed behind Mammy Joe's store, uncovered a gun he had hidden in the hay, and shot himself" (McCray 112–16).

Perhaps the most tragic reality of the quiet storm of suicide is the inevitable and anticipated response of life. In Randall Kenan's poignant and deeply resonant first novel, *Visitation of Spirits,* a tortured youth, a black boy for whom the requisites of race and sexuality finally overwhelm, finds resolution, if not redemption, in suicide. "Whether or not the malevolent spirit existed is irrelevant, in the end. For whether he caused it or not, the boy died. This is a fact. The bullet did break the skin . . . the blood did flow. . . . His heartbeat slowly decreased. Whether or not the demon was a ghost of his mind or a spirit of the netherworld, this did happen. And the man screamed, a helpless, affronted,

high-pitched, terror-filled scream . . . a sobbing, mournful wail, incon-
solable and primal" (253). And, perhaps as difficult as the loss of this soul
is the response to his sudden absence: "Most importantly, the day did
not halt in its tracks: clocks did not stop. The school buses rolled . . .
dishes were washed . . . food was eaten. And that night the sun set with
the full intention of rising on the morrow" (254).

3

Soon I will be done with

the troubles of the world.

— Traditional

The Ends of Days

"My memory stammers, but my soul is a witness"

It was 1959, and a generation of African American girls who accompanied their mothers to movies and drive-ins to see the just-released *Imitation of Life* saw their mothers crying. Most had no idea why a film would provoke the great heaving sobs and wet hankies (mothers still carried handkerchiefs in the 1950s), but clearly understood that some mighty experience had moved mothers to tears.

"Annie" — as played by Juanita Moore in Douglas Sirk's film — had died in cinemascopic splendor. Her deathbed moment and her funeral services, accompanied by Mahalia Jackson's rendering of the spiritual "Soon Ah Will Be Done," were to become singularly important in African American film history and in African American households as well. Later, Sirk was to comment on the funeral and Mahalia Jackson's role in it. "It's strange," Sirk explained to James Harvey in an interview about *Imitation of Life* in 1978. "Before shooting those scenes, I went to hear Mahalia Jackson at UCLA, where she was giving a recital. I knew nothing about her. But here on the stage was this large, homely, ungainly woman — and all those singing, beautiful young faces turned up to her, and absolutely smitten with her. It was strange and funny and very impressive. I tried to get some of that experience into the picture. We photographed her with a three-inch lens, so that every unevenness of the face stood out" (Harvey 55). Sirk also commented that he knew the funeral scene was highly emotional, "but I was surprised at that effect" (Harvey 55).

The emotion begins to build in Annie's bedroom, where she wearily lies on her deathbed, the end obviously near, despite "Miss" Laura's (Lana Turner) protestations. Seeing that death is near, Laura wailed, "God, No!" Annie struggles, opens her eyes, and replies, "Hate to dispute you Miss Laura"—then goes on about the business of her dying, "well" as some elders would have claimed. Before she goes, she has an opportunity to pronounce her judgment that "our wedding day and the day we die are the great events of life." To make certain this will be the case for the latter occasion, Annie takes matters into her own hands. First, she directs the disposition of her worldly goods, telling those gathered round her death bed who should get a little money, her mink stole, and other belongings. But, as to her funeralizing, this she has already made a formal text, written out in detail. She directs Laura's beau, "Mr." Steve (John Gavin), to her dresser:

> *Annie:* . . . and my funeral—Mr. Steve, you'll find what I want in the drawer over there.
> *Steve:* I've got it Annie.
> *Annie:* I want to go [*breathing laboriously now*] . . . the way I planned—especially the four white horses, and the band playing. No mourning, but proud and high stepping, like I was going to glory.
> *Laura:* No! I won't listen! There isn't going to be any funeral, not for a long, long time. You can't leave me!
> *Annie:* I'm just tired Miss Laura, awfully tired.

Despite Laura's command, Annie does indeed die. Four low, somber, and ponderous piano tones confirm the moment, and the scene shifts from her bedroom to a church sanctuary. The camera pans upward and finds Mahalia Jackson, perched high in the choir balcony, where she sings the old African American spiritual: "Soon I will be done with the troubles of the world. Going home, to live with God!"

Imitation of Life resonated throughout the African American community. It had publicly dramatized a private black narrative of passing: when African Americans who were light enough "passed" as white and

Funeral scene from *Imitation of Life*.

left the black community to lead lives across the color line. The movie was especially poignant to black women, not in small part because of its dramatic funeral scene, in which the errant, light-skinned prodigal daughter Sara Jane, who had left her dark-skinned mother behind, returns for Annie's grand funeral just in time to throw herself with hysterical sobs of "Mama! I'm sorry, Mama!" past the bearers and onto her mother's casket as it was being borne from the church and placed into a magnificent carriage. Severe critiques—similar to those that Fannie Hurst's novel of the same title had generated when it was published in the 1930s—argued against its authenticity and its daring representation of these "family matters" of African America to "public" (white) audiences. But the dignity and control that Juanita Moore brought to that deathbed scene, and the ornate funeral that she had authorized and directed, provoked the teary-eyed bonding of a generation of mothers and daughters.

Many who had not done so before, or who had not incorporated this nineteenth-century cultural practice into personal habit, were persuaded to write out their own funeral instructions, just as Annie had done in the film. Countless numbers of envelopes were carefully placed in dresser drawers with these poignant instructions written on the outside: "To be opened on the occasion of my death." As African Americans were less likely than most to prepare wills, the instructions in these envelopes did not constitute legal documents, nor did they serve as formal dispositions of goods or personal effects. They were, instead, notes that specified the ceremony for the funeral service. One such letter from A.M., shared with me by one of her daughters, began with a carefully typed list of directives.

—please don't buy a **New Dress**
—use the pink or white already here.
—don't put **any jewelry or make-up** on me except a little powder.
—put one pink rose in my hand.
—please don't **load** my casket **with flowers**—they did not give them to me while I was living!

She also included a handwritten addition to the list: "If you're going to give me anything, give it to the homeless." Anticipating the disarray of the event of her dying, and in a final helpful gesture to her family, A.M. appended a list of names and telephone numbers of "people to let know I passed."

Whether this kind of letter writing occurred or not, African Americans of a certain generation were often quite clear about the second "great event" of one's "lifetime." In a conversation, Sharon G. spoke to me of her mother's plans.

"Mama is real clear about what she wants. Everything has got to be blue. Blue dress, blue flowers, blue casket. Even the blankets and stuff inside the casket—blue. She sits us down and tells us all the time, make it all blue, even my hat."

"A hat, too?" I asked.

"Yes," Sharon replied. "My mama has got lots of hats, always did like hats. She wants to wear a blue hat, and she also said put my mink coat in there with me."

"In the casket?" I asked. "You mean she wants to wear it?"

"No," Sharon explained. "She just wants it in there . . . it's not blue—she don't want to wear it, just wants it in there with her. She told us, that's a real mink coat, put it in there with me."

Sharon and her brother and sisters plan to honor their mother's wishes. Sharon doesn't like funerals and has never attended one — even when her own grandparents died. Although she's not certain she will be able to go to her mother's funeral when the time comes, she assured me that it will all be blue.

In Tina Ansa's 1994 novel, *Ugly Ways,* a recently deceased mother lingers past the moment, commenting on the plans her three daughters have for her burial. Ansa's character made a powerful argument for following last wishes (and indicated that blue might not be for every body):

> From the looks of this here dress they bought to bury me in — went out to the mall and bought it out at Rubinstein's too, know they paid good money for it, the price tag is probably around here somewhere — you can tell they holds a grudge for something though. What in God's name would possess them to go out and spend good money on this navy-blue monstrosity — and they know navy blue is not my color, they know how pretty I look in pastels — when I had all those beautiful bed jackets at home. Hell, some of my old stuff might be a bit outdated, since I ain't had any need for street clothes in a number of years, but even it look better than this shit. They ought to be ashamed. Knowing how those girls love beautiful clothes, I can't believe they weren't trying to say *something* by picking this thing for me to lie in for all eternity. Them girls got ugly ways about 'em sometimes. (Ansa 37)

It is clear that the inherent pathos of the deathbed and funeral scene — not to mention the dramatic effect of having a private dimension of black life loom large on the silver screen — were in large part responsible for the emotional cultural response to *Imitation of Life.* However, even without this dramatic text, the fact is that African American deathbed stories often not only collect the particulars of an individual's life but visibly display the shared narratives of a culture's colored experience. Sometimes, our cultural identification with the racial events even displaced the truth of the actual event.

For many years, for example, the facts surrounding the death in 1950 of Dr. Charles Drew, who died of injuries sustained in an automobile accident, were displaced by what seemed to many to be a perfectly credible narrative — that Drew had been the victim of discriminatory medical treatment following the accident. Drew and three colleagues were driving from Washington, D.C., to an annual medical clinic at Tuskegee, Alabama, the morning of the accident. Because of a late speech the night before, they did not leave Washington until after midnight. Early in the morning of 1 April 1950, Drew fell asleep at the wheel as he crossed the Virginia border into North Carolina. The car went off the road and crashed. Drew, the most seriously injured of the occupants, was taken immediately to the nearby Alamance General Hospital in Burlington, North Carolina. Although the fact that he was transported to the hospital in a white funeral home's ambulance may seem ironic, it was commonplace, especially in the South, for funeral home hearses—black and white—to serve as medical transports. These cars were manufactured and designed as "combinations," reflecting the community's need to transport the barely living as well as the definitely deceased. (Reportedly, the McClure ambulance was the first of several to arrive at the accident site, although some accounts question the order of arrival of the combinations from both black- and white-owned businesses that rushed to the scene. Black-owned Sharpe Funeral Home and Hargett and Bryant Funeral Homes also sent "vehicles" [Love 272].)

Drew's foot was trapped under the brake pedal and his leg was nearly severed. He sustained massive internal injuries—the car had rolled over at least twice—and he was immediately treated at the closest hospital by physicians who were aware of his renown. In *One Blood,* Spencie Love reported that when Drew was wheeled into the emergency room one of his colleagues, Dr. Johnson, who had accompanied him in the McClure car, recalled that " 'He was still alive, periodically gasping.' . . . [A] tall, ruddy, brown-haired man [Dr. Carrington] in a long, white coat came in the emergency room and observed the patient. He asked in astonishment, 'Is that Dr. Drew?' . . . Johnson recalled Carrington's reaction: 'In a commanding voice he ordered emergency measures. At his request, fluids were assembled and attempts were made to place a tourniquet. . . . Concurrently, I was escorted from the emergency waiting room' " (20).

The most specific memory of the severe nature of the injuries came from Lucille Crabtree, a white nurse who was present at the scene and who was unaware of Drew's identity.

> I didn't know they were doctors till later in the day. . . . It was early in the morning. . . . [T]he emergency room called; they wanted me to come immediately. I didn't wait for the elevator. I ran down the steps. . . . Dr. Drew was on the main operating table. Right away I tried to get

an open airway. Another attendant tried to get an IV going. It wasn't even an hour till he was dead. His chest was crushed; his head was crushed and broken. There was nothing anyone could do—*even Duke*. He was torn up too bad. . . . His brains were coming out of his ears. . . . In my opinion he could not have been saved. (21; my emphasis)

Johnson recalled the moment he learned of Drew's death: "A doctor came and reported to us that Dr. Drew had expired. He said, 'We tried. We did the best we could. We started fluids but our efforts were unrewarding'" (23). The required medical treatment and the nature of his injuries were especially ironic, given that Drew was responsible for the discovery of a process for storing blood plasma and enabling blood transfusions. Indeed, this irony and its coincidence fueled the decidedly dramatic, albeit untrue, narrative that emerged. His death certificate listed three causes: brain injury, internal hemorrhage in the lungs, and multiple injuries to his extremities.

Two stories that circulated in the African American community reported this tragedy somewhat differently: one indicated that he had been denied entry to the nearest hospital; the second suggested that he had died because local doctors refused to give him a transfusion as they did not have any "black" blood on hand. The latter scenario had its history. During the war years, despite the pioneering work Drew had done to make blood plasma available for battlefield injuries, the Red Cross had notoriously refused blood donations from African Americans, later modifying this policy to "merely" segregate such donations. The Army was complicit in this segregation, and black soldiers suffered the consequences of this prejudice. In part due to the Red Cross policy, there was an especially bitter and bloody history attached to Drew's life-work, a history that ultimately became confused with the story of his death. Thus, although Drew's colleagues denied both of his death stories vigorously in the years after his death, their protestations were neither as believable nor as sustainable for African Americans as the history of racism that made those stories seem credible. The drama of the imagined narrative was simply too persuasive, given the prevailing racism and segregation of the day.

Equally influential was the factual history of hospital prejudice that informed the legend. Later in the year of Drew's death, for instance, young World War II veteran Maltheus Avery was returning home to

Highway marker
and memorial at
the site of Charles
Drew's accident.

Henderson, North Carolina, from A&T College in Greensboro, a city within fifteen miles of Burlington, when his car side-swiped a truck and careened into a ditch. Avery's car was completely demolished, and Avery was trapped inside, unconscious (Love 218). Doctors at Alamance Hospital, where Avery was first taken, decided that his injuries merited and could sustain transportation to the better-equipped facilities at Duke University Hospital in Durham, North Carolina. Crabtree had speculated on exactly that possibility of a transfer to Duke Hospital for the mortally wounded Drew. However, on his arrival at Duke, Avery was refused admission because Duke's quota for "Negro" beds was already filled. Turned away from the nearest and best-equipped facility because of his race, Avery was taken to a local black hospital—Lincoln. There, shortly after his arrival, Maltheus Avery died.

The two stories, so similar in locale, circumstance, and history, fused in many resident's memories. Love concluded, however, that "the Mal-

The *Carolina Times* implicates Duke University Hospital in the death of Maltheus Avery. *The Carolina Times.*

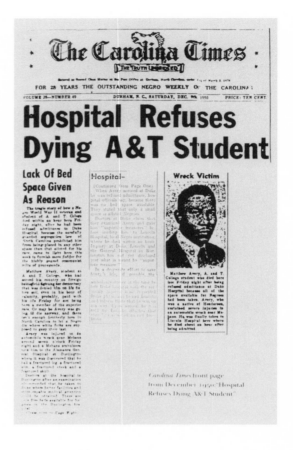

Carolina Times front page from December 1950, "Hospital Refuses Dying A&T Student"

theus Avery story did not by itself spark the Charles Drew legend. The rumor of Drew's refusal was already circulating for a multitude of other historical events had already laid the foundations for this legend. But the Avery episode at Duke University Hospital—and similar ones before and after—gave the Drew rumor additional credence" (227).

Stories like these were so pervasive that one white man who traveled the south in the disguise of a black man claimed, "Every time we had a close shave with another car, I could see myself riding around in a Jim Crow ambulance, hunting a Jim Crow hospital while I slowly bled to death." In his 1949 book, *In the Land of Jim Crow,* Ray Sprigle included an entire chapter, titled "White Hospitals and Black Deaths," on stories like that of the athletes of Atlanta's Clark University track team who traveled over one hundred miles, over the course of five hours, looking for medical treatment after a serious accident. They were refused admission in three hospitals. One of the athletes, Joseph Brown, died of his injuries (Love 277 n.62).

Among those African Americans who were inaccurately but believably portrayed as victims of such "medical" rites bias were Bessie Smith, who died in a car accident in 1937 in Alabama, and prizefighter Jack Johnson, whose 1946 automobile accident near Raleigh, North Carolina, and whose subsequent death at Raleigh's black hospital, St. Agnes, fueled stories similar to the one constructed for Drew. Love noted that Hazel Avery, mother of Maltheus Avery, "had told her children about Bessie Smith being refused treatment at a hospital and bleeding to death during their childhood. . . . But she obviously had not believed that such a tragedy could happen to one of her own children. . . . It was one thing to pass such a story on, another to experience it firsthand" (248).

At the end of the century, Hazel Avery's story to her children about Bessie Smith being refused treatment still had its believers. Bessie Smith *was* killed in an automobile accident in 1937, and the rumor—circulated largely by musicians and devotees—that she bled to death because a white hospital would not admit her was accompanied by the many other dramatic stories that surrounded her life.

There was, for example, the story that she was kidnapped by Ma Rainey and compelled to tour with her. There was what was for some the titillating fact of her bisexuality. So, it was difficult not to believe the legend of her death. In one story (told to me and represented as fact by a Chicago dramatist who still believes it to be so), the ambulance driver who came to the accident scene took her, knowing she was alive, to a funeral home rather than a hospital. It is likely that this misrepresentation has something to do with the use of the ambulance-hearse combination.

Actually, Bessie Smith lost quantities of blood sufficient to end her life before she ever arrived at a hospital. Her arm was nearly severed in the crash on U.S. Route 61 near Clarksdale, Mississippi, on 26 September 1937. She was with her friend and lover, Richard Morgan, who was driving her from Memphis to Darling, Mississippi, for a scheduled performance. Their car crashed into the back of a truck. White Memphis physician Hugh Smith encountered the accident scene, administered emergency treatment, and summoned an ambulance. During the interim, another automobile arrived on the scene. This one, according to

Bessie Smith's biographer, carried a "partying white couple" that crashed into the singer's disabled car. That incident and the white couple's "hysteria" added to the confusion at the scene and contributed to the conflicting accounts. When the deputy sheriff and the first ambulance arrived, Smith and Morgan were transported to Clarksdale to the "Negro" hospital—the G. T. Thomas Hospital at 615 Sunflower Avenue—where she died of shock following the surgical amputation of her arm.

The ambulance driver, knowing the Jim Crow politics of the day, had not even attempted to take her to the white hospital (Albertson 215–26). The distance between the two institutions seems irrelevant here, as they were barely a mile apart. Whether it would have made significant difference in her care is unknown. Given the era, it is not unreasonable to believe that the equipment for treating trauma would have been better at the white hospital. But, in this case, no effort was made to assess where she would get the better care—the only care available was at G. T. Thomas. Despite the fact that Smith was treated, the nuanced truth of racism that hovers over that incident—and over countless other stories constructed from that event—did not rest with merely the "known" of that event but depended heavily on African Americans' experience and clear understandings of the dangers of being black and needing emergency medical care.

An actual precedent for the legends surrounding the accidental deaths of Drew and Smith occurred in the 1930s. Juliette Derricotte, dean of women at Fisk University and a renowned figure in racial and community politics, died as a result of injuries in an auto accident in November 1931, in Dalton, Georgia. Although Derricotte's injuries were life-threatening—to the extent that one doctor, while waiting to arrange hospitalization, even called on a "local Negro undertaker" to prepare a room for her—white physicians who treated her in Dalton knew that their local hospital, like the hospital in Mississippi, did not "receive" colored patients. Consequently, they transported her fifty miles away to Chattanooga, Tennessee. But this delay was critical, and both Derricotte and her injured traveling companion were forced to endure the drive to Chattanooga. Her companion died without regaining consciousness before reaching Tennessee. Juliette Derricotte died the following evening at Walden Hospital in Chattanooga (Lerner 390–96).

The north was not much more reliable. In New York City, in March 1937, "the wife of W.C. Handy, composer of the St. Louis Blues, lay critically ill in an ambulance more than an hour before the doors of Knickerbocker Hospital while the hospital officials debated whether or not a Negro should be admitted" (Ottley 273).

While not all deathbed and medical-intervention stories bring racial politics to the fore, even the last journey of statesman and educator Booker T. Washington was not free of a racial politics. In this particularly damning situation, the narrative depends on the intimate nature of his illness. Washington's declining health was known to some of his relatives and friends, but mostly he kept the matter of his health a private affair. Biographer Louis R. Harlan commented that Washington's last travels were "probably" designed to "work his way toward the Mayo clinic" for evaluation and treatment, but Washington was unable to schedule a visit. Instead, he was examined at St. Luke's hospital in New York City, where a variety of physicians consulted on his condition. One of those physicians was Walter Bastedo, whose public comments following the examination were indiscreet and extremely problematic. He told reporters, "Dr. Washington has been suffering from severe headaches. . . . [T]here is noticeable hardening of the arteries and he is extremely nervous. *Racial characteristics* are, I think, in part responsible for Dr. Washington's breakdown. . . . [H]e is in no shape to go back to Tuskegee" (451–52; my emphasis).

Bastedo's comments about "racial characteristics" were at the core of this breach of professional ethics. Harlan noted that the phrase "made possible a whole circus of interpretation by press and public" (452). Knowing that the disease pathology of syphilis includes arterial complications, Washington's personal physician, Dr. George Hall, was specific in his outrage, saying, "that expression means a 'syphilitic history' when referring to Colored people" (452). In insisting that his patient, so far as Hall was aware, "had not had a Wassermann test," Hall attempted to defuse Bastedo's malicious and wounding statement. Hall may also have been sensitive to lingering public awareness of a curious visit—which did not last much more than an hour—that Washington had made some years earlier to an apartment in a "disreputable" white neighborhood in New York City. There, Henry Ulrich, a local resident of the neighborhood, unhappy with and suspicious of Washington's presence, took a stick and chased the distinguished statesman down the street (Donaldson and Donaldson 3:244). Washington's reasons for having been at that apartment and whom he may have been visiting were never made completely clear. It is possible that the memory of and public suspicions and rumors about that event added an uncomfortable dimension to the indelicate story that emerged during his final days. Biographer Harlan put the crux of this controversy into some perspective.

> Did Dr. Bastedo indeed mean to refer to syphilis when he spoke of "racial characteristics," or did he instead merely indulge in a white-supremacy stereotype of black nervous distress in the face of crisis? If he did signify syphilis, was the doctor on the scene, though indiscreet, more to be trusted than the discreet doctor far away, who had treated the patient for years but was a personal friend? Was it significant that the doctor consulted after Dr. Bastedo's examination was Dr. Rufus Cole, who happened to be an expert on gonococcus infections . . . ? The voluble Dr. Bastedo's statement could be construed as a hint of syphilis but certainly not a diagnosis of it, and it might in that race-obsessed era have been simply a white man's racial hyperbole. (453)

Harlan's comments, tactful as they attempted to be given the delicate subject and the formidable statesman under scrutiny, nevertheless left the weight of the judgment with the syphilis implication. Both Washington's consultation with the gonococcal specialist and the "extreme nervousness" and "breakdown" were left to stand without a persuasive counter-explanation. Their injudicious public airing encouraged an unfortunate private speculation.

Two days after public news of his illness broke through the veil of privacy, Washington, determined to go home to Tuskegee, boarded a train at Pennsylvania Station in New York. The heroic statement he made on the occasion was carried across the wire services: "I was born in the South, I have lived and labored in the South, and I expect to die and be buried in the South." He could not be persuaded to forego the journey, even though his physicians had predicted that he would only live a short time, perhaps even the space of a few hours. Thus, despite the dire predictions and without receiving a public apology for the unfortunate racial cast Bastedo's pronouncements on his illness had added to these last days of his life, Booker T. Washington walked to his berth on the train without the assistance of a wheelchair — giving credibility to his doctors' surprise at "see[ing] a man up and about who ought by all the laws of nature to be dead." When the train reached North Carolina, his

The dignified funeral of Booker T. Washington. The honor guard in Tuskegee Chapel was one of the very few concessions to "pomp" during the ceremonies. The profusion of flowers was another.

wife sent a wire to Tuskegee requesting that an ambulance and an escort meet them in Alabama. When he reached the station at Chehaw, Washington was aware enough of his surroundings to inquire after the well-being of his grandson. However, by early morning, just before 5:00 A.M., he died. The local student papers reported on his illness by saying that their beloved scholar was "completely worn out" and had succumbed to "nervous exhaustion and arteriosclerosis." In Tuskegee, there was no mention of "racial characteristics."

Washington's stature assured his dignified death, despite the cast of colored politics that nearly tainted his final days. Two years later, on April Fool's Day, 1917, ragtime musician Scott Joplin would succumb to syphilis—this time unambiguously indicated on his death certificate as "dementia paralytica—cerebral form," with the contributory cause being listed as "syphilis." Certainly, dementia could also be characterized in more particular circles as a "breakdown." Those who reported Washington's death as a heart attack and "arteriosclerosis" may have skirted the issue as well—during the secondary phase of syphilis, acute myocarditis, a scarring of the layers of the aorta, is common. Scott Joplin's case had no Washingtonian veil of doubt. Nor was there the veil of privacy and privilege that had surrounded Washington, protecting that "race man" from rumors and innuendo that could have had a devastating effect on the causes he advanced; in fact, for Joplin, the nature of his profession, with its particularly intense and intimate public scrutiny, afforded him no privacy at all in reference to his illness. Joplin's "classic symptoms" were an uncontested reality. Biographer Edward Berlin noted that the disease's symptoms included memory loss, erratic behavior, and irritability, followed later by "exalted emotional periods and delusions of grandeur alternating with periods of . . . melancholia . . . speech defects, tremors and discoordination of the fingers," which recalled fellow-musician Eubie Blake's description of "Joplin's feeble attempts to play the piano and . . . his inability to speak. [Joplin's wife] Lottie said that, toward the end, he destroyed manuscripts." Joplin, aware of his disease and its prognosis, "slipped into madness." Perhaps anticipating his own death, or perhaps with some faint hope of recuperation, Joplin attempted to leave New York to go to his sister's home in Chicago—but he never left the city. Instead, he was hospitalized at Belleville, transferred to and physically restrained in a mental ward in Manhattan State Hospital where he died "a horrible death" (Berlin 238–39).

Washington and Joplin experienced fame and renown differently, and circulated in environments that required different levels of confidentiality and caution. The public nature of Joplin's illness seemed to characterize entertainers' vulnerability to public performances of even the most private concerns. Consider the death of Billie Holiday, the artist who had seared the lyrics of "Strange Fruit" into America's cultural memory. The story of her death offers a different, but ironically complementary, perspective on the issues of privacy and the consideration accorded to different kinds of stature. There was no equivocating the nature of her illness. It was so well known and so intimately connected with the narrative of her performances that her illness and her performances seemed to develop alongside each other. Music and drugs conspired to form the legend of "Lady Day," a legend in progress even before her death.

Holiday was both brave and beautiful in her death, according to long time friend and newspaperman William Dufty. Dufty told *New York Times* columnist Nat Hentoff that "At the slightest rattle of the oxygen tent, she lunged forward, dukes up, and barked out . . . 'Don't be in such a hurry!'" Dufty reported that although she was breathing with difficulty, when "she wasn't fighting the pain, her face was beautiful." He was there when she died and told Hentoff about her final moments. "She was asleep, but seemed to rally. She was looking strong but [was] breathing very deeply, struggling for air. . . . Then her face relaxed. The nurse felt her pulse. 'She's gone,' she said" (O'Meally 194).

After her death, there arose two stories concerning the matter of approximately $750 she had in her possession in her final hours, money earned from a story she had sold to *Confidential* magazine editors who were eager to supply their readers with titillating details of the star's sordid experiences. First, there was Dufty's version. Dufty reported to the newspapers that, just *before* Holiday's death, a nurse had brought him the *Confidential* cash, rolled up in a cigarette-like tube, and that she claimed to have found it taped to Holiday's thighs during a medical examination. Then, there was the version presented by Robert O'Meally in his 1991 biography of Holiday. While O'Meally confirmed that Dufty did indeed get this roll of bills before Holiday's death from a nurse who had found it during an "examination," O'Meally believed that the money had been inserted into her vagina not taped to her legs. The thigh story, he felt, was constructed for the newspapers.

Donald Clarke's 1997 biography, *Wishing on the Moon: The Life and Times of Billie Holiday,* repeated O'Meally's money-in-the-vagina story and also accepted that the nurse had presented the money to Dufty just before Holiday died. Clarke added, perhaps by way of explanation, that the nurse had found it while "bathing" Holiday and that (ostensibly after the bath) "A nurse came out and said, 'Are you Bill?' " According to Clarke, Dufty worried that the nurse had found more drugs, but then she gave him the roll of bills along with the explanation that she had found it while "bathing" (!) the comatose Holiday. Reportedly, Dufty behaved in an honorable manner, refused the money, and asked that it be placed with Holiday's personal effects.

Although both stories seem to be neatly constructed—whether one accepts the bath or the examination, the thigh or the vagina—the medical facts raise doubts about both of those scenarios. Holiday was hospitalized with heart and kidney problems. All were aware that her grave condition indicated that death was imminent. Gently put, it would have been unusual to perform a vaginal exam at this time. Nor is it likely that, with a comatose patient nearing death, a nurse would have decided that this would be a reasonable occasion for a bath. And, finally, vagi-

Crowd at Billie Holiday's funeral. *Bettman/CORBIS.*

nal examinations were not performed by nurses. It is, however, a traditional hospital practice for nurses to prepare a corpse for transport to
the hospital's morgue. Further, it is usual and customary medical practice during this preparation to pack the body's orifices — the vagina and
rectum included — with cotton batting to prevent the effects of gravity
(i.e., leaking fluids). Considering these medical realities, it is more likely
that the cash Holiday hid in her vagina was not discovered until *after* her
death, following the preparation of her body to leave the hospital. At that
time, the cash would have been placed with her personal effects (where
Dufty said he directed the money). Clearly, when a body is headed to
the morgue, neither privacy nor dignity is a manageable issue.

Still, there have been more somber and dignified occasions in the history of twentieth-century African American death and dying. Consider
the quiet example of Bill "Bojangles" Robinson, whose public career was
followed carefully by whites and blacks. Toward the end of his life, however, he largely retreated from the public's view and was no longer working regularly. Indications are that the difference between the visibility of
his film and theater days and the comparative shadows of his final years

was difficult for him. His performances always stressed emotional control, and he never let the audiences see anything but that control. If any emotional residue lingered from the years when his magnificent skill and talent were eclipsed by race or when he was viewed as a humorous sidekick to a little-girl actress with a carefully regulated number of curls, no one was the wiser.

But early in 1949, the year he died, friends caught a glimpse of his sense of sorrow and mortality. Although Bojangles had negotiated a racialized terrain that publicly expressed his consummate artistry, he had done this primarily as an accompaniment to the white child-star Shirley Temple's imitation of his every tap-danced move. He was never allowed to do more than grin at the little dancer whose career he shadowed. Although one movie did have Bojangles and Shirley Temple hand-in-hand, tap-dancing up a set of plantation stairs so that she could go to bed, the image "intimated a relation so taboo that the dance sequence had to be cut from the film" when it played in southern cities. Temple-Black explained in her autobiography, "To avoid social offense and assure wide distribution, the studio cut scenes showing physical contact between us" (duCille 17).

So, at the end of Bojangles's career, when a young black tap dancer appeared on the Ted Mack Amateur Hour dancing like Bojangles, the irony may have been too dramatic. At the end of the child's well-received act, Robinson himself suddenly appeared on stage. Given the circumstances, someone had to have alerted him to what was planned for the day and had likely staged the meeting of the two. But, reportedly, both studio personnel and the audience were shocked to see him, as he had not been scheduled or announced on the show's line-up of guests. Regardless of the construction of the event, Bill Robinson joined the young dancer on the stage and, in a moment of overwhelmed and tearful emotion, embraced the young performer—something he could never have done with Shirley. One can only imagine the constellation of emotions that must have assailed Robinson as he held this youthful imitator—this time, one who looked like him. In a biography by James Haskins and N. R. Mitgang, Bojangles's friends remarked that "he looked tired. He looked sick." It was as if he recognized that "he was handing over his crown." It was "like him saying, 'This is my good-bye.'"

After that public breakdown, he rarely left his Brooklyn home, except to see his doctor. His wife, Elaine, said that he would "dance up the steps to the doctor's house. . . . [H]e said . . . if he danced, he could get up there quickly and feel a little lighter." In November, after having been admitted to Columbia Presbyterian Hospital following a heart attack, Robinson's condition worsened. His wife described his last moments: "I touched his hands and they were very cool. They asked us to leave the room. Then, the next time they asked us back in—it was maybe three minutes later—she said he was gone. I remember how he laid there so stiff with a blank expression. I said, 'What do you mean, "he's gone"? His feet are still moving.'" Mr. Bojangles was sixty-seven years old (Haskins and Mitgang 300–305).

When Louis Armstrong died, his professional artistry also accompanied his death story. Armstrong had had a series of heart attacks, but biographer Laurence Bergreen reported, "For a time, he seemed to rally. On his ceremonial birthday, July 4, 1971, television crews and interviewers came to visit him. . . . In a soft voice, with Lucille at his side, he declared his intention to resume performing as soon as he was able. The next day, he told the All Stars to prepare for a rehearsal. He had another gig coming up, and he was very excited about it." The anticipation did not last the night. "At 5:30 the next morning, July 6, 1971, Louis Armstrong died in his home, in bed, in his sleep" (Bergeen 492–93).

Literary renderings of these final moments not only retain their drama but also often embellish it through "poetic license." Zora Neale Hurston recalled her mother's death in her autobiography, *Dust Tracks on a Road,* embroidering it with folkloric detail. This was no surprise, given Hurston's literary and scholarly career as a novelist and anthropologist, but it was also illuminated a touching and important personal story. Hurston remembered:

It was not long after Mama came home that she began to be less active. Then she took to bed. I knew she was ailing, but she was always frail, so I did not take it too much to heart. I was nine years old, and even though she had talked to me very earnestly one night, I could not conceive of Mama actually dying. She had talked of it many times.

That day, September 18th, she had called me and given me certain instructions. I was not to let them take the pillow from under her head until she was dead. The clock was not to be covered, nor the looking-glass. She trusted me to see to it that these things were not done. I promised her as solemnly as nine years could do, that I would see to it. (62)

Although Hurston was notoriously unreliable about her own age at any given time of her life, it is now fairly clear that Hurston was, in fact, nine years old in 1900. The story she told about her mother's final hours detailed practices associated with African Americans, especially in the first part of the century.

I had left Mama and was playing outside . . . when I noted a number of women going inside Mama's room and staying. It looked strange. Papa was standing at the foot of the bed looking down on my mother, who was breathing hard. As I crowded in, they lifted up the bed and turned it . . . so that Mama's eyes would face the east. . . . And now, Death stirred from his platform in his secret place in our yard, and came inside the house. Somebody reached for the clock, while Mrs. Mattie Clarke put her hand to the pillow to take it away. "Don't!" I cried out. . . . "She said she didn't want it!" Now I know that I could not have had my way against the world. The world we lived in required those acts. Anything else would have been sacrilege. . . . My father was with the mores. He restrained me physically from outraging the ceremonies established for the dying. (62–64)

Mirrors and photographs did get turned to the wall or covered to keep the spirit from being captured in the glass as it departed from the body. The practice of stopping a clock was a way of record keeping, and clocks stopped at the appropriate hour were even placed on gravesites as memorials and tributes. The pillow's removal eased the departure of the soul from the body. The eastern orientation of the deathbed (as well as of the positioning of the head in a graveyard casket) was to assure that the feet were pointed in the soul's desired direction toward its rebirth. The women who attended Hurston's mother, Lucy, knew the history in these practices.

Tragically, Zora Hurston's dramatic literary historicizing could not be put to use for the moments when the veil descended on her own life. Not much of a story remains of Hurston's own lonely death in a welfare home in St. Lucie County, Florida. That which we do know has been reconstructed by her biographer and by Alice Walker, with other detail being provided by statements recorded on her death certificate.

In her last years, Hurston's health was greatly compromised by diabetes and hypertension. A tropical fluke, acquired during her Caribbean travels, eventually compromised her liver function, and she suffered from ulcers and a diseased gallbladder, as well. Friends described the once-vibrant Hurston—who in earlier days had invaded New York's Harlem literati scenes draped in dramatic red scarves, trumpeting her arrival as "Queen of the Niggerati"—as dispirited, "worn out and distracted." She entered the St. Lucie County welfare home in October of 1959 and did not last through the first month of the New Year. During the night of 28 January 1960, Zora Neale Hurston died of hypertensive heart disease. She had been dependent on the county welfare office for money to pay for her prescriptions and, prior to moving to the welfare home, for food vouchers. As she was penniless at death, her friends collected enough money to bury her—nearly four hundred dollars according to biographer Robert Hemenway, who wrote that a "group of students who remembered their substitute teacher collected $2.50 in small change." The other moneys came from her friends, her various publishers, and her family. Hemenway wrote that "the services were held in the tiny chapel of the funeral home and . . . the body was placed in an open casket. Zora was dressed in a bright pink dressing gown; fuzzy pink mules covered her feet" (347–348). Although the "full couch" casket—which accounts for our knowing what she wore on her feet—was not the ordinary casket displayed for Southern traditions, neither was its occupant.

The cultural expectations around observing traditions that eased a death were strong in the twentieth century, but because hospital beds eventually replaced family bedsides and because the scattering of family from traditionally insular communities became common, the practices that were anathema to Hurston waned. There were, however, family traditions that remained important and inscribed their own ritual on these deathbed moments.

Pamela A. described how she and one of her sisters, who grew up with "the strain that can exist between sisters separated by many years and different childhood experiences," shared a ritual that helped them deal with their grandmother's death—their sisterly bond was spiritually renewed by touching their grandmother's hair. Pamela explained that the women in her family "were all known for having long hair" and that getting their hair plaited on their grandmother's porch in Hamlet, North Carolina, was a family tradition. Mama G., their grandmother, had "wonderful, long, silver braids" that the grandchildren loved to comb and plait. "Often a cousin would stand on each side of Mama G.'s chair and race to see who could finish a plait first. After the plaits were done, we'd wrap them in circles to make flat buns near her ears."

> When Mama G. died, my sister and I decided we really had to plait her hair so it would look right. This was not an easy decision, but we knew we had to do it. Neither of us knew what to expect. We didn't know what emotion would accompany us: fear of a dead body? Overwhelming grief? I don't recall which one of us initiated the idea, but I remember the day we drove to the black funeral home of this small Southern town with the comb, brush, large hair pins, and a jar of blue hair grease. My sister took a last draw on a cigarette to calm her nerves and we went in. Then we stood outside the embalming room for a few seconds, each asking if the other was okay. She seemed small and was on a metal table, not the comfy chair from the front porch that we knew as children. We asked the funeral parlor employee to leave us alone. This was a personal, private time, and we knew Mama G. would not have wanted him in there with us. We each completed a plait and rolled it into the perfect bun she favored. It was a sacred experience.

There was a similarly sacred and sisterly sharing of grievous loss when Betty Sanders Shabazz, wife of the Malcolm X, died in a 1997 fire. The fire was tragically set by her grandson Malcolm, a child for whom poet Maya Angelou had perhaps the most loving and the most forlorn understanding when she described him as a child caught in "the clutch of circumstance." Shabazz's daughters—Attallah, Qubilah, Gamilah-Lumumba, Ilyasah, Malikah, and Malaak—gathered to cleanse and wrap their mother's body in preparation for her funeral and burial, following the traditions of their Muslim faith. Their incomparable sorrow, first shared privately in that soul-wrenching act of love, was then declared publicly as they gathered their tenacious spirits and their fierce love to speak at the funeral services of the woman called Dr. Betty, but whom they knew as "Mommy." They were quite literally the family left from the loving union of Malcolm Little and Dr. Betty Dean Sanders Shabazz. Her funeral and burial, like those of her husband thirty-two years earlier, was a state occasion. But, with the involvement, incarceration, and institutionalization of young Malcolm, theirs was a mourning story without conclusion.

Some dying stories told about prominent African Americans of the twentieth century were even more dramatic than those told by Shabazz's daughters. Richard Wright's passing on 28 November 1960 was striking enough for both fiction and fact. In *The Man Who Cried I Am* novelist John A. Williams wrote the fictionalized rendition. Wright, whose disaffection with the United States led to his eventual expatriation, had been well known for his communist sympathies. According to Williams's account—a version corroborated by some of Wright's biographers—there was enough mystery surrounding Wright's death to suspect the involvement of the CIA. Williams's fictional character in *The Man* is named Max, and his demise occurs soon after the secret service learn of his clandestine activities, which involve encouraging black America's armed resistance to what he anticipated would be the country's inevitable race wars. Max is killed with an overdose of morphine, administered covertly by a secret service agent (Edwards) who had been dispatched to arrange his assassination. "Edwards quickly pulled Max's body into his car and bent him over the steering wheel. He . . . found the morphine. . . . Without hesitation, he attached the needle to the syringe, then withdrew the morphine. He pushed up Max's sleeve and hit the big vein in the arm. Like the old days with the Narcotics Department he thought. . . . Jazz musicians in Europe dying of overdoses administered by agents getting tired of chasing them" (Williams 401–2).

Another biographer, Michel Fabre, indicated that Wright's profile in the United States had not diminished in the last month of his life, despite his Paris residency. He was well known for his acerbic judgments on this country's race relations. Fabre reported that although Wright was in France in November, word of a lecture he had given early in the month made news in the *Chicago Defender*. In that lecture, "The Situation of the Black Artist and Intellectual in the United States," Wright noted how black artists were often constrained in their revolutionary ideologies, for fear of governmental reprisals. The *Defender*'s article was headlined "Richard Wright Hits US Racial Hypocrisy, Country is Rapped" (Fabre 518). Wright's death at the end of the month came as a surprise to all who had been in communication with him at the time—including his wife, Ellen, and author Langston Hughes. For some, it was difficult not to engage the suspicion that the report of his continuing racial activism and the press notices at home were somehow involved in his death.

Fabre acknowledged that there were legitimate and "various questions raised by his sudden death," and, given the government's wariness about Wright's activities and political profile, "it would certainly be possible to write two contradictory but reasonably convincing conclusions" about the event. One of these conclusions, he continued, could be that "political intrigue had forcibly" intervened in Wright's final hours. Fabre chooses to believe, however, that he died as the result of a natural heart attack, convinced in great measure that Wright's public profile was not significant enough to lead to an event as dramatic as assassination. However, Fabre "did not consider it unreasonable" to assume the government's direct intervention in provocative attacks on Wright, the tension and stress from this close surveillance possibly leading to a heart attack.

Margaret A. Walker offered a more dramatic version of events—a midnight visitor, carrying a lethal injection. Walker, author of *Jubilee* and once intimately associated with Richard Wright, wrote a caustic and temperamentally uneven biography of Wright, filled to a great extent with her meagerly disguised personal and professional bitterness about this man. (In a personal conversation, Fabre suggested to me that jealousy compromised Walker's interpretive frame for Wright's death.) For Walker, the "seeds of suspicion were planted in my mind" after hearing at a conference that Wright might have been murdered, allegedly by "that woman." "The rumor is that he was murdered by a woman. The question is what woman? . . . Was she his mysterious visitor between ten P.M. and midnight? Or was there a woman posing as a wife or mistress in order to enter the hospital room? Was it the nurse who last saw him alive? Why would such a woman commit murder? For money or sex? Was there a sexual encounter shortly before death? Not likely, but if so, was he killed during that encounter or did that act of love in fact kill him?" (344–45).

Walker's odd histrionics continued, her tone increasingly strident. She raised questions about the Russian doctor, the choice of clinics, the nature of his illness, and the state of his finances. But her objective fixation, it seemed clear, was the woman: "The late night visitor may have been a mistress, a woman paid to act swiftly and fatally. But there was also a nurse who had seen him laughing and talking. Did the telephone call he received alert his killer? Did Medusa, the monster woman, show her face one more time? Was she wearing a mask, the fatal look of death? Either money or sex as a motive or bait may have been used. Whatever happened, Wright was surprised to see the frustrating face of Medusa one more time, and this time she was wearing the frozen face of death!" (Walker 345).

Walker repeated Constance Webb's accounting of the medicines Wright was taking during his "last illness"—an array of drugs that Walker speculated may not have been warranted. Continuing to stoke the fires of rumor, Walker also repeated Fabre's comment about an injection of some sort having been administered to him: "he might . . . have been disposed of at the Eugene Gibez Clinic where he did, in fact, die shortly after having been given an injection at a time when his health was apparently better" (Fabre 521; Walker 342). Walker's damning compilation of questions and statements, and her frequent and regrettably inaccurate citations, did add a certain fictive vitality to her recreation of Wright's death—although Walker's speculations tended toward the lurid rather than the political. In any case, neither the hyperbolic indulgences of the biography nor her account of Wright's death did much to relieve the black community's collective doubt about whether or not he had a natural death.

Whatever the fact of Richard Wright's death, its story was compellingly recast by his biographers and by the novelist Williams. His passing was thus not only significant for African American literary history, but its not-so-sotto-voce theme of retribution for racial activism left a trace, if not a specific mark, of black death.

In comparison, Wright's reluctant literary legatee, James Baldwin, died a quiet and unremarkable death, which is notable in the context of his own relentless testifying about the terror of black death in African America. Writing with stinging clarity and precision about the black children who were murdered in Atlanta during the latter third of the century, Baldwin made clear the associative nexus between black memory and the experience of black death: "memory makes its only real appearance in this life as this life is ending—appearing, at last, as a kind of guide into a condition which is as far beyond memory as it is beyond imagination" (*Evidence* xiii). What has this to do with the murdered, missing children of Atlanta? "It has something to do with the fact that no one wishes to be plunged, head down, into the torrent of what he does not remember and does not wish to remember. It has something to do with

the fact that we all came here as candidates for the slaughter of the inno-
cents. It has something to do with the fact that all survivors, however
they accommodate or fail to remember it, bear the inexorable guilt of
the survivor. It has something to do, in my own case, with having once
been a Black child in a White country. My memory stammers, but my
soul is a witness" (xiii).

Unlike the postmortem drama and loneliness associated with
Wright's passing, Baldwin died quietly and with dignity, with his
brother, lover, and friends nearby. Baldwin biographer David Leeming
wrote of the final hours, when "Jimmy," dying of liver cancer, was surrounded by a caring company of men. He died imagining the company
of a lifetime of friends coming to wish him a final farewell, and being
comforted by those who were there to keep him company:

> [E]ven as he was dying Jimmy insisted on his role as a witness and lived
> his prophecy. . . . He woke up during that evening and asked David
> whether he could see Simone and other friends passing along the wall.
> . . . Lucien had been sitting with Jimmy all day and into the night. The
> others were talking at the table when Lucien called David, saying he
> thought it was time. David sat on the bed and took Jimmy's hands,
> Bernard squeezed water from a napkin onto his lips. Jimmy looked at
> them and seemed to drift away. David and Lucien both had the sense
> that they were taking the journey with him as far as they could go. It
> was after midnight. They all kissed Jimmy. David said, "It's all right
> Jimmy; you can cross over now," and Jimmy passed. (Leeming 385–86)

"And I said that this is my son, this is Bobo"

An intersection between two Chicago stories reveals the poignant narratives of mourning and loss, and of black death. In the former, one parent
recalled bringing her child to the edge of the bier where another youngster lay dead, because she wanted him "to see what they do to us, and
how his life and his youth were meaningless." It was early in September 1955 when this youngster joined crowds of other children and their
parents at the Roberts Temple Church of God in Christ and saw the
maliciously mutilated remains of Emmett Till. In 1955, fifteen-year-old

Emmett left Chicago to visit family in Mississippi. The story of what happened there is murky. Was the provocation a whistle or a lingered glance? Or, was it a casual and flippant comment—"Bye, baby"—to a white woman that was enough to condemn the youngster? Some encounter of eyes, voice, imagination, and riotous white rage left Emmett's corpse tangled in the debris on the banks of the Tallahatchie River. His violently abused body was all that remained to reveal whatever story there was of his death and dying. When he was returned to Chicago for burial, the arrangements were handled by the A. A. Raynor Funeral Home in the city's South Side. Emmett's mother had demanded that the casket not be closed, so that the world, she said, could see what had been done to him. Her insistence made certain that the ravages of racism, etched into her Bobo's poor, dark body, would inscribe the cultural moment. Myrlie Evers, widow of civil-rights leader Medgar Evers recalled that Emmett's death taught that "even a child is not safe from racism and bigotry and death" (Powledge 49).

Nearly half a century later, again in an early September, again at a Church of God in Christ, and again in Chicago's South Side, another black parent declared at another black child's funeral, "I brought my grandson here to see what can happen. . . . [T]hat's a baby in there and I'm scared to death for mine" (Kendall 1). Once again, in a ritual that came to be darkly familiar to black youth and their families, children were brought to see a body that looked like them. The brutality of the 1990s was barely different in degree or kind from that directed toward Emmett in the 1950s. But it was critically different in its magnitude and its familiarity.

In August 1994, the body of eleven-year-old Robert Sandifer (his grandmother called him "Yummy") was discovered, dead, by Chicago police. He had been shot twice in the back of his head. No white racists had lynched this youngster. His fellow Black Disciple gang members, determined to keep Robert away from police questioning, had committed the crime. Days earlier, in a drive-by shooting, Robert's random gunfire had struck and killed his fourteen-year-old neighbor Shavon Dean. Knowing that Robert was a suspect in this killing and determining that any interrogation of him would endanger the security of the gang's activity, the Disciples decided to eliminate the liability by shooting him. In the short space of a week, Chicago mourned the deaths of two ado-

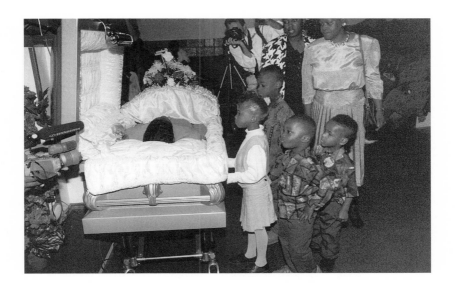

A group of children views the body of eleven-year-old Robert Sandifer. *Photo by Charles Bennett. The Associated Press.*

lescents—Robert and Shavon—and absorbed the loss of all of them, the killers and the killed.

Like Emmett, Robert was funeralized in early September. About four hundred people attended Yummy's funeral, far fewer than the estimated crowds of between one hundred thousand and six hundred thousand who filed past Emmett Till's open casket. One newspaper account noted that his body, lying in the casket, looked as if it belonged to a seven year old playing dead in his big brother's tan suit. In contrast to Bobo's mutilated body, Yummy's seemed almost pacific in its pose. Whereas the racist violence of Klan-era America led to Bobo's murder, the pathology of street violence, crime, and urban deprivation and denial led to Yummy's. Whatever the circumstances, though, three children were buried too early.

Stories that emerged from African American children's deaths brought the morbid experiences of African American communities into sharp focus. The death of children should be unexpected events in the life-death cycle. But, from the fact that such occasions had become familiar—and even anticipated—emerged a perspective of black com-

Children find a grave space in the scenes of black death.
News and Observer

munity life that told a larger story than the single, pitiful event of one child's dying and burial. Stories like Emmett's haunted our fiction, appeared in autobiography and memoirs, and became our folk and news stories.

"The" *Jet*—a magazine that since 1951 has helped engrave such narratives into the memorials of the black community—printed a photograph of Emmett's disfigured corpse lying in his casket. My grandmother always tried to hide the magazine from my sisters and me. She felt that the bathing-beauty photos and the crime scene reports were inappropriate for our consumption—although she and my grandfather kept a subscription all their lives. I knew that she hid them in the basement bookshelves. And I always read them cover to cover. I will never forget the summer that I saw Emmett. I even think I remember where it was—on the bottom of a left-hand page. I know I remember his face. Or, what was supposed to be his face. I see it as clearly today as if I were still in my grandmother's basement, frozen at the moment I glimpsed down and saw him. Author John Edgar Wideman recalls, as well, the moment he came across Emmett's Till's photograph in *Jet*: "I certainly hadn't been searching for Emmett Till's face when it found me, I peeked quickly,

This embalming product for "delicate" tissue is often used for children's bodies.

focused my eyes just enough to ascertain something awful on the page, a mottled, grayish something . . . something I registered with a sort of simultaneous glance at and glance away" (Wideman 126).

Such photographic images of children pitifully recalled their vulnerability. The fact that their bodies were similarly fragile was also a business concern to chemical-company representatives like Geary Powell, whose Arlington Chemical Products markets a special product for the embalming of children. He and Allie Freeman, President of Bondol Laboratories in Madison, Arkansas, are two of only a handful of black businesses—"of any consequence," according to Freeman—in the embalming-products market. Arlington has been in business since the early 1920s, and Bondol since 1938. Their products have responded to the shifting markets of demand for industry products, including the necessity, as they perceive it, for a special fluid that is recommended for use with "delicate" tissue. Its targeted marketing was not unrelated to the high rate of death among African American children.

Children's stories persist long past their passing on. For example, Emmett Till's story appears briefly in Nobel laureate Toni Morrison's

These three occupy different spaces before the bier of a child killed in the Birmingham church bombing. Each, however, participates in this ritual of black death, their own vulnerability creating the shadow images of this scene.

novel *Song of Solomon*. And, even though Morrison's narrative is fictive, there is barely a pause at the wonder of Emmett's factual presence in this novel. In Morrison's novel the remembrance of children is kept company by the specter of a murdered and mutilated Emmett Till. Till slipped from narrative to narrative, appearing not only in *Jet* and *Song of Solomon* but also in a Bebe Moore Campbell novel—all cultural commemorations that belied the assumption that our children were farthest away from the trauma of death. Instead, they were pitifully and despairingly near.

Even children, for instance, did not escape lynching. In Georgia, early in the century, two children fatally scuffled over a gun they were playing with. "Little" T.Z. McElhaney, a sixteen-year-old black child from Wynnton, accidentally shot his white playmate Cedron Land. T.Z. was taken from the Muscogee County courthouse on 13 August 1912 "by a mob of unmasked, well-known white men, including several from the family of the dead white boy, taken for a ride on a trolley car and shot some 50 times" (Winn). In his study of lynching, historian William Brundage documented a memo found in the NAACP archives of "Sandy Ray, 17 years of age, short-trousered, lynched in Georgia and the fourteen year old Andrew Dudley, lynched in Richmond, VA in 1904" (105n.49).

The ephemeral presence of four little girls who were killed on a Sunday morning in Birmingham, Alabama, seared their tragedy into our memories and our stories both, making certain that their story is placed among the sorrow songs of black deaths and dying. Again in *Song of Solomon,* children's dying in fact became a fiction. The 1963 assassination of Cynthia Wesley, Addie Mae Collins, Carole Robertson, and Denise McNair, murdered in a bomb blast during a summer Sunday-school service, haunted the text of the following passage: "Every night now Guitar was seeing little scraps of Sunday dresses—white and purple, powder blue, pink and white, lace and voile, velvet and silk, cotton and satin, eyelet and grosgrain. The scraps stayed with him all night . . . bits of Sunday dresses that . . . did not fly; they hung in the air quietly, like the whole notes in the last measure of an Easter hymn. Four little colored girls had been blown out of a church" (173).

Jazz, blues, and protest singer Nina Simone's artistic response to the loss of the Birmingham children led to her composition "Mississippi Goddamn." She recalled that moment in her autobiography:

> I was sitting . . . in my den on September 15 when news came over the radio that somebody had thrown dynamite into the 16th Street Baptist Church. . . . Later in the day, in the rioting which followed, Birmingham police shot another black kid and a white mob pulled a young black man off his bicycle and beat him to death, out in the street. It was more than I could take. . . . The bombing of the little girls in Alabama and the murder of Medgar Evers. . . . I suddenly realized what it was to be black in American in 1963. . . . [I]t came as a rush of fury, hatred, and determination. (89–90)

After an initial period of rage, during which she tried to make a homemade gun (a zipper gun), Simone realized that a response true to her own spirit would be artistic instead. "An hour later I came out of my apartment with the sheet music for 'Mississippi Goddamn' in my hand. It was my first civil-rights song and it erupted out of me quicker than I could write it down. I knew then that I would dedicate myself to the struggle for black justice, freedom and equality under the law for as long as it took, until all our battles were won" (90). Simone's delivery was passionate and raw, and the lyrics, "I think every day's gonna be my last," echoed the rage and fear embedded in that era. The twentieth century's African American music shared, participated in, and reflected the rage against American racism and black vulnerability. Simone's song, in particular, had significant impact on the singer's career and on the cooperation of the aesthetic with political outrage against black death in the United States. Simone explained that her audiences "knew I was making sacrifices and running risks. . . . [M]y music was dedicated to a part of this struggle . . . to the fight for freedom and the historical destiny of my people. . . . I felt a fierce pride when I thought about what we were all doing together" (91).

African American narratives are scripted out of the ways of our remembering our bodies and the conditions of dying. Giving bodies back to grieving mothers, being taken to bodies by anxious grandparents, or anticipating the graphic photos of *Jet,* we inscribed these mourning stories into our national culture until they told us, surely and consistently, about the quality of our living and the quantities of our dying. Emmett's story was not distant enough from Yummy's to disclaim the resemblance. Each of these deaths moved Chicago toward a familiar ritual and toward a familiar language.

The parent who brought her child to see a body followed a tradition grown out of an experienced ritual—a passed-on narrative for the African American community. "I came to bring my son," said one father. Another explained that he planned to bring his children back to the funeral home to let them understand "you're not too young to die." "I wanted the world to see," said Emmett's mother. "I brought my child because I wanted him to know," said a mother who stood in line at Yummy's funeral. This series of interchangeable statements from Bobo's and Yummy's funerals—separated by forty years but joined by a cultural mooring place—construct a familiar language.

Five years after Emmett's death, Richard Wright published *The Long Dream.* An early scene in this novel echoes Emmett Till's death. The character Fish's father, Tyree, is an undertaker who gets the badly mutilated body of Chris, Fish's best friend. Like Emmett, Chris is lynched

Emmett Till.
Bettman/CORBIS.

after an encounter with a white woman. Chris's mother is brought to identify her son's body. Wright's story describes the scene this way: "Mrs. Sims opened her eyes and saw her son's broken body and screamed and lunged forward, flinging herself upon the corpse. 'Chris baby, this ain't you!'" (75). In *The Long Dream,* Wright clearly recognizes the American tragedy of color and youth here, writing the following soliloquy for Chris's mother: "Gawd, *You* didn't do this! You *couldn't*! And You got to do something to stop this from happening to black women's children! . . . Lawd, we ain't scared to die. BUT NOT LIKE THIS!" (75).

In *Your Blues Ain't Like Mine,* Bebe Moore Campbell's fictionalized account of the Till story, the imagined text for that same moment in the funeral parlor was equally wrenching. "Delotha stared at the battered and swollen body of her son, spread out on the funeral parlor table. A strange odor she couldn't place hovered in the air. . . . The director of the funeral parlor, Mr. Willie McCullum, a light-reddish man with sandy hair and the only colored man in Hopewell to wear a suit during the week . . . said . . . 'These the coffins I have,' and pointed to several wooden caskets propped up along the wall. 'You need to make you a choice'" (Campbell 55).

No fiction, however, could displace the pathos of the actual moment, here recalled by Emmett Till's heartsick mother, Mamie Till Bradley: "I didn't want that body. . . . That couldn't be mine. But I stared at his

Mamie Bradley at her son's gravesite. *Bettman/CORBIS.*

feet and I could identify his ankles. I said, those are my ankles. Those
are my knees. I knew the knees . . . and then I began to come on up
. . . until I got to the chin and mouth . . . those were Emmett's teeth,
and I was looking for his ear. You notice how mine sort of curls up . . .
Emmett had the same ears. . . . [T]he one eye that was left, that was definitely his eye, the hazel color confirmed that, and I had to admit that
that was indeed Emmett and I said that this is my son, this is Bobo"
(Thomas 5).

These issues of our flesh, its way and its wounding, inscribed a cultural narrative whether told as fiction or fact. In *The Long Dream,* after
Chris's mother identifies her son, Tyree explains to his son his funeral
business: "Fish, you know how I make my living? I make money by

gitting black dreams ready for burial. . . . Most folks on this earth don't even have to think about dying like that. But we do" (80).

Children's deaths made apparent both the persistence of memory and the necessity of memorial. Whether they come in the form of Polaroid shots sifted between family photos in an old black-page album, or in the formal work of professionals like Van Der Zee and Richard Samuel Roberts, photographs of dead black children serve as a particular means of memorial. The great migration of the 1920s dramatically affected African American's experiences with death and dying. In this era, the dead were disproportionately young. In Harlem, for example, during the 1920s and 1930s some funeral directors recall a seemingly "endless" procession of small white caskets that became ordinary as black children succumbed in disproportionate numbers to the tuberculosis epidemic and the pneumonia—called "consumptive disease"—that ravaged the community. An 24 October 1929 article in the *New York Times* led with the headline "Congestion Causes High Mortality" and detailed a death rate 40 percent higher in the crowded neighborhoods of Harlem than in the rest of the city.

Harlem photographer James Van Der Zee, who was well known for his documentary pictorials of Harlem lifestyles, was celebrated as well for the powerful photographs of mourning that he took early in the century. Van Der Zee explained that these photographs were sometimes the only possible way for some families to memorialize a child. In one, a wife leans over her husband as he sits cradling their dead infant in his arms. Both are smiling down at their child as they pose in a domestic setting. The dead baby, dressed in white garments like those worn for a christening, is nestled in his father's arms. He looks as though merely asleep. The parents, whose affect suggests an eerie peace, look down on their dead baby with a calm that belies the still-life story constructed for the photographic occasion. Van Der Zee explained that the picture was taken not in their home but "in the funeral parlor. [A] radio was in the picture to make it look more homelike. It belonged to the undertaker anyway. It was my suggestion to have them hold the child while the picture was being taken to make it look more natural." When asked how the parents felt about holding the dead child he replied, "Well it was their baby. . . . Most of these babies they all died of pneumonia; chest gets filled up with colds because they were living in cold flats. It was a common thing in those days for people to be without heat" (Van Der Zee 83).

These parents intend a different memory than the fact of their infant's death. The domestic scene is betrayed, however, by the shadowy presence of the mortician's assistant in the upper-right-hand corner. *Photo by James Van Der Zee.*

Accounts written at the time suggested that the most dreaded disease in the densely populated projects of Harlem was pneumonia. But tuberculosis as well took its toll. A 1934 survey of 20,000 residents of Harlem revealed that 3 percent had pulmonary tuberculosis. Dr. Louis T. Wright, then chief surgeon of Harlem Hospital, reported that the disease was so pervasive that one city block was known as the "lung block." Because most hospitals in the city that were treating tuberculosis refused to admit "Negro" patients, blacks were squeezed into the wards of Harlem Hospital, just as they were packed into the blocks of Harlem's streets and tenement houses. Both kinds of congestion contributed to the virulence of the disease, hence the high rates of black morbidity and mortality. Harlem Hospital was referred to as the "morgue" in the community, and there was great distrust of its facilities. The story in the streets was "you go there to die." And, pitifully, there was sufficient cause for distrust. In December 1938, New York Department of Health and Vital Statistics reported that twice as many people—men, women, and children—died at

In *Jazz,* Toni Morrison reconstructs this young girl's passed-on narrative, naming her "Dorcas." *Photo by James Van Der Zee.*

the black Harlem Hospital as did those in the white wards of Bellevue (Greenberg 31).

Included in Van Der Zee's collection of Harlem photos is one of a young girl who "was shot by her sweetheart at a party with a noiseless gun" (Van Der Zee 84). Van Der Zee often placed inserts into his pictures—images of Jesus rising over the body in an open casket, flags inserted into the corners of veteran's funeral photographs, biblical scriptures etched into a corner, and angels hovering over caskets were not unusual. He explained, "I just put them in to take away the gruesomeness of the picture, to make it look more like 'suffering little children to come unto me and I'll give you rest'" (Van Der Zee 84). In the photo of the gunshot victim, an image of Jesus cradling a lamb peers through one of the lace curtains above the casket. The young girl lies with a bouquet of flowers across her chest—full couch (that is, with the casket completely open) as was traditional for northern funerals. Van Der Zee recalls the story this way: "She complained of being sick at the party and friends said 'Well, why don't you just lay down?' and they taken her in the room and laid her down. After they undressed her and loosened her clothes, they saw the blood on her dress. They asked her about it and she said, 'I'll tell you tomorrow, yes, I'll tell you tomorrow.' She was just trying to give him a chance to get away. For the picture, I placed the flowers on her chest" (Van Der Zee 84).

Toni Morrison imagined a text for this event in her 1994 novel, *Jazz*. Her narrator explains how, having "lived too much in my own mind," all that was left was to lament the absence and loss of body. In the novel, Morrison named the woman whom Van Der Zee photographed "Dorcas." The husband of Violet, another character, was the shooter. At the moment of dying—which Morrison made parallel to Van Der Zee's recollection—Dorcas thinks, "I ought to be wide awake because something important is happening" (192). Indeed. After Dorcas dies, Violet, whose husband was in love with Dorcas, seeks revenge and goes "to the funeral to see the girl and to cut her dead face" while she lay in the coffin.

Although neighborhood and community funeral homes became practiced in handling remains from their own neighborhoods and communities, those who died in the North were very often buried and funeralized in the South—reflecting the facts of generation and origin of black communities in the United States. Black morticians became adept at accommodating this migration. In the last century, a good deal of their business was "ship-in" or "ship-out." A story from Dwayne Walls's social narrative of the migration is characteristic, even in its overlap of birth and death: "Lessie was midwifing the birth of her fourth great-grandbaby when the telephone rang. . . . [A] minute later she heard Blanche scream. . . . 'Omega's been stabbed, 'Mega's dead.' Her scream was interrupted by her granddaughter's cry for help, and Lessie knew that life must be celebrated before death. [After the baby's birth] she sat numbly on the side of the bed, holding her new great-grandson and mourning her dead son" (68).

Omega had gone north, to Philadelphia, following the allure and promise of work and economic freedom (it was the 1960s). In Omega's hometown of Kingstree, South Carolina, the largest black funeral home was Dimery and Rogers. Walls explained that "a good portion of its business, maybe twenty-five or thirty funerals a year, is ship-in business. The other two [black] places get some ship-ins, too. The bodies for Kingstree and surrounding small towns come into the Kingstree station at the rate

Mamie Bradley meeting her son's body at railway station.
Bettman/CORBIS.

of 300 or so a year. Last weekend alone, there had been eight shipped in, mostly from New York and Newark and Philadelphia and Rochester, New York" (68–69). These deaths—of the children who died during epidemics, of the young who were victims of violence, of the citizenry that was vulnerable to riot and disease—were linked in the experiences of black funeral homes who practiced their crafts with anticipation of the quantities of ship-ins they would negotiate. Southern and northern black communities found a sorrowful ritual enacted at train stations whose box cars brought back the bodies of residents, bodies that retraced the journeys, back and forth, of migrating black families.

As the twentieth century ended, persistent occasions of urban violence deeply affected the improvisational rituals of death in Chicago and Los Angeles. In metropolitan centers across the United States, the generational music of young African Americans reflected their striking sense of vulnerability. Charlotte Hunter, a former publicity agent for rap groups Public Enemy and L. L. Cool J, labeled the music of the 1990s as "mourning music" and explained that the "hip-hop generation, much like any other generation, has its sorrow . . . but for them, Mr. Death is always looming" (Marriott). African Americans participated so often in the ritual of death that it was distressingly ordinary to find contemporary memorials that doubled as urban artistry and cultural critique.

All too often, these memorials were created for familiar faces.

"John Scarborough IV pulled into the parking lot of his father's funeral home and walked in, past the faded yellow vinyl couches, past the double doors that lead to the chapel, past the photographs of his father, his grandfather and his great-grandfather. Stepping toward the back of the building, to the rooms where the embalmers do their work, he stopped to look down at a body bag on the table. When the embalmers unzipped it, Scarborough found himself staring at one of his childhood friends, who had been shot to death in Richmond, Va." (Chen 1E). The crisis that Scarborough's generational cohort faced was reflected in the lyrics of 1990s musicians, including the Houston-based rap group Geto Boys, whose CD *The Resurrection* lyrically expressed their fear and anticipation of death, as well as its public rehearsal.

> And every morning I wake up I'm kinda glad to be alive
> Cause thousands of my homeboys died
> And very few died of old age
> In most cases the incident covered up the whole page.

The cover of the CD featured a series of open caskets—one for each of the artists. The inside-cover photographs that showed them within the caskets was haunting, because it was not quite surreal enough. It was an image that was intimately understandable to funeral directors.

> "He was arguing with someone over something," says Scarborough. "And he just shot him. They just did an autopsy. . . . When I saw him I just shook my head, 'Damn, my man's gone; he's really gone.' But my dad says it's just the spirit that's gone, and all you can do now is make him look presentable to the family. A dead body is still a dead body, but it doesn't bother me now. I've seen four friends that I grew up with die, and we buried them. Right now it doesn't bother me no matter how grotesque it is or what type of death it was." (Chen 1E)

Elaborate rituals evolved for gang deaths in Los Angeles—testimony to the familiarity of this particular dimension of cultural death. A cottage industry evolved to furnish floral tributes draped in gang-colored ribbons and to create sweatshirts and T-shirts with the deceased member's name in a variety of fonts and with a choice of texts like "R.I.P. Homie." Streetcorner memorials, with children's toys stacked on a sidewalk, poetry sketched on building walls, and declarations of love and goodbye messages scrawled on sidewalks became familiar, if transient, urban landmarks. The backlog of children's deaths made weekday rather than weekend funerals an ordinary event in some cities and led funeral directors in other cities to refuse to handle the funerals of children because, as one funeral director in Buffalo, New York, said, "they come in here with guns and all, and they act up."

From Buffalo to Boston, the fear was the same. In 1992, Boston's black clergy gathered to express their grief, outrage, and disbelief at the scene that shook the congregation and the community following the funeral services for twenty-year-old Robert Odom. Before his mother "had the chance to say 'farewell' to her only son . . . young hoodlums who can never be classified as men destroyed that last chance" (Hernandez A1). Odom had been the victim of a drive-by shooting, and the church was filled with teenagers whose gang memberships clashed. The *Boston Globe* described the scene:

> Teen-agers from the Mission Hill and Bromley-Heath housing developments arrived, adding to a crowd that had grown to the point that folding chairs had been set up in the aisles.
>
> Then a group from Castlegate Road came, which "caused some anguish" among the Vamp Hill, Bromley, and Mission Hill groups. A confrontation occurred in the front of the church. (Hernandez A1)

Gunshots were fired; youth fled through the church, almost tripping over the casket; a group of young people "mauled" another youngster. The minister in charge described a "wave of hysteria and chaos" at the scene, and those who gathered on the next day expressed shock and outrage. "I've never seen anything like it in my life," said Jimmy Johnson, deacon at the Morning Star Church. "It was degrading. It was a blow to the community. Where do we go from here? What happens when you can't even find comfort in your own church . . . [when] there's blood, blood in the church?" (Hernandez A1).

In Los Angeles, one young adult speculated about his own funeral as he planned the services for his girlfriend and their thirteen-month old son, who were "gunned down outside a liquor store by gang members retaliating against Williams after a soured drug deal." Enraged and drugged into a murderous rage following that event, Williams and his "homeboys" "got drunk, smoked some PCP and started doing drivebys"—they couldn't remember how many. The next day, Williams took care of the familiar and tragic business of planning the funeral of his girlfriend and daughter. He arranged a $7,000 funeral service, paying for the cost "by dealing dope." Eight hundred people attended, but there was no way to keep the violence of retribution from shattering the peace of the burial and the normally serene cemetery grounds. As the caskets were about to be lowered, a thirty-second barrage of gunfire shattered the solemnity. Williams recalled that "cars drove by and started shooting up the place. . . . I fell to the ground, grabbed my gun and started shooting back." Reflecting later on the psychological consequences of his participation in these ongoing rituals, he said, "You know, I still dream about the funerals I've been to, the drivebys, the people I've hurt. I have nightmares." He thoughtfully constructed what would be an appropriate epitaph for all the youth and young adults conquered by this familiar violence: "I'm trying to shake it, I'm trying to shake it, but it's like I'm in mourning all the time" (Wilkinson and Chavez A15).

Despite a trend toward violence that seemed primarily contemporary, there were stories from earlier in the century that indicated the troubling history of youth crime. In 1945, in New York City, a local district attorney spoke about the violence between two rival gangs that had "its membership graded and named according to age as Tiny Tims, kids, cubs, and seniors." A feud between two Harlem youth groups, the Sabers and the Slicksters, resulted in the deaths of two sixteen year olds in September 1945—ten years before the Till lynching and fifty before Yummy's murder. The youths were stabbed with "a three foot bayonet, an ice pick and an ornate 'ranger' dagger." The district attorney described the other gang weaponry as "zipper guns." In one episode that resulted in a child's death, the bullets from a gun wounded a "girl passer-by," giving Shavon Dean's 1995 story a disturbing historic parallel (Schoener 97).

In "City of Specters," journalist Lynelle George wrote of death in Los Angeles.

In junior high school we went to more funerals than weddings. . . .
These deaths were often careless accidents; macho posturings or ran-

dom, mercuric moves made in fits of anger, that most times followed a red blur of words. Best friends played fatal games with loaded guns. . . . The first funerals my classmates attended were for close friends, all under eighteen. "I didn't go to an old person's funeral until my grandfather died," J. recalls. By then it was a ritual grown darkly familiar. For shortly before her grandfather slipped away, her stunned family buried her older brother, the summer of his sixteenth year. (159–60)

Too many African American children anticipated their own deaths and dying and participated in the adult ritual of planning their funerals. A junior high school student in Washington, D.C., discussed his plans with descriptive detail to a *Washington Post* reporter, saying, "'I don't want my hands like this,' he said, folding them across his chest. 'I want to be buried with peace signs. And I don't want my funeral to be in a church. I want it at Rollins Funeral Home, and I want to be buried at Harmony [Memorial Park]. I want to wear sweats and tennis shoes. I don't want to be buried in a suit'" (Brown A1).

With the innocent informality of a child and the tragic vision of an adult, another junior high schooler detailed her plans and explained how she wrote out her funeral: "On the top of the page I wrote my name a couple of times. . . . I like to write my name. . . . Then I wrote the songs I want sung. Then I wanted a tape of me talking, telling everybody I'm all right. I'm real dramatic, you know. But I was serious. Then I wrote who I want to talk. . . . I told my mother what to wear" (A1). In a forlorn reversal of the anticipated generational process, the reporter noted, "she sealed the envelope and gave it to her mother."

A psychologist at Hahnemann University Hospital, Douglas Marlowe, commented on the youngster's desire. Noting that children "often become fascinated with death in adolescence," Marlowe indicated that making plans for a funeral is "extremely fatalistic. . . . Once [children] start planning their own funerals, they have given up" (A1). Another youngster, elementary-school aged, told the reporter that she wants to be buried in her sixth-grade prom dress if she is murdered. Her childish perception belies the somber occasion of her thoughts: "I think my prom dress is going to be the prettiest dress of all. . . . When I die, I want to be dressy for my family" (A1). Michele Marriott wrote for the *New York Times* that "through much of the 1990s, inner-city teenagers and young adults have been confronted with staggering death rates among their families, friends, and neighbors, the causes ranging from infant mortality to AIDS to substance abuse to homicide. As a result, some elementary aged children plan what they will wear to their funerals, their older siblings mark their dead on memorial walls . . . and grow increasingly listless about their futures."

Despite the gruesome and sometimes imaginative humor that funeral-industry insiders use to dispel the weight of their daily undertakings, not all have the solace of professional distance. Children in the Ida B. Wells projects in Chicago need no imagination to think about death. Its familiarity is perhaps the most grievous tragedy of their childhoods. In 1993, five-year-old Eric Morse—a.k.a. "Shorty"—was dropped from a fourteenth-floor window in the projects, because he would not steal candy for two other youngsters, only ten and eleven themselves. Two youngsters later interviewed Eric's ten-year-old cousin, Donell, about the loss. *Our America* (Jones et al.), their book about living and dying in Chicago's Ida B. Wells Projects, records their conversation:

> *LeAlan:* Anybody home? Anybody home? ghost town.
> *Lloyd:* Shorty fell from way up here! . . . I know Shorty was scared when he was falling. He was wondering, "Will I die?"
> *LeAlan:* I wonder how he felt falling from fourteen stories? What the hell would go through your mind?
> *Lloyd:* I'd be thinking about how I'm going to land and if I'm going to survive. I'd be thinking about how it is in heaven. But I know I won't have that much time to think.
> *LeAlan:* How long do you think it took for him to drop? Maybe four or five seconds? . . . Man, I don't know what I'd be thinking about. I probably just would have said a prayer or something.
> *Lloyd:* That's all you could have said. . . .
> *LeAlan:* You think they got a playground in heaven for those Shorties?
> *Lloyd:* Nope. They don't got a playground in heaven for nobody!
> *LeAlan:* But what's Shorty gonna do up there? He wasn't old enough to do anything bad enough to go to hell. So what could he do up there? . . . Shorty was nothing but five. So what's he gonna do up there—chill with the grown-ups? Or is he reincarnated? Maybe he's a little bird or something. . . .

This tragic mix of the somber situation and their youthful imaginations matched the pitiful irony of a child's death. And the interview they eventually gained with Eric's cousin continued this agonizing disjunct:

LeAlan: What is your relationship to Eric Morse?

Donell: He's my cousin.

LeAlan: How does it make you feel that your cousin is gone?

Donell: It makes me feel bad. I cry every night when I go to sleep. I just want him to be here now.

LeAlan: How much do you miss Eric?

Donell: More than I miss my own self. . . .

Fare thee well.

Fare thee well.

If I never ever see you any more, fare thee well.

I will meet you on the other shore.

—Traditional

4

Funeralized

THE REMAINS OF OUR DAYS

Sanctuary

It is critical to understand the role of the twentieth-century black church in African America and the significant task it had in bringing appropriate context and closure to African American lives lived, as W. E. B. Du Bois would argue, within the veil of race. The church honored its historical role of bringing final perspective both to those lives lived long and courageously despite challenged circumstances and to those lives cut short often, too often, because of those same circumstances. The church also insisted on a public acknowledgment of this role. From its earliest iterations, the church's role was to carve out a space for redress and question, for balm and solace for black folk who gathered, as they so often did, because of their race. Pushed out of doors or to the backs and balconies of white churches in nineteenth-century America; preached at by slave masters and their ministerial minions who told them their lot was different from and lesser than those who enslaved them; denied bodily integrity, dignity, and ownership of self; blacks welcomed the construction of this critically racialized and sacred space, which served as an always ready site for cultural redress and spiritual reclamation.

At the turn of the twentieth century, Du Bois called the black church the "social centre of Negro life," the place for "various organizations—

the church proper, the Sunday-school, two or three insurance societies, women's societies, secret societies, and mass meetings of various kinds. Entertainments, suppers, and lectures are held. . . . [E]mployment is found for the idle, strangers are introduced, news is disseminated and charity distributed" (140). In *When We Were Colored,* Clifton Taulbert explained that the black church was "more than an institution, it was the very heart of our lives. Our church was . . . beyond the welfare of whites. . . . [It] provided the framework for civic involvement, the backdrop for leadership, a safe place for social gatherings, where our babies were blessed, our families married, and our dead respected" (91, 94, 105–6).

Throughout the twentieth century, the church continued to serve the black community with some variety and combination of these occupations. Its consistently close association with the business of black folk, and the nation's continued encouragement of what Martin Luther King Jr. spoke of as the most segregated hour in America, assured the church a critical position in determining the shape and articulating the contours of black culture. It was to this matrix that the church brought its exquisite refinement of the rituals of death and dying.

While not each funeral nor every burial ritual was equally culturally coded, the interesting dichotomy between the rituals in black and white churches is inscribed by the differences between specific moments in the black church history. In the way that the black funeral home engaged a racialized history, the cooperative ritual between the black funeral home and the black church encouraged a necessary cultural dialectic between sacred aspiration and secular experience.

In the United States, the driving force of capitalism within the burial business imposed surprisingly similar structures on what were, in effect, discrete church traditions. The similarities between American deathways are notable in a country of various ethnicities and cultures. What one discovers as homogeneity among these practices is the direct result of the influence of the funeral industry and the rituals that it influences, which confer social solidarity. Cultural anthropologists Peter Metcalf and Richard Huntington argue, "Given the myriad variety of death rites throughout the world, and the cultural heterogeneity of American society, the expectation is that funeral practices will vary widely from one region, or social class, or ethnic group to another. The odd fact is that they do not. The overall form of funerals is remarkably uniform from coast to coast" (93–194).

Nevertheless, however similar the industry's practices, what did emerge as culturally distinct variables in twentieth-century funeral practices were the consumers' conduct at these services and the dependably shared perception and anticipation of that divergence. Social solidarity as cultural practice conditioned the unique expectations and performance of the black burial service. And, to the extent that mortuary businesses and the church maintained their segregated practices, the expressive and experiential sociocultural universe that was brought to the black church and funeral industry underwrote a culturally distinctive preaching and practice. Cultural conduct within these realms bestowed various complexions on admittedly uniform American burial practices of "rapid removal of the corpse to a funeral parlor, embalming, institutionalized 'viewing,' and disposal by burial" (Metcalf 194).

The popular image of the black church—present as a kind of cross-cultural "common knowledge," whether one has intimate or distant knowledge of these institutions—portrayed a place where preacher and parishioners engaged in a dramatic and performative display of movement, speech, and song. Theorist Hortense Spillers described the minister's "passional" sermon as "an instrument of collective catharsis," a "gamut of emotions . . . whose end is cathartic release"; and biblical scholar William Pipes noted that "the chief purpose of old-time Negro preaching appears to be to 'stir-up'; to excite the emotions of the audience and the minister as a means for the escape from an 'impossible world'" (Hubbard 7, 13).

When asked in a not-at-all-scientific survey about the differences between black and white churches, citizens both elderly and young, black and white confirmed this perception of the black church as theatrical. One twenty-three-year-old African American—who has attended southern black Baptist churches and black Methodist churches, and who has been a member at two white churches (one in the south and one on the west coast)—explained the difference as "dynamic versus sedate. . . . In the black churches there is more movement and more noise. . . . White churches are not participatory in the same way black churches are. In the black churches, the preacher moves to emphasize his exhortation." Her sentiment was shared by a sixty-year-old white male who described "more congregational participation in black churches—more talking back to the preacher." A sixty-year-old African American woman felt similarly, saying "black churches are more apt to express emotions, to shout and cry; they are not afraid to express themselves." Another black woman of similar age noted that, in her experience, "black churches seem to shout more, holler more, and sing louder. It becomes a way to relieve or vent problems for black people. With white churches, they are a little bit different, *I think because they have different problems to deal with*" (my emphasis).

Exactly. These "different problems" do make a difference. So many blacks died untimely deaths that funeral anguish came to be rehearsed as a dimension of the culture's engaged ritual rather than as the reason for the occasion.

Black church drama was no insular, community secret. Late in the twentieth century, some Harlem churches became official tourist sites for foreign visitors. Busloads of European and Asian tourists stopped by, promised an opportunity to see and to photograph the worship services of African American parishes. They were there to audit the expressive passion of music, of ministerial call and congregational response. The *New York Times* reported on the phenomenon.

> A decade-long influx of foreign tourists visiting Harlem churches has swelled considerably . . . to the point where Harlem on a Sunday morning has been transformed into something of an ecclesiastical theme park. Charter buses roll in by the dozens, lining the avenues. Tourists spill out by the thousands, pointing cameras at churchgoers like paparazzi swirling around celebrities at a movie premier. . . . "People don't just go there for the religion," said Patricia J. Williams, a black professor of law at Columbia University. . . . "They go for a show; there's this sense of whites being on safari. All that's missing is the hats."
>
> In this country there is a long history of white fascination with black worship. . . . [R]eligious rituals are often seen by tourists as one of the most accessible and theatrical windows into a different culture. (Bruni)

Although there was every reason to anticipate ethnic variation of religious practice within the black church, even to the extreme of anticipating a "show," it is important to note that some black churches had —sometimes quite intentionally in order to avoid the racial marker— shifted away from offering culturally specific (tourist-worthy) sites to creating comparatively generic social spaces in which their services differed very little from those of white congregations. Nevertheless, despite some degree of black social assimilation toward white religious practice, the perception of cultural specificity persisted to the end of the twentieth century, nourished by a healthy number of examples.

A monologue by Richard Pryor in the 1970s caricatured this perception in a way that is helpful in explaining its resonance in the United States. In a comedic riff on black churches before a largely white audience, Pryor used as a specific text what Americans believed to be the difference between funerals in black and white churches. His narrative dramatized white funerals as occasions in which one might anticipate quiet and restrained sniffling and a few barely audible sighs that escape from the whispered voices of friends and family in mourning. He then characterized black funerals as events where people fall out, grief-stricken, in the aisles, scream and weep loudly, and shout with unrestrained anguish and despair. His audience laughed appreciably and in knowing agreement. Interestingly, Pryor began that monologue with the general—the difference between black and white congregations. In and of itself, that juxtaposition was enough to encourage hearty and sustained laughter from his audience. But, when he moved to the specific text of a funeral as the urtext of the distinction, he tapped into his audience's implicit understanding of an absolute association between the cultural experience of black death and the particular drama of the black church.

In their own way, my survey respondents echoed Pryor's assumptions. When I asked about the perceived differences between black and white funerals, I received comments like "the character of the funerals is consistent with what I described as the differences in the church traditions—dynamic vs. sedate." Or, in "the white funerals" there is no "atmosphere of weeping." Black funerals "are often open casket and one may even touch the deceased. . . . Loud weeping is characteristic." One white participant, however, noted that there were class and regional differences among white funerals, recalling that in white, southern, rural communities (in which cultural historians and linguists have documented crossover behaviors of black and white cultures) there are white burial "events where you see which relative can cry the loudest." But, 97 percent of my respondents shared sentiments such as these: black funerals were "more lively and interactive"; "white church services and funerals were staid and passive"; "black churches are just more emotional and expressive.

. . . [T]here is more touching—even kissing—of the bodies, at the white churches it was more subdued and proper; at the funeral, they were less likely to (openly) express grief, they refuse to break down." The sixty-seven-year-old African American respondent encapsulated the stereotype:

> Blacks seem to grieve more, funeralwise, sometimes, we go crazy. White people give it up easier than blacks do; we are less willing to put the dead away, we want to hold and grieve more. Also, black people spend more, financially, to put their dead away—even if they can't afford it as much. When my brother died, his family were being a little tight, but I said, "Why?" But black people keep the dead out longer. Sometimes, we keep them out for a week, to wait for people who have to get off from work or find the money for the trip or to wait for people to get home. Whites bury sooner. . . . [B]lack people hang around the area where they keep the body longer.

The day-to-day experiences of living black in America, experiences that were brought to the church and shared within its walls, urged a particular shape to the character and text of the minister's sermonic call and the congregational response. Echoing the verbal contours of the call-and-response practice of West African cultures, African American spirituality found a racialized resting place embedded in the salvational promise of Christian faith—"losing the joy of this world, [the Negro] eagerly seized upon the offered conceptions of the next" (Du Bois 144). In *Blues People*, poet and essayist Leroi Jones (Amiri Baraka) recalled the "African dictum" that "the spirit will not descend without song," claiming the black church as a "church of emotion" shaped through "the call and response of the worship service" (40–41). Throughout the century, the pulpits of black churches were the socially accepted spaces for congregation and instruction. The racialized messages delivered in these places, whether early abolitionist or later civil rights, meant that the experience of black folk would constitute the church's sustainable and memorable text, and that an expressive spirituality would be its vehicle. As the church became a site for redress and reconciliation and—more important—as the experiences brought to the sanctuary were draped in the anguished dramas of race in America, the emotive substance of the racialized experiences of its parishioners nourished the passion and drama that characterizes black churches. As one survey participant suggested, "they have different problems to deal with." Another respondent explained that "the church has been our sanctuary," even as she regretfully acknowledged the carnage that some of these spaces have encountered as black bodies return to our churches for burial. "But even there," she noted, "we haven't always been safe."

Paradoxically, while the black church was a haven from the outer world, it was, at the same time, vulnerable to white hatred and resentment. In addition to holding the sacred service of the Sabbath, black churches served as daily meeting places for the business of the race—where sit-ins were planned, voting tactics discussed, school matters decided, and health issues reviewed. But the church's visibility, coupled with society's understanding of its racial affiliations and advocacy, made the edifices of worship themselves susceptible to racial hatred. Throughout the twentieth century, black churches were assaulted—the targets of bombs, arson, and vandalism, specifically because of their racial activism and racial identification.

Little wonder, then, that the emotion and purpose from one congregational meeting leaked into the next. Within these sanctified spaces, the text of race, common to sacred as well as to secular days, found a certain, specific, and shared cultural expression. Thus, black churches came to contain the vigorously engaged debates of civil rights and civilities, as well as the passionate embrace of Sunday morning services of celebration and salvation.

The voice of the black preacher as "God's Trombone" gave sound and sense to the institution of the church. Du Bois wrote of the black preacher within this "first Afro-American institution," as a "healer of the sick, the interpreter of the Unknown, the comforter of the sorrowing, the supernatural avenger of wrong, and the one who expressed the longing, disappointment and resentment of a stolen and oppressed people" (141–42). Given that much of the sociological drama of race had as its source the untimely death and dying of black folk, and given that the sacred space of the black church was the site where these dramas were brought to conclusion, it was almost predictable that the already engaged intensity of the social and sacred within the black church would express itself as well in services for the dead.

In his novel, *The Avenue, Clayton City*—which recalls life in the black Alabama town of his birth—religious scholar, poet, and novelist

Black churches were targets of white rage and riot throughout the century. This one was destroyed in the Greenwood neighborhood of Tulsa, Oklahoma, in the riot there in 1921. *The Tulsa Historical Society.*

C. Eric Lincoln described the funeral of one of his characters. Reverend Rusoe's sermon follows a black preacherly tradition. In its message about houses and housing patterns, about lives lived in service, and in the way that its preacher's call gains a dramatic congregational response—both in voice and in conduct—this text signified racially.

> This was, he declared, a sad day. Sad because one beloved of the church and the City of Clayton had laid down her burden and gone home. There was a scattering of "Amens!" But it was also a day for rejoicing, because she had gone to live in the City of Eternal Peace. A celestial city. . . . She wouldn't have to wash no more dirty overalls! Scrub no more kitchen floors! She wouldn't have to wonder how she was going to pay the groceryman. She wouldn't have to hide because she didn't have a dime to give to the insurance man. "Her insurance is all paid up, and Sister Lucy's gone home to collect her dividends." This time

Exterior view of bombed church in Birmingham, Alabama.
Bettmann/CORBIS.

The remains of a sanctuary of a black Presbyterian church in North Carolina. Investigators linked it to black church arsons. *Associated Press.*

there was a strong chorus of "Amens!" and a rumbling of feet to let the preacher know his message was being heard. . . .

"Now some folks'll tell you that the preacher can *preach* you into heaven [ah-ha!], they say the preacher can ferry you over to the *kingdom.* [Ah-ha!] Across the moat of perdition. [Well, ah-ha!] Around the rocks of retribution. That's what they say. . . . Ain't that what they say? You've heard 'em say that!"

"Yass, Preach! Preach on! That's what they say!"

"Well, let me tell you one thing, brothers and sisters: The preacher cain't *preach* you nowhere! Can't *send* you nowhere! You got to go there for yourself! You got to stand the test for yourself!"

"Help me Lord!" somebody screamed. "Help me!"

"Where you going when you quit this vale of tears, the preacher ain't got nothing to do with it. The preacher can *review* your life [Ah-ha!] but he cain't reprieve it. Your record is already on file. [Ah-ha!] In the Registry of Deeds. On *file!* [Ah-ha!] In the Book of the Judgment! You can't add nothin, [No Jesus!] an' you can't take nothin' away."

"Preach on! It's on file! Preach it like it is! Preach!"

"The white folks can't change it!"

. . . Several of the women began to moan and shout and rush about the church. They were restrained by black-clad assistants, who roamed the aisles with cardboard fans, trying to anticipate where the next outbreak of the spirit would come. . . . Some of the women began to sob and shake. . . . The preacher . . . leaped nimbly over the rail and strutted back and forth between the casket and the weeping, shouting congregation; then suddenly he whirled and leaped over the rail and was back in the pulpit again. "Hallelujah! Hallelujah!" he cried. A large woman directly in front of him fainted, and the ushers carried her out to be revived.

"Hallelujah!" shouted Reverend Rusoe. "Hallelujah! In the name of Jesus! She's comin' home! Open up the mansion house! Give Sister Lucy her key to her celestial apartment. Ain't no three-room shacks in heaven. Ain't no railroad tracks running through the front yard. Every house they got up there is a mansion. *Jesus* said that. Every heavenly residence is on the celestial avenue. And the avenue is paved with gold. . . ." (252–57)

Lincoln was part of a tradition of black writers who found the text and performance of the black preacher—particularly at the moment of a funeral sermon—the most persuasive and compelling way to articulate the passion and performance of the black church and its text of blackness. This racialized text invaded the cultural construction of the church and its rituals—especially the sermon. Ralph Ellison's *Invisible Man* powerfully literalized this conflation of "blackness" and text in a storefront preacher's sermon titled "Blackness of Black."

And a congregation of voices answered: "That blackness is most black, brother, most black . . ."

"In the beginning . . ."

"At the very start," they cried.

". . . there was blackness . . ."

"Now black is . . ." the preacher shouted.

". . . an' black ain't . . ."

"Black will git you . . ."

". . . an' black won't . . ."

This southern funeral scene characterizes the formal role of the church. The women in white, whether they are the choir or "nurses," craft the drama of the funeral.

"Black will make you . . ."
". . . or black will un-make you."
"Ain't it the truth, Lawd?" (9–10)

Dolan Hubbard explains the tradition, noting, "The preacher stands between racism and injustice, and between racism and poverty. . . . The form of the black sermon issued directly out of the content of black life" (18, 19). Arguing a similar interpretation of the cultural text, minister and theologian Henry H. Mitchell explained that "'black preaching' is conditioned by sociology, economics, government, culture — the whole ethos of the Black community" (124). Given this cultural exegesis, the sermonic production itself contained and imparted the expressive and performative spirit of the race, delivering the emotive urgency of a century of civil-rights struggle up to a sanctified space.

Little wonder, then, that black churches engendered a particularly fervent reaction when they engaged the facts and experiences of black death. In addition to encouraging reflection on the racialized circumstances of one's own life, African American funeral rituals also exalted and amplified the social solidarity that accompanied the cultural experience of race. And, as these rituals were conducted in spaces that issues of race had exposed to danger, the "passional" response characteristic of the black church experience was further amplified. The lamentation in the black funeral is akin to a Biblical weeping and wailing—loud, strong, and unrelieved. The hovering presence of "nurses"—the church deaconesses or church mothers in white (sometimes black) who stand nearby the family with tissues and fans, ready to escort a prostrate mourner out or ease the fall of the faint—embody the cultural anticipation.

> After many admonitions to "sinners" and much praise of Sister Backler, the pastor ended his sermon, the last soloist sang, and the church prepared to see Sister Backler for the last time. Two assistants to the funeral director went to the casket, arranged the interior lace in its appropriate place. Then they stood on either end of the casket while two other assistants accompanied by a church nurse, took each member of the immediate family to view the body. . . . After all the family had viewed the body, leaving the members of the church distraught by their emotional outbursts, all the rest of the congregation stood and formed a line and marched around to view Sister Backler. They touched her, kissed her, embraced her, and frequently had to be restrained in their emotions. (Irish 57)

If this funeral scene seems constructed by the funeral home personnel and the nurses to encourage the passion, it was. Last rites in African American churches had a century of cultural expectation that encouraged emotional display. Whether this seemingly uncontrolled sentiment arose from centuries of cultural anguish and found sweet release in death, which enslaved Africans saw as the only sure liberation from the slavery's sorrow, or whether the moment occasioned the collective grief of a community whose deep cultural sense understood that their black lives had been, as Langston Hughes expressed, "no crystal stair," the one consistent cultural marker of African American death was the dramatic and emotional intensity of the funeral service and the way in which congregations gathered absolutely in need of the certain balm of that cultural text. When the community came together for a funeral, there was a collective expectation for the moment. It served, in a sense, as a periodic catharsis for the weight of living black in the United States.

For much of the twentieth century families took the responsibility of funeralizing very, very seriously. Black culture's attention to this ritual was, however, susceptible to the century's turn toward a lesser degree of formality. Some members of the NFDMA felt that they were particular witnesses to shifts in cultural mores and codes. Even as they experienced a gradual eroding of their black clientele base, they noted a similar shift in the attention given to rituals of burial. Some of these changes, they felt, were regional. One Louisiana mortician's perspective summarized this fairly widely held sentiment: speaking of African Americans who have left the South but who have elderly family still "down home," he told me that "people from up North and California, they'll come back home as quick as they can, pay cash or credit card for their departed, and then they're on their way back from where they come from the next day. People that have been up North, they'll call me, their mother is down here with us and they'll call and say, 'I'll be down there—you pick out the casket and get everything ready.' And then they come down, they pay for it, and they are out of here." On the other hand, "people in the South, they want you to hold Mama until Saturday or whenever. . . . She may have died on the Saturday before that, but we have to wait until Great Aunt Sis or whoever can come down from New Jersey until we can put Mama away." If the lessons of the century had been instructive at all, those mourners were likely to find, once they "come down," that Mama had some ideas of her own about how she wanted to be "put away."

"The way in which you go out is important, very important."

On a clear and crisp February morning in 1915, in Nashville, Tennessee, a prominent pastor of the Primitive Baptist Church died of pneumonia. He was sixty-six years old, barely a month away from his sixty-seventh birthday. The disease had ravaged his lungs; their elasticity, fully compromised, left them unable to inflate or deflate completely. The pastor never became comatose, so shortly before he died he was able to laboriously "breathe the last speaking words of comfort to his children and friends" who had gathered at his bedside. He died on a Saturday, the twenty-seventh day of the month. The normal business-day bustle of Nashville's city streets had shifted to the less-hurried stroll of its weekend shoppers, just reaching their peak as the day neared noon. The weather was a typically mild Nashville winter's day — although the temperature had started out just hovering at the freezing mark, by noon it had reached a comfortable fifty degrees. Reverend Luke Mason's kin would eventually move north, to Jeffersonville, Indiana, and Louisville, entering "the business" to become the twentieth-century proprietors "Mason and Sons." But Luke Mason died in Nashville, just before the morning moved toward noon, at 11:15. The mild weather cooperated in allowing his many friends and parishioners to fan through the neighborhoods and city streets to spread the word of his passing. "Elder Mason," as he was called within the church, had been a formidable figure in the black Nashville community, and the notice of his death and forthcoming burial and funeral services attracted considerable notice. A small pamphlet — which church elders published in his memory, celebrating his life and detailing the moment when he "answered the final call" — offers an important glimpse into the practice of funeralizing in the African American community.

Luke Mason had been intimately involved with the "Negro" community in Nashville, working especially as spiritual adviser to young black men who faced execution. The congregation's memorial pamphlet recorded some of his interventions, which spanned two centuries, for "Ben Brown who murdered one Frank Arnold and was hanged in March. . . . for Robert Ford, a youth of 18 who murdered Allen Oakley and was hanged in April 1895. . . . He was with Dan Harris who killed his femesole in 1898 and also with Petway and Thompson who murdered Miller in 1901, hanged in the spring of 1902. The last two colored men who went to the death chair in 1912 he interceded and begged executive clemency, but had to bow to the strong arm of the law, thus they died." These sad details reveal how, as the leader of a black congregation, he found his pastoral mission consistently involved in the bereavement and grief counseling for families whose brothers and sons faced execution and death at the hands of the state. Mason's ministry thus found a specific cultural occupation in black death. The esteemed church elder was "always among the first Negro men sought and sent for" when it came to the need for "public schools for Negroes, or T. B. Hospitals for Negroes." Because he had given such service during the most grievous occasions for the families in his community and had earned such racially defined prominence, it was predictable that when Elder Mason died, "as soon as the breath had left the body the news spread like wild fire over the city and . . . all who looked upon him as a father began to gather at the home to express their sympathy to the members of his family" (Mason 25).

The first formal gathering of friends and family that happened after his death was the wake, or "settin-up"—a funeral tradition that African America easily adopted and that served to reconvene the family and its community to rehearse the situations and events of black death. Although some folk stories claim that the origins of the wake lay in fears of premature burial, custom had it that certain illnesses mirror a deathlike state, so family members gathered to watch the body in case it a*wake*ned. (There have been wakes, festivals, and ceremonies of various sorts around the world, and documented in Europe since the 1400s.) As much as this practice is shared across cultures, the particular kinds of racial conversation and memorializing that recurred within African America on these occasions imbued them with some cultural particularity. For Luke Mason, those who convened in his home following his death recalled him as a "race man," a "counsellor of the distressed and a champion of the oppressed. There were mothers present who had in days past sought Rev. Mason to intercede for their boys; there were those who had on many occasions accompanied him to the jail to advise some man condemned to be hanged" (Mason 17). Since Tennessee's executions of black men between 1880 and 1930 averaged nearly ten each year, Mason's ministrations to these families were not an uncommon dimension of his pastoral care. The community recollections brought to the occasion of his wake illustrate the community narratives that surround these individual moments.

As in the United States in general, in the particular communities of African America, the wake is the appropriate first occasion to extend comfort and assistance to the bereaved family—and the food served at this time is as important as the conversations and remembrances that friends bring with them to the family home. Throughout most of the century, the amount of food and the quality of attention given to its preparation were important and notable signals of respect to the bereaved family, as well as a commentary on the manners of the bearer. Bringing store-bought food to the house was once sure to invite a cynical aside and a "tsk! tsking!" from those who knew better and expected that you should as well. But, in the last quarter of the century, the traditions of food preparation shifted—including the cultural parameters of the recipes. Fried chicken, for instance, had been nearly de rigueur on these occasions. (In fact, food preparers and volunteers often began with, "And who's going to bring *the* chicken?" because it was a given that *somebody* would.) But with the advent of fast foods, specifically fried chicken outlets, the labor in family kitchens was rapidly replaced by a bucket from the Colonel. It could be argued that Kentucky Fried Chicken buckets actually paved the way for foodstuffs other than those prepared in neighborhood kitchens to work their way onto the tables of bereaved families.

Black class differentials accounted for some dimensions of late-century codes of funeral conduct. In her novel *Linden Hills,* Gloria Naylor incorporated the changing cultural sense of decorum, calling attention both to traditional practice and to novel behaviors emerging in the newly installed and very modern black upper class of Linden Hills, who signaled their status with the fancy and expensive display of a catered meal.

> Luther Nedeed came into the dining room carrying a cellophane-wrapped cake. He was the only guest Willie had seen bringing food that night, and it surprised him. He knew that his family always fried chicken and baked stuff for a wake [but] it was the last thing he expected to see done in Linden Hills. Willie lingered in the upstairs hall a moment and watched Luther as he hesitated in front of the buffet. There was not space for his bundle next to the ornate array of catered food.
>
> "Nice of you to come, Luther." Parker got up and took the cake from him.
>
> "I guess I have to become accustomed to these modern ways." Luther seemed embarrassed. "In my time, friends and neighbors always supplied the food for these types of occasion. . . . My wife baked this." (135–36)

The tradition of providing meals to a grieving family cycles through the entire bereavement process for black folk, starting with the wake and concluding with a formal meal after the funeral services. Toni Morrison described the "funeral banquet" as a peal of joy after the thunderous beauty of the unreal. It was like a street tragedy with spontaneity tucked softly into the corners of a highly formal structure. The deceased was the tragic hero, the survivors the innocent victims; there was the omnipresence of the deity, strophe and antistrophe of the chorus of mourners led by the preacher. There was grief over the waste of life, the stunned wonder at the ways of God, and the restoration of order in nature at the graveyard. . . . [T]he banquet was the exultation, the harmony, the acceptance of physical frailty, joy in the termination of misery. Laughter, relief, a steep hunger for food. (*Bluest Eye* 142–43)

Even as the twentieth century came to a close, a majority of mourners in African America still ended up where the ceremonies began—at the church, where they would be served dinner in the recreation hall or church-school rooms. There, "church ladies" served the family meals they had prepared. These were the same elders—deaconesses and nurses—who passed out fans (conveniently marked on the back with the funeral home's logo) and hankies during the funeral. Their role was an evolution of the caretaking and attention once extended to families within lodges and burial societies.

While it is true that some no longer returned to the church and that for some the hands that prepared the food were no longer intimate, the cultural flavor of funerals, especially in the American South, was still tied to the familiar "funeral banquet." Professional caterers stepped in to take advantage of this market. Windsor Jordan, of Mary Jordan's Catering Service in Atlanta, Georgia, provides a modern version of the church meal as a catered service. He notes that "when a brother passes, we cater a lot of meals. Folks are emotionally exhausted and hungry, so we give them a solid menu: barbecued ribs, hot catfish, fresh pork ham, *baked* chicken [not fried—this is, after all, a "catered" affair], turnip greens, pasta salad, mushrooms, sweet potato pie and cheesecake. A gospel song says you'll get to heaven 'in golden shoes and high-heeled slippers with angels singing,' he says. We start [celebrating] here on earth" (Patureau 2; my emphasis).

So, as was traditional, after Elder Mason's death, "the house was never empty." The "members of his church and a host of friends" gathered, brought food, wept, remembered, and held "special services" all night. In the tradition of early-century wakes, Mason's body was "laid-out" in the family home, and the gathering fulfilled one of its important purposes—to plan and direct the funeral service. Anticipating final ministrations, Mason had left instructions as to how he wanted his body to be prepared for burial, "and they were carried out to the letter. The body was wrapped in an immaculate white sheet from head to foot, and he looked like one asleep and not dead" (Mason 26).

Nashville was one of the cities in the United States that had had black undertakers since the late 1800s. Like many black preachers, Mason had a close association with one of the black undertakers in the city. And, like many undertakers, this mortician was also a minister. Mason's body was "carefully prepared by Elder Preston Taylor, the progressive undertaker at 449 Fourth Avenue North, Nashville, Tenn." This was the same Taylor who had arranged the impressive funeral for the black firemen back in 1892. Taylor had been friends with Luke Mason for twenty-eight years, and "Elder Mason had sent for Elder Taylor on Thursday evening, Feb. 25, before his death Saturday morning and told him every detail about his funeral, even to the wrapping of his body in a linen winding sheet, as he had seen himself in a vision, years ago."

Elder Mason's body remained at the family home until, at the time of the service, it "was removed to the church on Lewis Street." Other families and communities had their own settin-up rituals: while some rural South Carolina black families held a pig-pickin after a night-long roasting of the animal, others had the body brought to the family church where a vigil would commence at dusk and last throughout the night. As the funeral business became more regularized, however, funeral parlors began to provide an on-site space where people could view the body before the services and pay their respects to the family, a development that made the shift from family home to funeral home desirable. Under a professional's direction, the settin-up—still called a wake or sometimes a "family hour"—moved to the funeral home. After the family arrived (in company limousines) to view the newly embalmed body, friends gathered, first stopping at the traditionally open casket, then moving on to greet and console family members. Mourners and visitors typically stayed in the viewing room of the funeral home for only a short period of time, especially if the family members were present.

This funeral-home event was generally a period of quiet reflection—although some funeral directors told me that in recent years, respect for the dead has diminished, and it has been known to get noisy and raucous as the hours pass. Directors try to limit the family's stay to a contracted time, not only so they might better control the hours they charge to the family's bill and the costs of the personnel they have to pay to be present, but also to minimize the casualness and even the violence that invaded some of these visitations in the last decade of the century.

Casualness and violence began to spill over to the funeral itself. For example, the *Los Angeles Times* reported that Reverend David Moore was "nervous" when he presided at the funeral for a gang member. He had just signed up to serve as a $75-a-service minister at the funeral home, and it was his first gang funeral. "I got an inkling that this was not going to be an ordinary funeral when I drove into the parking lot and saw that young men were drinking." The death-care industry had to adapt to this dimension of the changing cultural scene, sometimes by bringing security into their establishments. Sergeant Bill Shortley of the LAPD reflected that "years ago, we didn't have to cover every funeral. It was the exception rather than the rule when you had trouble. Now, because of the volatility of the gangs, we pretty much have to cover them all" (Wilkinson and Chavez A15).

Perhaps reflecting the postfordian state of America's consumer culture, and certainly reflecting the dramatic and embellished display of performative cultural rituals, a black company, Thornton's Mortuary in Atlanta, debuted the country's first "drive-through" funeral parlor in 1968. It "had five viewing rooms, draped and carpeted and bathed in soft fluorescent light. Each room had a large plate glass window facing a carved gravel drive, so that the mourner paying last respects could do so without leaving an automobile. The curtains would open to reveal the deceased. Outside each window was a box, as in a drive-in bank, for cards and signing in" ("Drive-Through Funeral" 11). Although this innovation did not become a trend for black mortuaries (or any others), there were some who took on the challenge of this kind of innovation and pushed the concept forward. Just as the century ended, Gatling Funeral Home in Chicago opened its own version of drive-through viewing, which acknowledged late-twentieth-century technology. Its facilities featured a curved driveway fronting its Halsted Street facilities that was covered with green indoor-outdoor carpeting. Cars could come into this driveway and proceed to a television monitor. With a microphone alerting personnel inside, the monitor could be activated to select one of the six parlors in Gatling's to view the deceased on closed-circuit television. A box was available near the outdoor monitor to leave condolences. But, the traffic on the busy South Side Chicago thoroughfare became so congested with cars lined up to view the bodies that Gatling had to shut down the service until they could make plans for relieving the resulting traffic nightmares.

Each of these carefully orchestrated innovations was linked to offering specific services with potentially billable expenses that profit the funeral business. Earlier, wakes at home, and even "settin-ups," relayed no particular income to funeral directors, unless perhaps the directors were to provide some service like bringing in folding chairs for the family's anticipated guests. But, as embalming practices were refined and moved into the business establishment and out of the bedrooms of the deceased; as the funeral industry's reach into all aspects of service, ritual, and ceremony became more pervasive, it began to make commercial sense to control this dimension of mourning as well. Within the black community, it was also important that the (indoor) visitation parlors of funeral homes provided an arena large enough to stage some of the rituals associated with the burial associations, lodges, fraternal, and sorority organizations. Because these were not sacred ceremonies, and because some pastors felt the secularism of such ceremonies competed inappropriately with the church's sacred mission, the funeral home provided an important alternative site for the traditional enactment of social functions and rituals significant to many African American families.

One of Andrea C.'s earliest memories was of a ceremony like this. She was taken to a funeral home by her mother, a member of Alpha Kappa Alpha Sorority. It was the 1950s, and mother and daughter were appropriately attired in Sunday church-wear for the visitation. As with church attendance, the cultural code of conduct mandated that funeral home visits, too, require formal dress. It was not a casual occasion. Andrea recalls that

> We walked together up a long sidewalk to a building that looked just like a house. My mother was uncharacteristically quiet. I don't recall if she told me where we were going ahead of time, but when we went into a room filled with flowers, I knew immediately where we were.

Nobody was talking, and people were seated on those wooden folding chairs we had in the church basement. My mother held my hand and took me up to the casket. I was too short to see inside of it, and I remember that I tugged at her hand because she was just standing there and I was ready to go. I must have been just tall enough to reach her wrists, because I remember the smell of the starch in the white lace of the cuffs she had attached to her dress before we left home.

When we finally sat down with the other people. I could see I knew a lot of them, including my teacher who disappointed me greatly by not speaking. It was as if I were invisible. Suddenly mother, my teacher, and the other women got up and walked back up to where the casket was. I noticed that all of them were wearing white dresses, and somebody was passing out small sprigs of ivy. I remember thinking there must have been some signal for them to all get up at once and together and I chastised myself for missing what I was sure was a secret signal. They stood so close together that I couldn't see the casket anymore, just smell the flowers. The candles that were beside the casket were lit and all the ladies began to sing the most beautiful song. Each lady tucked her ivy into the casket. By that time everyone still seated was crying. Later, my mother told me that it was a ceremony for an "Ivy Beyond the Wall." For years after that, whenever I saw my mother's Ivy Leaf pin, or heard the sorority hymn, I recalled as well the heavy scent of flowers.

At the annual national and regional conventions, members of this sorority replicate this local service—holding an "Ivy Beyond the Wall" ceremony commemorating all of the "sorors" who died in the intervening year. A designated member of each chapter brings an ivy vine to a candle-lit table as the departed member's name is read. The service concludes with the somber singing of the sorority's national hymn. The importance of this ritual is so thoroughly engaged by its members that when my own mother died and I asked to participate in that ceremony with them (Mother and I had both, as undergraduates, pledged into the same Talladega College chapter), members of her sorority chapter told me that I could of course participate—*if* I had brought a white dress with me. I had not, having been occupied, as might have been expected (and appreciated), with the overwhelming issues of my mother's illness and impending death. Although I was mightily chagrined at the imposition of this regulating ritualistic symbolism, which loomed larger for the membership than did the fact that this was *my* mother for whom they were planning the ritual, my irritation did dissipate during the actual ceremony, which was quite beautiful and moving. I sat with my family in the church pews while my mother's sorors filled the aisles of the church and surrounded her coffin. Just as their ceremony came to its conclusion, one of the members came to me with the last ivy vine and asked me to place it in the casket. By that time, I was overcome with the grief and memory, as well as the not-insignificant impact of the impressive presence of nearly a hundred women (all wearing white) and of the ivy that, in its abundance, was nearly spilling from the coffin where my dearest and beloved mother lay. And I walked forward, and tucked the last leaf into the soft folds of fabric where she lay.

African American cultures depended on and labored over the effect of such symbolism and excess. When a prominent person died, the period of "visitation" or "viewing" lasted a great deal longer than usual, and considerable attention was given to the often elaborate visual presentation of homage. For example, when 30,000 Chicago mourners filed past singer Dinah Washington's body after she died in 1963, they "saw her laid out in a solid bronze casket [with] a glittering tiara on her head, a white mink stole around her shoulders, a yellow chiffon dress and $200 rhinestone shoes" (Sanders 147). There was precedent for the movie star's elaborate set up. Nearly forty years earlier in Harlem, when the beloved dancer and singer Florence Mills died, the community came to a standstill. Mills had performed in Sissle and Blake's *Shuffle Along* in 1921, and her fame spread from that moment to her celebrated appearance in the Broadway musical *Blackbirds,* which ran for a short time in Harlem and sustained a European tour. In England, the Prince of Wales was said to have seen the performance nearly a dozen times. It was on this tour, after she had become the "darling" of Harlem, that she became ill. Jervis Anderson recalled the event in *This Was Harlem,* writing that Mills had died following an operation shortly after she returned to New York following the European tour of *Blackbirds.* Before the day of her death had passed, floral tributes said to exceed a hundred thousand dollars flooded the hospital and chapel at Howell Undertaking Parlors at 137th Street and 7th Avenue. Mills lay "in state" at Howell's for a week, her body draped "in swathings of shimmering silk and spidery lace" and lying in a "massive casket of hand-hammered bronze," which the *New York Age* reported to be a replica of Rudolph Valentino's casket.

> Nearly 150,000 people lined the streets and crowded windows above the streets as the funeral procession moved to Mother A.M.E. Zion church, a "silent host that stood in awed reverence." A uniformed group of lodge members formed an escort, following the band, and then nine automobiles laden with the most extensive and gorgeous floral display Harlem has ever seen. An immense bleeding heart, made of deep red roses, with broad white satin ribbons fluttering from the top was the tribute sent by . . . the husband. . . .
>
> Another floral offering that attracted much interest was a vast tower of red roses, four feet wide by eight feet high, which bore the simple inscription, "From a Friend." All that was known of its source was that cabled instructions came ten days ago from London for its presentation, and there was a persistent report to the effect that the Prince of Wales . . . had sent it. . . . The casket was covered by a blanket of red and white roses. . . . Eighteen flower girls followed, each bearing a floral piece. . . . (Anderson 181–84)

For Elder Mason, who was a man of stature in Nashville's Negro community, the matter of how he would appear during the formal presentation of his body was not insignificant. While his body was still in his home, it was shrouded simply in the "immaculate white" linens that he had "seen in a vision." But, by the time his body was brought to the public arena for the funeral, it was clothed in a "black prince albert suit [and lay in] a royal purple casket, trimmed in dull silver and a steel maxwell vault, the gift of his son William." The formal display of Mason's body and its striking attire had its desired effect on the thousands of mourners who came to attend the funeral ceremony. "Early Tuesday morning, the people began to gather at Ryman Auditorium to pay the last tribute. . . . They were there from all quarters. Every morning train brought its quota of out-of-town friends and acquaintances. Many thousands of Nashville's best people, irrespective of denominations or religious inclinations, were on hand" (Mason 26).

African American funerals during the twentieth century depended on the spectacle of the moment to involve the community of mourners as fully as possible in the emotions and the ceremony of the event. Community involvement in the African American funeral ceremony took its significance (if not its actual practices) from West African cultures that attended to death and burial as an important, public, elaborate, and lengthy social event.

"The bell tolled and tolled." Historian John Hope Franklin's voice grew distant with this recollection. "I remember this like it was yesterday." Professor Franklin was sitting across from me at dinner when he shared this story of his childhood memory of his home in Rentiesville, Oklahoma. His son leaned forward to listen as well. "Whenever there was a death in the community, the bell tolled. I can remember it waking me up. You couldn't go back to sleep after that. You knew somebody had died and you didn't know who it was then; but you knew it would be somebody you knew." I began to tell him how I had included the Tulsa story in this book, knowing that Rentiesville was nearby and that his father, Buck Colbert Franklin, had been one of the lawyers who went to Tulsa following the destruction of Greenwood to try to legislate reparation for those whose citizenship had been so abused. But Franklin emphatically interrupted. "No! No! This wasn't about Tulsa and the riot there. This was the bell tolling like it did whenever *any*body died. I can hear it now." His son, John Whittington, spoke up then and told his father that that was exactly what had happened in the small community he had lived in for about seven years after graduating from college. The bell tolled to announce a death there, as well. Villagers explained to him that it was a tradition as old as anybody could remember. "Just like you're saying about Rentiesville, Dad," he said. "That's exactly the tradition of the village I lived in on Goree Island, Senegal."

The cultural continuity of these rituals is difficult to ignore. The funeral ceremony was the family's opportunity, as well as its responsibility, to announce to the attendant community, through the quality and length of the services and mourning, that the decedent's family was giving proper respect and attention to the moment. In *The Joys of Motherhood*, Nigerian novelist Buchi Emecheta described one such occasion in her homeland.

> She let out a loud cry to tell the world that her father . . . had gone. People woke and rushed in and Agbadi's widows all took up the cry. Cannons . . . were fired into the air. Soon the whole of Ibuza and the

174

neighbouring towns as well knew that an important person had left this earth to go to his ancestors.

The mourning and dancing and the wake went on for days. . . . With a great deal of dancing and festivities, Obi Nwokocha Agbadi was set up on his Obi stool and sat right there in the grave dug inside his courtyard. The coffin, a sitting coffin, was very long, for he was a tall man. He was dressed in his chief's regalia. . . . [H]e sat there as if he were about to get up and speak. (154)

One may reasonably suspect that the length of African American funerals — traditionally longer than those of white Americans — had some generative relationship to those West African traditions. But, most important and most specifically generative were the traditional call-and-response and the performative and participatory dimensions of the black funeral service.

Those traditions of West Africa — the "mourning and dancing" that Emecheta describes — had perhaps their strongest corollary in twentieth-century black America in the jazz funerals of New Orleans, ceremonies heralded by the music of legendary brass bands. Kongolese slaves who had been brought to Louisiana would "vent the soul's sorrow with customary weeping and wailing" before they accompanied the dead to the burial sites "with much rejoicing." Decorum required that the "mourners sing, beat the drum and tambourine, and dance the soul to its new home" (Osbey 104).

The bands were formed from the social clubs and benevolent societies — those informal organizations that, as discussed in the previous chapter, provided burial insurance to black communities.

Midcentury, the traditional New Orleans jazz funeral was at its heyday. A "grand marshal," a member of the club or society of the deceased, "set the tone. He wears the face of sorrow and solemnity. His dignified attire [complete, usually, with white gloves] and demeanor elicit respect from the waiting crowds. His rhythmic strut, from heavy-footed marching to hopping sidesteps, will signal for all the soul's departing. It's a privileged position" (Touchet). (Many black funeral directors still, in a tradition at least visibly linked to the black marshals of the jazz funerals, wear gloves during the service, sometimes distributing them as well to pall-bearers, signaling the solemnity of the occasion, and representing the ceremonial cultural link.) New Orleans native Brenda Osbey re-

Jazz funeral. *Bettman/CORBIS.*

called that the grand marshal would signal his leadership by carrying a
baton or walking stick. "Shoes were spit shined to a dull glow and the
bearing appropriately, even theatrically, grave. . . . In the old days, the
bands prided themselves in their appearance. They dressed in black suits,
starched white band shirts, crisp bow ties. . . . On all sides there would be
a deep hush, with only sporadic words of admiration for the dignity of
the whole procession." In Touchet's *Rejoice When You Die,* jazz trumpeter
Ellis L. Marsalis Jr. described the ceremony.

> . . . the band meets at the church or funeral parlor where the dismissal
> services are being conducted. After the service, the band leads the pro-
> cession slowly through the neighborhood. . . . The mood is generally
> somber, and musical selections are taken from Christian hymns such as
> "Amazing Grace" or "Just a Closer Walk with Thee" commonly sung
> in black Protestant churches. While playing the hymn(s), the musicians
> indulge in virtually no improvisation.
>
> The distance the band walks today may be only a few blocks, since
> burial sites are not always within walking distance of the church or
> funeral parlor. If the cemetery is nearby, the band accompanies the pro-

cession to it. When the interment ceremony is completed, the band leads the procession from the gravesite without playing. When a respectful distance from the site has been reached, the lead trumpeter sounds a two-note preparatory riff to alert his fellow musicians. At this point the drummer begins to play . . . [and] the band now sheds its solemnity in favor of music more conducive to lively, even joyous activity on the part of family, friends, and other celebrants—the group affectionately known as the "second line." Out come umbrellas, many of them elaborately decorated, that seem to be more about styling and profiling than protection from nature's elements.

When a returning brass band is heard in the distance, that sound announces the impending arrival of a public celebration. Those who are willing and able will fall in behind the band, next to the band, between the band members, affecting the body language of a dance, a strut, a "booty bounce" to the music of the second-line beat. (2, 3)

The funeral marches and jazz band parades through New Orleans communities gave that community considerable experience with public black burial services. Tourists habitually gathered there, flocking to its cemeteries, hoping to catch its musical strains and glimpse its celebrants and mourners. Claude Robin, the French naturalist, was in New Orleans at the time of its sale to the United States and remarked, "I have noticed especially in the city that the funerals of white people are only attended by a few, those of colored people are attended by a crowd, and mulattoes, quadroons married to white people, do not disdain attending the funeral of a black" (Roach, *Cities of the Dead* 59). Although cultural anthropologist Joseph Roach argued the jazz funeral as "a space for memory as improvisation," ritual patterns of memory emerged and dominated the performative space of the black funeral, whether it was a New Orleans jazz ceremony or a less public occasion of black mourners gathered. Marsalis described a New Orleans tradition whose late-century conduct seemed merely a riff on the earlier practices, noting that "much of this has changed. . . . Although the jazz funeral is very much a part of New Orleans' black culture, some of the younger brass band players are either unfamiliar with or indifferent to the traditional music . . . and the stately march to the gravesite is becoming a thing of the past: often now the livelier music begins at the church doors" (2). As the century came to a close, observers familiar with the earlier traditions observed that the bands themselves were different: their membership no longer specifically attached to the old-time societies and clubs, and even their names—Dirty Dozen, Soul Rebels, Algiers—told the tale of the shifting times. Osbey commented on the shift, stating that she

> mourns the apparent and apparently inevitable passing of the traditional jazz funeral. But in my discontent, I have taken note . . . that more and more, jazz funerals are becoming the purlieu of the young. And when the very young die, it is almost always at the cost of violence. And so I begin to think that perhaps it is not merely all right but appropriate that the very young mourners of the very young dead begin *their* celebration as soon as the casket is removed to its hearse. Their own lives being so susceptible to the same fate, who knows when they might have the chance to "do it up right"? (101)

Some specifically black funeral traditions, however, did persist. One hallmark of the culture's specific behavior, for instance, lay in the sheer length of a service, which lasted long enough to inscribe whatever cultural or familial memory was important. Even formal ceremonies for such luminaries as Supreme Court Justice Thurgood Marshall and Commerce Secretary Ron Brown—which were clearly state events—retained their cultural inflection as black memorials. By midcentury, the funerals of statesmen had become nationally broadcast public occasions. The filming of funeral ceremonies for President John F. Kennedy and later Martin Luther King Jr. made it possible for every American with a television to witness their final rites. Although a national mourning was engaged and orchestrated with these state occasions, the services for King, Marshall, and Brown did not lose their black specificity, which was apparent in the music (including the "Negro National Anthem" and "Lift Every Voice and Sing") and the lengthy orations.

The four-hour-plus funeral service for Clinton-administration Commerce Secretary Brown surprised not a few whites in attendance (including the c-span camera crew who filmed the entire service for its viewers) who had anticipated the traditional brevity of a public, state funeral. The eulogizing of Brown continued for hour after hour, despite admonitions and pleas to adhere to a time constraint that program organizers had hoped would prevail. What became evident was the way in which cultural practices of African American eulogists demanded a dif-

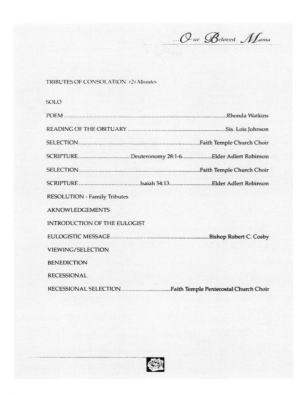

...*Our Beloved Mama*

TRIBUTES OF CONSOLATION *(2) Minutes*

SOLO

POEM ....Rhonda Watkins

READING OF THE OBITUARY ....Sis. Lois Johnson

SELECTION...Faith Temple Church Choir

SCRIPTURE.....................Deuteronomy 28:1-6................Elder Adlert Robinson

SELECTION...Faith Temple Church Choir

SCRIPTURE...........................Isaiah 54:13..........................Elder Adlert Robinson

RESOLUTION - Family Tributes

AKNOWLEDGEMENTS

INTRODUCTION OF THE EULOGIST

EULOGISTIC MESSAGE...Bishop Robert C. Cosby

VIEWING/SELECTION

BENEDICTION

RECESSIONAL

RECESSIONAL SELECTION........................Faith Temple Pentecostal Church Choir

Note the time constraints suggested in the upper left of the funeral program. This reminder carries little authority with those called on to memorialize. In fact, it drama-tizes the moment in making clear that time has no dominion at these ceremonies.

ferent kind of recognition. The brief attention span of a typical television audience would not be an appropriate signal of respect for the black dead. Ron Brown's funeral program indicated that there would be several speakers who would engage different parts of his life and career— from its beginnings in Harlem to his diplomatic days in Washington. No programmatic admonitions expressed verbally or by some cautionary language within the funeral program itself could constrain those speakers from making clear their admiration, love, and respect for his accomplishments. Race was not an insignificant difference separating those speakers who were brief in their comments and those who were not.

Printed funeral programs had been introduced into wide use mid-century and were one means of (or at least an effort toward) formalizing the length of the services. And, although the funeral programs sometimes even prescribed a time frame for tributes, the cultural admonition and expectation was that taking one's time was an indication of honor and respect.

When Rosemary Redmon Cosby, founder of Salt Lake City's Faith Temple Pentecostal Church was funeralized in the late 1990s, the funeral program itself signaled the likely course of the service — it was thirty-four pages long. It not only indicated the order of the service but included several full-page colored photos of the minister lovingly known as "Mama" at different stages of her life, as well a series of testimonials from local and state politicians. Although the service and program specified that there would be "two minutes" allotted for tributes, there was no such restraint at that point in the service, nor at any other. According to one congregant who wrote me about the ceremonies, the funeral was to have begun

at 10:00 A.M., but it did not. The viewing, weeping and wailing lasted for hours. Then the praise service with lots of dancing and shouting followed. Finally, the choir . . . jogged in and the band went into action. They had come to send Mama home and they were going to do it in style. . . . All I can say is that those folks got to dancing and shouting so hard, Mama's body was literally jumping up and down in the coffin. Now if they had come from the [islands] there would be some wonderful folk myth created about Mama dancing with the congregation during her going home ceremony.

I thought everything would be over by 1.00; I left at 2:50. . . . I later learned the procession — miles long — got to the cemetery after 7:00 P.M., in the dark. . . . Needless to say, practically no one was there to meet them except a lone agent who took the body and locked it in a safe room for the night. I think Mama was finally buried some time on Monday. . . . This took place in Salt Lake City, Utah, right in the shadow of Founder Joseph Smith and Prophet Brigham Young, who I am sure turned over in his grave when the shouting from Faith Temple rose above and beyond Temple Square and the Mormon Tabernacle. Who said there is only one choir in Zion? Black culture is alive along the Wasatch!

Despite the effort to enjoin against long speeches and tributes, a lengthy service was perceived to be an honor to the deceased — a testimony to the great impact of his or her life. Consider the 1996 funeral of Bishop David Ellis Sr., pastor of Detroit's Greater Grace Temple of the Apostolic Faith, whose services stretched over three days. His body was laid to rest in a $30,000 gold-plated casket that was "propped at an angle in the church aisle so mourners could see his body resting on red velvet cushions" (Henderson A1). Academy Award–winning actress Hattie McDaniel's 1952 funeral had 5,000 mourners and a procession of 125 limousines and twenty-four vans just to transport the flowers from the church to the cemetery. And, when Harlem finally finished viewing the elaborate display of the young Florence Mills, she was funeralized and buried with similarly lavish touches.

> The church . . . was jammed with at least 3000 people. . . . An orchestra . . . played the Chopin Funeral March as the body was borne up the aisle, the preacher intoning the scriptural passage, "I am the way and the life." . . . [T]he mournful hymn of consolation, "Come Ye Disconsolate" was sung by the regular church choir. . . .
>
> After the service, the funeral procession moved up 7th Avenue to Woodlawn cemetery, where the body was interred. . . . A low-flying aeroplane flew in slow circles overhead and released a flock of blackbirds which fluttered and flashed in the afternoon sun, recalling one of the songs made famous by Miss Mills, "Goodbye Blackbirds." (Anderson 181–84)

Twentieth-century African Americans also implicitly understood that, at this final moment, when there is literally no time left, to take the requisite time to honor and dignify a life is a determinative form of final tribute. Elder Mason wanted to make certain this would be true for his funeralizing. The undertaker-preacher Preston Taylor, served as master of ceremonies and told the crowds gathered at the Ryman auditorium in Nashville of "the desire of the family and the church that the wishes of the deceased be carried out . . . and that Rev. Mason desired that his friends have a word to say at his funeral and that they *should not be rushed through*" (Mason 28; emphasis mine).

For many it was important to note the procession of cars and prominent numbers of mourners. Their visual excess expressed a story that African America otherwise had difficulty illustrating—that these were lives of importance and substance, or that these were individuals, no matter their failings or the degree to which their lives were quietly lived, who were loved. Charles Drew's funeral was held at the nation's capital in a black church that was more than a hundred years old, the age of the place signifying both the historical weight of the black cultural presence in that important American city and the stature of Drew in that community. In these situations, it seemed less important to have room enough for the mourners than to select a room that by its capacity or prestige indicated a moment that even the space could not contain. "Hundreds came" to Drew's funeral, and "when the funeral procession stopped at Nineteenth and E Streets, near where [the brothers Charles and Joseph] had lived and played as boys, the cars stretched back three blocks, all the way to Pennsylvania Avenue. Policemen were posted at every corner." One of Drew's sisters was "impressed with the magnitude of the funeral," and said, "It seemed to me that only Franklin Roosevelt's funeral was bigger in D.C. . . . The florists in Washington were sold out of flowers." Her proud memory was also painful. She recalled as well that when she passed by her brother's open casket, she could see his hands and that they had been clearly "mangled" in the accident (Love 28–29).

In contrast to these extraordinary funerals was that of Booker T. Washington, who specifically requested that the bereaved "keep the exercises absolutely simple," so that the monument of Tuskegee could serve as his memorial. Still, commentary on what was *not* done threw into relief exactly what *would* have been standard procedure for memorializing the death of such an esteemed race man, even in 1915. In Washington's ceremony, it was noted, there was a "lack of studied pomp and ceremony . . . no labored eulogies; no boastings of his great work; no gorgeous trappings of horses; no streaming banners; no mysterious ceremonies of lodges" (Holsey 454). One report of the funeral managed to make clear, however, with its prosaically generous descriptors of who was there and what did occur, that a significant moment and man were being remembered.

> If there was aught out of the ordinary it was the great crowd of negro leaders from all parts of the continent, the hosts of whites, the multitudes of the simple country folk whom Dr. Washington loved so well, the flowers and plants sent in offering to the dead, a casket before which student guards changed watch every few minutes during the entire service and the tears which fell from all faces. . . . A guard of forty-four officers of the student battalions [and] thousands [who] gazed into the casket where the dead chieftain lay.
>
> But the most pathetic of all was the sight of the humble and unlet-

tered colored people of the cotton fields who literally packed the school grounds. . . . One old couple, themselves near the sunset of life, walked a long, long distance to be here. Piteously the man approached one of the instructors and, with trembling lips and eyes that overflowed, asked: "Do you reckon they will let us see Booker? . . . We have come so fur jes' to see him de las time. Do you reckon they will mind us looking at him?" They were escorted to the casket and given their heart's desire. . . . (Holsey 454)

A similar drama, garnered not from opulent show or luxurious appointments, was felt by those congregated for James Baldwin's funeral. It came instead from the collective synthesis of cultural sense and sound in the immense New York City cathedral where his body lay. Instead of being left with a recollection of the display of place, funeral-goers experienced the congregational spirit and purpose that enveloped his mourners and that gave occasion to the weight of his words and presence in America's social and cultural history. At Baldwin's funeral, a collocation of culturally explicit moments and *materia*—drummers, the speakers and singers, the draped casket, his mother's mournful cries, and his own voice—all contributed to the aura of solemnity and momentousness.

> The coffin, draped in black, stood at the cathedral crossing in front of the high altar. The procession of the family and the honorary pall-bearers, led by Baldwin's grieving mother [Berdis] in a wheelchair, moved down the long aisle to the African drumbeats of the Babatunde Olatunji Ensemble. The cathedral choir . . . sang the psalms. The words of the King James Bible provided a strange contrast to the drums and suggested, like the mix of the congregation, Baldwin's role as a prophet to the *whole* nation. . . .
>
> Odetta sang the congregation through the first moments, during which Berdis Baldwin's mournful moaning echoed through the cavernous church. . . . There were moving tributes from Maya Angelou and Toni Morrison, who spoke of Jimmy as a "brother" and as now an "ancestor." There was a jazz salute and then the main eulogy, a stirring speech by Amiri Baraka, who reminded the congregation of Baldwin's righteous anger and of the fact that "he lived his life as witness. . . ." Perhaps the highlight of the service was Baldwin himself on tape singing "Precious Lord, take my hand, lead me on." This part of the service

had been announced in the program, but, nevertheless, it startled the listeners. He seemed to be there, still witnessing. . . .

The pallbearers led the family and the coffin to the great west doors, which opened to give the witness back to his city, and a caravan of cars took him through Harlem, through the world of his childhood, a world that had never been out of his thoughts. . . . (Leeming 387)

What is remarkable in African America is that such symbolically rich display did not only matter for the wealthy and famous—but that the sense of a "special" funeral mattered to many who lived lives of less public acclaim. C. Eric Lincoln claimed that, even in a late-twentieth-century contemporary market in which "cremation and minimalist funerals" were the developing trends, he had "yet to meet any black people, whatever their status, who do not feel that the way in which you go out is important, very important" (Tilove 3E).

Indeed, as if in defiance of those trends, the opportunity to bury and funeralize someone with some measure of pomp and circumstance spoke to the ways in which those lives were racially constructed. The African American funeral director gave black folk a familiar, safe, uncritical space—a moment that the profession controlled, encouraged, and understood—and an opportunity to display something other than the selectivity that being black in America too often forced forward. Given the history of black memory and cultural expectation, it is difficult not to understand the emotional impact of Annie's passing in *Imitation of Life* and the effect that the elaborate funerals in the two films with this title seared into cultural memory. From the gardenia-draped casket to Mahalia Jackson's solo to the funeral cortege drawn by white horses and elegantly attired groomsmen, the expectations of both a theatrical Hollywood performance and a supremely articulated cultural tradition were enacted. "Going Home" was no time to cut corners. In Orange, Texas, local funeral director Wayne Sparrow fulfilled a woman's request that sounded as if it took its inspiration from that movie. She wanted to be buried in white garments and taken to the church in a casket on a caisson drawn by six white horses. The driver was to wear a top hat. Sparrow explained that "it was a big thing to that family" to have these final requests honored (Dart 7).

When gambler Flukey's son Willie was gunned down in 1983, his father arranged for his body to lie in state in a coffin that was shaped like

"Body by Fisher." *Bettman/CORBIS.*

a Cadillac, "complete with a steering wheel, blinking headlights and tail lights, a windshield, whitewall tires and 'Wimp' embossed on a plaque." One magazine ran the photo with the caption "Body by Fisher." Flukey's settin-up was no less grand. Seven thousand people came to see his body, some wearing T-shirts sporting the slogan "Flukey the Gambler Lives Forever." Flukey's body was in a glass-topped, $9,000 mahogany coffin. Its "powder-blue interior matched the occupant's double-breasted suit, tie, handkerchief and python shoes." In case color-coordination might not have had the full effect desired, the mortuary had placed "an ivory, slim-line telephone" in his hands, "similar to the car phone on which Flukey conducted his business" ("Forever Stylish" 172).

Although the ritual formality and spectacle of black funerals and burials were clearly deliberate attempts to make the "home-going" ceremonies of African Americans underscore or encourage a view of each life as important and notable, there were occasions when the struggle of black life and black event was instead the surviving message of the ceremonies. Recall the Boston funeral of Robert Odom and the mournful lament of "blood, blood in the church." In California, as another example, several youths were wounded in a gun battle at Rosedale Ceme-

The Biggie Smalls funeral procession winds through Harlem.
Associated Press

tery when two gangs, each attending simultaneous funerals for their murdered members, "came face to face." According to a counselor in the Crenshaw district of Los Angeles, "every funeral carries the threat of more mayhem and death. They are a 'keg of dynamite.'" Police there "cite a litany of horrors. Once, enemy gangs invaded a funeral home and stabbed a corpse. Another time, gangsters shot a body after stealing it from the mortuary" (Wilkinson and Chavez A15).

The funeral of late-twentieth-century rap artist Christopher Wallace (a.k.a. Biggie Smalls, or Notorious B.I.G.) began as a dignified, private affair. His body was displayed wearing a white double-breasted suit, and it was placed in a coffin of "African" mahogany. But, after the funeral procession left the church and, as was traditional, drove through the New York City neighborhood where he had spent his youth, there was a clash between police and bystanders that seemed to echo the violent manner of his death—he was the victim of a drive-by shooting in L. A.—and the aggressive lyrics in the rap music he helped to make famous. Just as the procession of the black hearse, eight stretch limousines, and thirty cars, some carrying "ornate floral arrangements," passed his childhood apartment—where a memorial of flowers, liquor bottles, and votive candles had been arranged by mourners and neighbors—teenagers "jumped onto several parked cars and began dancing . . . [and] police moved in."

The crowds had gathered in anticipation of the motorcade's route and had been waiting "in an almost festive atmosphere with people drinking beer and listening to music." But the subsequent police clash resulted in the arrest of ten people (Fisher). It seemed as if the disruptive character of Smalls's life and the manner of his death found last expression in the confrontation between police and onlookers in Harlem. Raheem Harris, a fourteen year old who witnessed the goings-on commented, "That's the way he chose to go. . . . You reap what you sow." When rapper TuPac Shakur died in a similarly violent way in 1996, the lyrics of some of his songs—"If I Die 2Nite" and "Death Around the Corner," for example—reminded even those for whom rap was not an interest that these young artists' music, message, and method of living were intimately connected with the not-surprisingly prescient sense of their vulnerability to black death.

The community ownership of and commentary on these events are haunting indicators of the way in which black death and dying envelope both a national and public space, as well as the more intimate, neighborhood spaces of black cultural memory. The territorial exchange of these narratives contributes to their permanence. They appear and reappear like an ephemeral but persistent remembrance, a ghostly embodiment of national and cultural memory.

The late twentieth century's evolution of the last rites, as displayed in Smalls's last driveby, was a phenomenon that could not have been imagined by Reverend Mason, whose advice to his congregation, repeated in the memorial pamphlet, was to "be clean and upright men of truth and to be sober-minded in all things and to wear this world as a loose garment." His funeral was certainly appropriately sober and disciplined and clearly a cultural affair. For the Elder Reverend Mason, "the Primitive Baptists, true to their customs and beliefs sang the songs of Zion as they are accustomed to sing. . . . [T]he thousands of voices made the very walls of the great auditorium echo—echo as they had never done before" (Mason 28). At his funeral, there was the requisite weeping; the "old members were stricken with grief over the loss of their shepherd" and there were even some white folk who came to the service. "Seated on the rostrum were all of the leading pastors of all denominations, business and professional men, *members of the City Commission, City Judge-elect Wells, Hon. Noah Cooper and several others of prominence*" (Mason 27; emphasis mine). The melees that sometimes occurred at end-of-the-century services for rap artists could not have happened then. The undertaker, funeral director, and preacher Preston Taylor "kept order and discipline at all times despite the many thousands in attendance." At the end of the obsequies, when each of Mason's friends, members of his family, and the assembled dignitaries had had requisite time to speak—without having been rushed or hurried, as the Elder had desired—"Reverend Mason was laid to rest in Mt. Ararat Cemetery in his family square, *beside his father and five children*" (Mason 30; emphasis mine). As if in final testament to the ubiquitous thesis of black death, the pamphlet thus concluded with its own subtextual mourning story as it revealed that each of these children had preceded their father in death.

As did our son.

We took the remains of our child back to his church. It was our first instinct and our only balm—to have his final rites pronounced in the church of his childhood, a black church and an institution whose historic role in comforting heartsick and weary congregations through the years of their lifetimes is intimately connected to its cultural vitality. We prayed that Bem's spirit would be received within that space, and that there, there would be the reconciliation and redemption he longed for.

5

The Promise
of Hope in a Season of Despair

A FUNERAL SERMON BY MAURICE O. WALLACE, PH.D.

The family has requested a sermon rather than a eulogy proper, a message generalized for us all, of course, but one which I hope will posture our spirits, nevertheless, to always remember the beauty of Bem.

May I call your attention, now, to a portion of the Old Testament located in the book of the prophet Isaiah?

The lament of Israel, in the ears of Isaiah, is no strange lament to us, centuries and centuries removed from Isaiah's writing. Theirs was the bitter cry of near-hopeless captivity in Babylon and the shrill objection to exile so familiar to us, of late.

The exiled Jews Isaiah sought to console were, like so many detained and dispossessed, geographically displaced. But more deeply than that, they experienced a loss of the structured, reliable world of sense and coherent meaning that was existentially home. In its place the vexed persistence of failed hopes, anger, wistful sadness, and forlorn resignation would come to hold forth, and despair would have its dominion.

For us who know little firsthand of the violence of exile or extradition, perhaps the condition of despair is more resonant. From an ecclesiastical point of view, I submit, it is the defining pathology of our day, and quite possibly the greatest threat to our spiritual strivings, to our unique capacity, that is, as people of faith, to be buoyant and keep singing in the strange, disorienting places of life.

So much despair and confusion. So much angst and hopelessness.

So much bewilderment and unending madness. It is enough to make the strongest among us throw up her hands in resignation, and hang her harp upon the weeping willows in Babylon.

"By the rivers of Babylon," a psalmist wrote, "there we sat down, yea we wept, when we remembered Zion. We hung our harps upon the willows in the midst thereof. For there they that carried us away captive required of us a song and they that wasted us required of us mirth, saying, Sing us one of the songs of Zion. How shall we sing the Lord's song in a strange land?" he wonders.

How can we sing, when our hearts refuse to make melody? How can we rejoice? When our woes defy words. And here? In Babylon? How can we sing here? In this place? Here, in this situation so hard and so despairing that praying seems futile and singing seems senseless? Sing? Here? How can we? How can *I* sing, of Zion anymore?

Well, the answer may be simpler than we know. I urge you that if Babylon be your lot, and storm clouds gather menacingly overhead; if you *must* sit down at river's edge and weep with the willows, well then you must. But whatever else the pressures of life have you to do, never, never hang up your harp. It is the sign and symbol of your dignity and endurance, your capacity to last still longer and conjure a song in the midst of your storm.

> Don't hang up your harp, even in the darkest day.
> Don't hang up your harp, it may be all you have, but it may be all
>   you need.
> Don't hang up your harp, lied on, cheated, talked about, mistreated.
> Don't hang up your harp, 'buked, scorned, talked about sure as
>   you born.
> Don't hang up your harp.

For as long as you've got a harp in your heart, God's got a hymn for your hurt. And as long as you've got a hymn, then you've got hope. For in seasons of despair, singing brings hope and despair is transformed into doxology, a hymn of praise to God for a victory won when situations of great trouble are transformed by His power and mercy.

Israel had been singing doxologies since the deliverance from Egypt. Every man, at his mother's knee, learned to sing about the decisive power and reliable commitment of Yahweh to intrude in life-giving ways in circumstances of ostensible defeat, disorder, or death. So it must be in our singing. When we sing "Farther along, we'll know all about it. Farther along we'll understand why. Cheer up my brother, my sister. Live in the sunshine. We'll understand it better by and by," then hope comes alive. And hope won't permit us to submit to the gods of fear or anger or despair. When we sing, "Come ye disconsolate, where e're ye languish. Come to the mercy seat, fervently kneel. Here bring your wounded hearts, here tell your anguish; Earth has no sorrow that heaven cannot heal," then hope is reborn. And it is hope which gives us spine and spunk, resolve and courage, energy and freedom. It is hope that affords us such freedom of imagination to discern an alternate reality, a countervision, to a present anguish.

When, in Isaiah chapter 40, Israel complains of God's indifference to her, saying "My way is hidden from the Lord," the responding hymn of the ensuing verses assert, rather, that Yahweh is the God of all generations, past, present, and future, and is not weary or faint or powerless but gives power to those who hope.

The power of hope, then, is the power to run and not be weary, to walk and not faint.

The power of hope is the power to trust that all things work together for good, to them who love the Lord.

The power of hope is the power to believe against logic that nothing shall be able to separate me from the love of God in Christ Jesus; neither death nor life, nor angels nor principalities, nor powers, nor things present, nor things to come, nor height, nor depth, nor any other creature.

The power of hope is the power to surrender to the almighty power of God, cognizant that if God be for us, well, then who can be against us?

The power of hope is the power to stand, when no one will stand with you, and having done all to stand, stand anyhow.

The power of hope is the power to improvise on the impossible; and transform what is only possible into what is probable.

The power of hope no longer asks the question "How shall we sing in a strange land?"

But rather it sings the new question, penned generations and generations later: "Why should I feel discouraged? And why should the shadows come? Why should my heart feel lonely and long for heaven and home? When Jesus is my portion, a constant friend is he. His eye is on the sparrow and I know he watches me." How can I sing in the strange land of trouble, you ask me? "I sing because I'm happy. I'm happy because I'm free. His eye is on the sparrow. And I know he watches me."

Finally, beloved, I leave you with the encouragement of a sprite gray-haired preacher portrayed in writer James Baldwin's ambitious blues novel, *Another Country*. To a sorrowfully rapt audience of mourners like us, Reverend Foster implores the bereaved: "Don't lose heart, dear ones—don't lose heart. Don't let it make you bitter. Try to understand. Try to understand. The world's already bitter enough, we got to try to be better than the world."

God bless you.

Epilogue

HARRIET TUBMAN DAVIS

"I had reasoned this out in my mind; there was one of two things I had a right to, liberty, or death; if I could not have one, I would have the other; for no man should take me alive."

I wandered for an hour trying to find HARRIET TUBMAN (1913). I didn't mind the time. I had grown used to these searches, and I came to depend on their quiet and solitude, feeling comfort and ease in these stilled cemetery spaces. They even became a necessary interlude—an intervention of sorts for the personal interviews that I conducted for this project, interviews that were challenging for an English professor more used to the quiet spaces of books than the characters that they imagined. Most of the time I traveled alone, but there were trips when my husband and daughter accompanied me. That time, my fourteen-year-old niece Aziza came along, persuaded to go on the two-hour drive from my parents' home in Buffalo to the Auburn, New York, cemetery if I would agree to listen to her Prince tapes while we traveled. It was an easy bribe: I wanted her company and I like Prince.

When we entered the cemetery gates on that Sunday summer morning, there was only one person stirring who might have some indication of where we could find Harriet Tubman. He guided his lawnmower neatly and carefully between the tombstones as if there were years of practice and respect for the grounds governing his labor. It's under that really big tree on the south side along the wall, he told us—not particularly happy, it seemed, with our distracting presence. So, we thanked him and walked there, following the wall's back route, Aziza asking at each gravestone, Maybe that one? And me thinking how each grave was reminiscent of Dickinson's "a swelling in the ground." Suddenly, a massive cypress emerged from the leafy vista that had obscured it, and there was Harriet.

Some years into the process of writing this book,

1915
Booker T. Washington

1917
Scott Joplin

1919
Madame C.J. Walker

1921
Pinckney Benton Stewart
   Pinchback

1922
Bert Williams
   (Egbert Austin)

1925
Homer Plessy

1926
Elizabeth "Bessie" Coleman

1927
Florence Mills

1929
Elijah McCoy

BILLIE HOLIDAY
"When I die people can maybe cry
for me because they know they're going
to start me off in hell and move me from
bad to worse."

I left behind the sense I was searching for tombstones. I was looking instead for Harriet, or Billie, or Richard. It became a personal, even an intimate, sojourn among my cultural kin. When we found BILLIE HOLIDAY's (1959) grave in New York City, the lyrics and melody of "God Bless the Child" moved from memory to mouth, and soon I was standing in full-voiced song before the tombstone she shared with her mother. An elderly white couple, tending a grave some rows down, left their work and came to where I stood with Billie and her mother and asked if I knew her. Before I could help it, I heard myself say, Oh yes, she's my great aunt. Of course, it wasn't at all true, but at that moment, I *felt* like kin. Well, we take care of her, they told me. Whenever we come to tend our parents' graves, we clear away any weeds in front of Miss Holiday's as well. I was touched by their neighborliness and told them so. I think I even said the family will be so grateful. I know I could have said this; it would have been easy. Poetic license.

I left a flower at the gravesite of each twentieth-century African American I wanted to memorialize with this project. And, despite all the various shades that have dimmed the past years of my own life, I can remember distinctly each moment when I discovered a grave. The shivering embrace of the chilled air on one fall afternoon in Paris is with me still. At Le Cimetiere du Pere-LaChaise, I walked, without sense of or concern for the time that was passing, down byways thickened with monuments. I did not know then that there was a cemetery map that would have led me directly to the columbarium and RICHARD WRIGHT's (1960) space there among the cremated.

It was only after reading hundreds upon hundreds of names that I found his square of black granite that, nestled in the corner where I knelt to reach it, reflected my own tear-filled eyes back at me, either the wind or the memory rising to my gaze. Its gold lettering was simple and clear—starkly projected against the dark stone. My hand trembled as I placed a pot of African

1930
Charles Sidney Gilpin
Pauline Hopkins

1931
Ida B. Wells
Daniel Hale Williams

1932
Bill Pickett
Charles Waddell
 Chesnutt

1933
Sissieretta Jones

1934
William Monroe Trotter

1935
Richard B. Harrison
Alice Dunbar Nelson

1936
John Hope

1937
Henry Ossawa Tanner
Bessie Smith

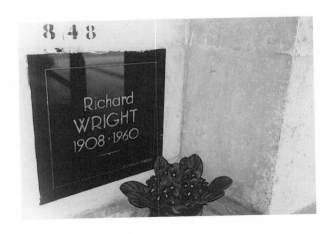

RICHARD WRIGHT

"He would have to purchase the wisdom of life
with sacred death."

LOUIS ARMSTRONG

"Once I cut out, forget it. . . .
Just the music, that's all I'm interested
in. . . . You have to have something
to die with."

violets at the base of the wall. And, then, I waited there, until the sense that the moment had done what it would passed. Before I left, I tucked just a few of the African violet's blossoms into the crack between the wall and Wright's stone. Poor Richard, I mumbled, remembering an essay with that name. I laid the flat of my palm against the stone and held it there. How shall you be remembered? I traced the deep etching of the bright letters in his name.

Later, I actually came to prefer to search without a map, to wander these serene spaces unguided, giving the imaginations I constructed about my grave meanderings time to develop. When the caretaker in Monaco told me that not one of Josephine Baker's children came to visit their mother's grave, my English "tsk tsk" echoed hers in French. Back in the United States, my husband Russell and I saw the tributes of coins on the gravestone of LOUIS ARMSTRONG (1971). A submarine sandwich had been divided, its halves placed on each of the in-ground markers that lay before the tombstone (one marking the space for Louis, the other for his wife Lucille). There was a soda on hers and a can of Fosters on his, the condensation on his can still apparent. We took the photograph quickly, not wanting to intrude on that loving gesture (which Josephine should have had from someone who cared at least that much). As we left, I looked back through the quickly dissolving haze of the early morning. And, as I walked away, it seemed as if the white marble trumpet atop his memorial had no foundation, that it hovered over the site, like his music lingers in our national memories.

That visit's haze and harmony was like another early morning visitation, this one as far south as the other had been north. In St. Louis Cemetery Number 1, near voudou priestess Marie Leveau and the Morial family vault is the vault of Homer Plessy, the litigant in the famous civil rights case *Plessy v. Ferguson,* which made legal the ethic, as well as the practice, of "separate but equal." Perhaps it was the jumble of spiritual

1938

Arthur Schomburg

James Weldon Johnson

1939

Benjamin Brawley

Ma Rainey
  (Gertrude Malisa Nix
  Pridgett)

1940

Robert Sengstacke Abbott

Marcus Garvey

1941

Jelly Roll Morton
  (Ferdinand Joseph)

Ernest Everett Just

1943

George Washington Carver

Fats Waller
  (Thomas Wright)

Robert Nathaniel Dett

1946

Countee Cullen
  (Countee L. Porter)

Jack Johnson (John Arthur)

Horace Pippen

1948

Claude McKay

1949

Harry T. Burleigh

Bojangles
    (Bill [Luther] Robinson)

Leadbelly
    (Hudson Ledbetter)

1950

Charles Drew

Carter G. Woodson

1951

Oscar Micheaux

Oscar DePriest

1952

Hattie McDaniel

Canada Lee
    (Leonard Canegata)

Charles C. Spaulding

1953

Adam Clayton Powell

1954

Alain LeRoy Locke

Mary Eliza Church Terrell

ARTHUR ASHE

"I do not brood on the prospect of dying. . . .
I think that we must do our best to face
death with dignity. . . . Thus far, I have been
steadfast."

energies in New Orleans, and especially in the cemeteries, that interrupted any individual sense of Plessy.
Instead, decades of jazz funerals and the tremendous
crush of sight and sound, movement and melody satu-
rated the thick New Orleans air. Later that day I wished
that Mahalia Jackson could be there as well. As aus-
tere and stately as her gated marble edifice might be,
at the edge of a cemetery just outside of New Orleans,
there was no way to recall her spirit to the noisy space of
her plot, which was too near the highway, power lines,
and a culvert of dirty water. I wished instead she had

been in the company of the surreal cities of the dead in downtown New Orleans.

I had no such regrets when I found ARTHUR ASHE. (1993) I was grateful for the decision of his family to keep him and his mother, Mattie Ashe, in the historically black cemetery Woodland. The family gated the small plot where tombstones of Arthur and Mattie now stand together. But the iron pickets that surround his and his mother's gravestones did not imply separation from others in that black cemetery in Richmond, although Arthur's is certainly a memorial of greater size and note than the others in its company, including hers. Instead, it seemed to lovingly enclose him and his mother, and I felt there a spirit of embrace rather than separation. I found both Woodland and Arthur's gravesite quite easily, as the caretaker I had called had assured me I would. He told me that I could not miss it on the left, as I drove up the short, winding road to the cemetery gates of that historical burying ground for blacks in Richmond.

The historical practice of maintaining separate graveyards for blacks and whites in this country was one that continued, in fits and starts, throughout the twentieth century, although in the later years of that century, after bias became a federal wrong, that practice persisted more as a matter of choice for both races. A 1930s black resident of Savannah, Georgia, explained that "ebrybody wannuh be buried in deah own town. An we nebuh bury strainjuhs wid our own folks. Ef a strainjuh die yuh, we bury em in duh strainjuh's lot" (Elizabeth Roberts 113). Outright bias, shameful conduct, and a generally quiet history of preference in the habits of many graveyards recalled the practices of the funeral homes and churches that brought them their dead.

Only three days had passed since Whitney Elaine Johnson, an infant, had been buried in Barnett Creek Baptist Church Cemetery in Thomasville, Georgia, when church deacons approached her obviously grief-

1955
Matthew Henson
Charlie "Bird" Parker
Walter White
Mary McLeod Bethune
Emmett Louis Till

1956
Charles S. Johnson

1958
W. C. (William Christopher) Handy
Angelina Weld Grimké

1959
Billie Holiday

1960
Zora Neale Hurston
Richard Wright

1961
Jessie Redmon Fauset
Charlotte Hawkins Brown

1962
Louise Beavers
Augusta Savage
William Stanley Braithwaite
E. Franklin Frasier

stricken mother and asked that she exhume her daughter's body and move her to a "cemetery that would accept blacks." Althought it was 1996, the Baptist fellowship at Barnett Creek was not quite ready to change a "lifetime" policy at their cemetery, which "had been segregated for as long as anyone can remember," even for a biracial child whom they had not identified as black until her father showed up to visit his daughter's grave. Fortunately, before the baby was exhumed, these deacons reversed their decision, succumbing, albeit reluctantly, to the glaring light of a curious and challenging media onslaught. Although the story of the deacons' request to preserve the all-white cemetery in Thomasville became public, there were many similar stories at the century's end that were successfully and privately buried. Thomasville, Georgia's, story just happened to be one that earned the attention of the press; others were able to quietly continue a history of separation under cover of the weight of tradition. Whitney's grandmother bemoaned this state of affairs in her hometown, saying, "this isn't the 1950's" (Bragg).

She must have known that era well. At that time, even a veteran's uniform could not break the code in some U.S. cemeteries. In 1952, Greenwood Memorial Park in Phoenix refused to bury Pfc. Thomas Reed, a nineteen-year-old soldier killed in Korea. His body lay in a mortuary vault, and Lincoln Ragsdale Sr. defiantly left him there, unburied, for three months until the cemetery trustees voted to rescind their racist policies. In the same era, black families in Michigan were also forced to contend with the issue of segregated cemeteries; according to a 1959 letter to Gordon Parks, for instance, black families in Flint "buried their kin in Saginaw because only one undertaker and one burial ground in their hometown accepted blacks" (Kruger-Kahloula 131). It wasn't until 1966, when the Michigan Court of Appeals upheld the case of J. Spencer, whose mother was denied burial in Flint's Memorial Park because she was African American, that the county cemeteries dropped their bans against nonwhites (Kruger-Kahloula 131–32). If one were to track the history of such stories, one might expect that perhaps African American Korean War veterans would have been the last to experience blatant racism and lack of respect from their countrymen. But, even in the Vietnam era, black veterans found a macabre kinship with their Korean counterparts. In Ft. Pierce, Florida (Zora Neale Hurston's final resting place), it took federal legislation to make room for a black Vietnam veteran. Despite the fact that he had been "given military honors at an armory," that veteran's 1970 eulogy characterized him as a "man without a country" (Kruger-Kahloula 132).

Although cemetery desegregation was juridically assured in 1968, when the Supreme Court ruled in *Jones v. Mayer* using an 1866 civil rights law that guaranteed blacks equal rights in making and enforcing contracts and purchasing personal property, local legislation was slow to acknowledge the impact of that ruling. The conduct of cemeteries toward African Americans often extended beyond belief and common sense. Not until midcentury did the national cemetery at Arlington begin accepting the bodies of loyal black veterans for burial. It did not matter that, during the last years of the Civil War, the Freedmen's Village of nearly 3,000 black people existed on what were the eventual grounds of Arlington National Cemetery. Nor did it matter that 2,700 members of that black population were already buried there. The United States maintained Arlington as a segregated national cemetery until 1948, well after the two world wars that filled both urban and rural cemetery plots with deceased black veterans. Little wonder that the prominent African Americans who are buried in Arlington today attract such respectful attention and notice.

THURGOOD MARSHALL's (1993) grave stands there, an American flag visible in the distance and, ironically, the great columns of the Robert E. Lee house, on a hill in the background, look much like the ones on the

1968

Martin (Michael) Luther
  King Jr.

1970

Jimi Hendrix
Benjamin O. Davis Sr.
Sonny Liston

1971

Whitney M. Young Jr.
Louis Armstrong
Ralph Bunche

1972

Mahalia Jackson
Adam Clayton Powell
Jackie Robinson
Roberto Clemente

1973

Arna Bontemps
Diana Sands

1974

Duke Ellington (Edward
  Kennedy Ellington)

THURGOOD MARSHALL
"I was appointed for life, and I intend
to serve out my full term. . . . I'm not
going to leave until I die."

Supreme Court building where Marshall labored over
the constitutional consequences of the nation's legal
doctrine for thirty-three years. Many of the twentieth-
century African Americans buried at Arlington had a
critical impact in the construction of the nation's cultural history. JOSEPH LOUIS BARROW's (1981) gravesite
is there as well, his classic pugilistic pose reaching out
from one side of the granite marker, enacting the de-
termination that characterized his life. Also in Arlington, just to the left of a massive sphere that identifies
the man buried beneath as the "discoverer of the North
Pole," is a particular black granite tombstone shaped

JOE LOUIS

"Your whole life is a funeral."

just like Arthur Ashe's. Like Ashe's, it is adorned with a bronze and gold relief and bears an engraving that effectively back-talks the site to its right. MATTHEW HENSON's (1955) tombstone guarantees that the story of his life, which did not gain respect and credibility while he lived, would be explicit after his death—it identifies him as the "co-discoverer" of the North Pole.

It was not always that explicit. I think that scientist GEORGE WASHINGTON CARVER's (1943) grave is sometimes overlooked, with his more-famous colleague, Booker T. Washington, often gaining the greater notice. Carver's gravesite at Tuskegee University was

MATTHEW HENSON
"So let me steal away gently. . . . So let me pass away peacefully, silently, only remembered by what I have done."

GEORGE WASHINGTON CARVER
"We need have no fear of death . . . if we concern ourselves with seeking His laws by which we unlock His storehouse of wonder."

ringed with plastic flowers when I saw it. I wanted to
remove them and leave something more dignified. The
faded plastic blossoms seemed less than this great agri-
cultural scientist deserved. But I found some measure
of contentment sitting on the curved bench that was
placed just at the foot of Carver's aged concrete marker
and that provided an appropriate place for pause and
consideration of his accomplishments at Tuskegee.

Not all gravestones properly indicate the era and
moment of the deceased. Although the historic grounds
of Oakwood Cemetery in Chicago seemed to promise an aged and period-appropriate stone for the gravesite of the antilynching crusader and feminist activist
Ida B. Wells, nothing in the marker that lies across her
grave indicates the era of her passing. Instead, she shares
a fairly modern granite tombstone with her husband
Ferdinand, a nod to a late-century decision to "im-
prove" her gravesite. Oakwood's current owners do not
rest on the distinguished history of its residents; they are
still in the business of drumming up patrons. When my
husband and I went in search of Ida B., the woman in
the cemetery office looked at us carefully, as if we were
auditioning to get the information we wanted, which
was simply the location of Symphony Shores, where Ida
was buried. But she surprised us by asking if we were
married. I said yes, wondering why that was in any way
relevant. When she followed up by asking if we were
interested in a plot for ourselves, I realized the business
of burial never concludes.

Perhaps one of the most poignant postmortem
stories of the twentieth century was told by MALCOLM
X's (1965) modest gravesite in Ferncliff Cemetery—the
story of a summer tragedy that echoed his own pro-
phetic words: "It had always stayed in my mind that I
would die a violent death. In fact, it runs in my family."
His gravesite had originally been marked with the small
brass plate, riveted flat against the ground to a concrete slab, characteristic of all plots in the cemetery in
Ardsley-on-Hudson. But, on a summer day thirty-one

1986
Ron McNair
Ella Josephine Baker
Sippie Wallace

1987
Bayard Rustin
Harold Washington
James Baldwin

1988
Jean-Michel Basquiat
Romare Bearden

1989
Sterling Brown
Sugar Ray Robinson
  (Walter Smith)
Huey P. Newton

1990
Sarah Vaughan
Ralph Abernathy
Sammy Davis Jr.
Pearl Bailey
Alvin Ailey

MALCOLM X

"It had always stayed in my mind that
I would die a violent death. In fact, it runs
in my family."

MARTIN LUTHER KING JR.

"We've got some difficult days ahead. But it doesn't matter
with me because I've been to the mountain top and seen the
promised land. . . . I may not get there with you."

years after his death, I looked for Malcolm, only to find that the site had been disturbed and his marker removed, temporarily replaced with a bouquet of flowers that withered in the summer's sun and a T-shirt with Malcolm's words emblazoned in red across black cloth. At first I was merely disappointed, but then I realized why his marker was gone, and the tragic generational vitality of his own prophecy brought me to tears. His marker had been taken away so that his wife's name, Betty Shabazz, could be engraved next to his. This was the summer of her death, which she had suffered in the hands of her grandson, Malcolm. Her body, but not her name, had already been placed next to his in the grassy, bronzed pathways of Ferncliff.

The stories of graveyards do not only point inward, toward the personal, but outward as well, to the public. Certainly, the dramatic difference between the final resting places of two men of the century's most significant stature and renown — Malcolm X and MARTIN LUTHER KING JR. (1968) — suggests a very interesting postmortem narrative. I did not look very long before finding a parking place near the city block in Atlanta, Georgia, that had become King's gravesite, mausoleum, museum, historical center, and souvenir site. It was early on a Sunday morning, and the city streets were not very busy. On the one hand, the megablock of King's memorial symbolized the constantly evolving postmortem capitalist construction of his unique legacy, an ever-expanding legacy that does continue to benefit African Americans. But, when that site is juxtaposed with the modest gravesite of Malcolm, who is buried in a *community* of gone-but-not-forgotten souls, the narrative of culture, capital, and memory is apparent. I felt as if I had made a requisite tourist stop as I stood staring at King's sarcophagus centered in the middle of a reflecting pool — but that was all I felt.

Although the century's years and its passing customs can only occasionally be discerned in the gravesites of African Americans, there were still, at the end

1991
Miles Davis

1992
Audre Geraldine Lorde

1993
Dizzy Gillespie
 (John Birks)
Reginald Lewis
Thomas Dorsey
Thurgood Marshall
Arthur Ashe
Roy Campanella
Marian Anderson

1994
Ralph Ellison
Cabell "Cab"
 Calloway III
Carmen McRae
Wilma Rudolph

1995
Elizabeth Ann "Bessie"
 Delany
Butterfly McQueen

1996

Barbara Jordan

A.G. Gaston

Ron Brown

Carl B. Stokes

Ella Fitzgerald

TuPac Shakur

Moneta Sleet

Benjamin Quarles

1997

Queen Mother Moore
  (Audrey Eloise Moore)

Samuel Proctor

Robert Weaver

1998

Eldridge Cleaver

Lois Mailou Jones

John Henrick Clarke

Dorothy West

Charles C. Diggs

Margaret Walker
  Alexander

Florence Griffith-Joyner

Betty Carter
  (Lillie Mae Jones)

Flip Wilson

Stokley Carmichael
  (Kwame Toure)

Henry Hampton

A. Leon Higginbotham

This shell-covered gravesite on Hilton
Head Island recalls West African
decorative rituals.

of the twentieth century, some southern black burial
grounds where one could find plots decorated with the
remnants of broken dishes, glassware, bedframes, and
shells—echoes of early traditions in West Africa and the
eighteenth- and nineteenth-century enslaved Africans
in America. The families of the deceased had nurtured
a belief in the spiritual lives of their loved ones and,
through the use of such decorative graveyard arts, broke
the connection between the two worlds, eased the soul's
transition from one world to the next, and gave the
traveling soul a place to rest. Even though the sculptural
art of William Edmondson—whose grave markers were
important additions to the gravesites of the "impoverished yet art-loving members of Nashville's 1930s black

The broken vessel is a way of urging the spirit's break with the world of the living. This cemetery is in Euchee Valley, Florida.

community"—shifted from cemetery to museum once he was "discovered" by a Harper's Bazaar photographer, the "urge to adorn," as Zora Neale Hurston put it, followed the African American cultural spirit and did not end with the funeral (Powell 84).

Those who gave shape and contour to African America in the twentieth century are not all here, within these pages, nor are they fully memorialized in the photographs I have taken of their gravesites. But those who are here, chosen from each of the century's decades, might appropriately stand in for the others. The very last gravesite I visited before I brought this project to its end had also been the first. I returned to Paris and Pere-LaChaise. My daughter Ayana was with me, and I wanted her to see Richard Wright. It was the summer of 2000, two years since the last gravesite trip I had taken. Ayana and I took the subway from our hotel on the left bank, easily changing stops at Odeon and Strasbourg-St. Denis. I knew the way back. It was early morning, and the cemetery gates reliably rose into view as we climbed the stairs from the Metro. The day was cool but bright and sunny, and we were in no hurry. We strolled casually, shifting back and forth between the stone paths that edged the cemetery's thicket of small mausoleums to the gravelly roadway that stretched out before and beyond them. We spoke only to remark on the chestnut trees that lined the road and the way the sun stretched and streaked between leafy vistas. I told Ayana how as a young girl I used to collect chestnuts on my walks home from school, then string them into necklaces. We were relaxed and at ease until we got to the site where those who had been cremated were interred. There I stopped silent, stilled but for the tears that clouded my sight. I thought of my child, our son, her brother, and I could go no further. And so, we left together, her hand in mine, turned toward home.

Bibliography

"AIDS Infects Blacks in U.S. at Record Rates." *Jet* 22 March 1999: 31.

Albertson, Chris. *Bessie*. New York: Stein and Day, 1972.

Anderson, Jervis. *This Was Harlem*. New York: Farrar, Strauss, and Giroux, 1982.

Ansa, Tina McElroy. *Ugly Ways*. New York: Harcourt, Brace, and Company 1983.

"Assisted AIDS Suicides Increase." *News and Observer* 11 July 1996: C3.

Axtell, Lillian and Max Meyers. *Treatment and Survival Patterns for Black and White Cancer Patients Diagnosed 1955 through 1964*. Washington, D.C.: U.S. Department of Health, Education, and Welfare, Public Health Service, National Institutes of Health, 1975.

Baldwin, James. *Another Country*. New York: Dial Press, 1962.

———. *The Evidence of Things Not Seen*. New York: Henry Holt, 1985.

———. *Go Tell It on the Mountain*. 1952. New York: Modern Library, 1995.

Barbeau, Arthur and Florette Henri. *The Unknown Soldiers: Black American Troops in World War I*. Philadelphia: Temple UP, 1974.

Barrow, Joe Louis, Jr. *Joe Louis: Fifty Years of an American Hero*. New York: McGraw-Hill, 1988.

Beeth, Howard and Cary D. Wintz. *Black Dixie: Afro-Texan History and Culture in Houston*. College Station: Texas A&M UP, 1992.

Bendann, E., *Death Customs: An Analytical Study of Burial Rites*. London: Kegan Paul, Trench, Trubner, and Company, 1930.

Bergreen, Laurence. *Louis Armstrong: An Extravagant Life*. New York: Broadway Books, 1997.

Berlin, Edward A. *King of Ragtime: Scott Joplin and His Era*. New York: Oxford UP, 1994.

"Black-White Disparities in Health Care." *Journal of the American Medical Association* 263.17 (2 May 1990): 2344.

Bogle, Donald. *Brown Sugar: Eighty Years of America's Black Female Superstars.* New York: Da Capo Press, 1980.

———. *Dorothy Dandridge: A Biography.* New York: Amistad, 1997.

Boone, Margaret S. *Capital Crime: Black Infant Mortality in America.* Newbury Park, CA: Sage Publications, 1989.

Bowman, Leroy. *The American Funeral: A Study in Guilt, Extravagance, and Sublimity.* Washington, D.C.: Public Affairs Press, 1959.

Bradford, Sarah. *Harriet Tubman: The Moses of Her People.* 1886. Secaucus, NJ: Citadel Press, 1997.

Bragg, Rick. "Just a Grave for a Baby, but Anguish for a Town." *New York Times* 31 March 1996.

Brandt, Nat. *Harlem at War: The Black Experience in WWII.* Syracuse, NY: Syracuse UP, 1996.

Broussard, Albert. *Black San Francisco: The Struggle for Racial Equality in the West, 1900–1954.* Lawrence: University Press of Kansas, 1993.

Brown, DeNeen L. "Getting Ready to Die Young: Children in Violent D.C. Neighborhoods Plan Their Own Funerals." *The Washington Post* 1 November 1993: A1.

Brundage, William Fitzhugh. *Lynching in the New South: Georgia and Virginia, 1880–1930.* Diss. UMI, 1988.

Bruni, Frank. "Drawn to Gospel, Foreigners Arrive by Busload." *New York Times* 24 November 1996.

"The Business Side of Bereavement." *Black Enterprise* 8.4 (November 1977): 55.

Campbell, Bebe Moore. *Your Blues Ain't Like Mine.* New York: G. P. Putnam's Sons, 1992.

"Cemetery Lawsuit Preparations Begin." *Los Angeles Sentinel* 13 July 1995.

Chen, Howard. "Scarborough and Son." *Raleigh News and Observer* 20 July 1997.

Chua-Eoan, Howard. "Black and Blue." *Time* 155.9 (6 March 2000): 24–28.

Clarke, Donald. *Wishing on the Moon: The Life and Times of Billie Holiday.* New York: Viking, 1994.

Cobb, James C. *The Most Southern Place on Earth: The Mississippi Delta and the Root of Regional Identity.* New York: Oxford UP, 1992.

Cohen, William. *At Freedom's Edge: Black Mobility and the Southern White Quest for Racial Control, 1861–1915.* Baton Rouge: Louisiana State UP, 1991.

Cole, Susan Letzer. *The Absent One: Mourning Ritual, Tragedy, and the Performance of Ambivalence.* University Park: Pennsylvania State UP, 1991.

"The Cult of Death." *Newsweek* 4 December 1978: 38–81.

Dandridge, Dorothy and Earl Conrad. *Everything and Nothing: The Dorothy Dandridge Tragedy.* New York: Abelard-Schuman, 1970.

Dart, Bob. "Funeral Industry Maintains Air of Dignity in Hard Times." *Atlanta Journal and Constitution* 16 August 1992: R7.

David, Jay and Elaine Crane. *The Black Soldier: From the American Revolution to Vietnam.* New York: William Morrow and Company, 1971.

Davies, Douglas. *Death, Ritual, and Belief: The Rhetoric of Funerary Rites.* London: Cassell, 1997.

Davis, Angela Y. *Blues Legacies and Black Feminism: Gertrude "Ma" Rainey, Bessie Smith, and Billie Holiday.* New York: Pantheon Books, 1998.

"Death Comes to the World's Richest Negro." *Ebony* October 1950: 65–70.

"Death is Big Business." *Ebony* May 1953: 17–31.

Dollimore, Jonathan. *Death, Desire, and Loss in Western Culture.* New York: Routledge, 1998.

Donaldson, Norman and Betty Donaldson. *How Did They Die?* Vol. 1. New York: St. Martin's Press, 1980.

———. *How Did They Die?* Vol. 3. New York: St. Martin's Press, 1994.

D'Orso, Michael. *Like Judgment Day: The Ruin and Redemption of a Town Called Rosewood.* New York: Boulevard Books, 1996.

Drake, St. Clair and Horace R. Cayton. *Black Metropolis: A Study of Negro Life in a Northern City.* 1945. Chicago: University of Chicago Press, 1993.

"Drive-Through Funeral." *Southern Funeral Director* April 1968: 11.

Duberman, Martin. *Paul Robeson: A Biography.* New York: New Press, 1989.

Du Bois, W. E. B. *The Souls of Black Folk.* 1903. New York: Penguin, 1989.

duCille, Ann. "The Shirley Temple of My Familiar." *Transition* 73: 17–37.

Dufty, William. *Lady Sings the Blues: Billie Holiday.* New York: Avon Books, 1976.

Ellison, Ralph. *Invisible Man.* 1952. New York: Vintage, 1982.

Ellsworth, Scott. *Death in a Promised Land: The Tulsa Race Riot of 1921.* Baton Rouge: Louisiana State UP, 1982.

Emecheta, Buchi. *The Joys of Motherhood.* New York: George Braziller, 1979.

Fabre, Genevieve and Robert O'Meally, eds. *History and Memory in African-American Culture.* New York: Oxford UP, 1994.

Fabre, Michel. *The Unfinished Quest.* Urbana: U of Illinois P, 1993.

Fisher, Ian. "On Rap Star's Final Ride, Homage is Marred by a Scuffle." *New York Times* 19 March 1997.

"Forever Stylish, Drug Dealer Flukey Stokes Goes Out with a Bang." *People Weekly* 8 December 1986: 172–73.

Fountain, John and Gary Marx. "Boy's Wake a Lesson for Roseland." *Chicago Tribune* 7 September 1994: 1.

Frazier, E. Franklin. *Black Bourgeoisie*. New York: Simon and Schuster, 1957.

Gaines, Ernest. *A Lesson before Dying*. New York: Knopf, 1993.

George, Lynelle. "City of Specters." *Sex, Death, and God in L.A.* Ed. David Reid. Berkeley: University of California Press, 1994.

Gibbs, Nancy. "Murder in Miniature." *Time* (19 September 1994): 54–59.

Giddings, Paula. *When and Where I Enter: The Impact of Black Women on Race and Sex in America*. New York: William Morrow, 1984.

Golden, Thelma. *The Black Male: Representations of Masculinity in Contemporary American Art*. New York: Whitney Museum of American Art, 1994.

Greenberg, Cheryl. *"Or Does it Explode?" Black Harlem in the Great Depression*. New York: Oxford UP, 1991.

Griggs, Sutton. *The Hindered Hand: Or, The Reign of the Repressionist*. 3rd ed. 1969. New York: AMS Press, 1905.

Habenstein, Robert and William Lamers. *The History of American Funeral Directing*. 3rd ed. 1955. Milwaukee: National Funeral Directors Association, 1995.

———. *Funeral Customs the World Over*. 4th ed. 1960. Milwaukee: National Funeral Directors Association, 1994.

Harlan, Louis R. *Booker T. Washington: The Making of a Black Leader, 1856–1901*. New York: Oxford UP, 1972.

———. *Booker T. Washington: The Wizard of Tuskegee, 1901–1915*. New York: Oxford UP, 1983.

Harris, Middleton. *The Black Book*. New York: Random House, 1974.

Harris, Trudier. *Exorcising Blackness: Historical and Literary Lynching and Burning Rituals*. Bloomington: Indiana UP, 1984.

Harvey, James. "Sirkumstantial Evidence." *Film Commentary* 14.4 (July/August 1978): 55.

Haskins, James and N. R. Mitgang. *Mr. Bojangles: The Biography of Bill Robinson*. New York: William Morrow, 1988.

Hemenway, Robert. *Zora Neale Hurston: A Literary Biography*. Urbana: U of Illinois P, 1977.

Henderson, Angelo. "Black Funeral Homes Fear Gloomy Future as Big Chains Move In." *Wall Street Journal* 18 July 1997: A1.

Hernandez, Efrain. "I've Never Seen Anything Like It: Four Men Arraigned in Melee at Funeral." *Boston Globe* 16 May 1992: A1.

Holland, Sharon Patricia. *Raising the Dead: Readings of Death and (Black) Subjectivity*. Durham, NC: Duke UP, 2000.

Holsey, Albon. "Last Speaking Engagements." *Booker T. Washington's Own Story of His Life and Work*. New York: J. L. Nichols and Company, 1915.

Honan, William. "Wilbert J. Oliver Dies at 89, Fought Funeral Color Line." *New York Times* 23 August 1999.

Horne, Gerald. *The Fire Next Time: The Watts Uprising and the 1960s.* Charlottesville: U of Virginia P, 1995.

Houston, Eric. "When Silence is Deadly." *Emerge* April 1997: 28.

Hubbard, Dolan. *The Sermon and the African American Literary Imagination.* Columbia: U of Missouri P, 1994.

Hughes, Langston and Arna Bontemps. *The Book of Negro Folklore.* New York: Dodd Mead and Company, 1958.

Hurston, Zora Neale. *Dust Tracks on a Road.* 1942. New York: J. B. Lippincott, 1971.

Irish, Donald P. et. al, eds. *Ethnic Variations in Dying, Death, and Grief: Diversity in Universality.* Bristol, PA: Taylor and Francis, 1993.

Iserson, Kenneth. *Death to Dust: What Happens to Dead Bodies?* Tucson: Galen Press, 1994.

Iverem, Esther. "Suicide: The Warning Signs." *Essence* July 1996: 74, 120–122.

Jencks, Richard. "The Press and Jim Jones." *Wall Street Journal* 12 December 1978.

Johnson, Thomas L. and Phillip C. Dunn, eds. *A True Likeness: The Black South of Richard Samuel Roberts, 1920–1936.* Columbia, SC: Bruccoli Clark Layman, 1986.

Jones, Barbara. *Design for Death.* Indianapolis, MO: Bobbs Merrill, 1967.

Jones, James H. *Bad Blood: The Tuskegee Syphilis Experiment.* New York: Free Press, 1981.

Jones, Lealan, Lloyd Newman, and David Isay. *Our America: Life and Death on the South Side of Chicago.* New York: Washington Square Press, 1998.

Jones, Leroi (Amiri Baraka). *Blues People.* New York: William Morrow, 1963.

Kenan, Randall. *A Visitation of Spirits.* New York: Anchor Books, 1987.

Kendall, Peter. "That's a Baby in There." *New York Times* 9 September 1994: A26.

"Kids Killing Kids Rekindles Plea for Action to Stop Black on Black Crime." *Jet* 26 September 1994: 16–18.

Kilduff, Marshall and Ron Javers. *The Suicide Cult: The Inside Story of the Peoples Temple Sect and the Massacre in Guyana.* New York: Bantam Books, 1978.

Klineman, George and Sherman Butler. *The Cult that Died: The Tragedy of Jim Jones and the Peoples Temple.* New York: G. P. Putnam's Sons, 1980.

Krause, Charles A. *Guyana Massacre: The Eyewitness Account.* New York: Berkley Publishing, 1978.

Kruger-Kahoula, Angelika. "On the Wrong Side of the Fence: Racial Segregation in American Cemeteries." *History and Memory in African-American*

Culture. Ed. Genevieve Fabre and Robert O'Meally. New York: Oxford UP, 1994. 130–49.

Kubler-Ross, Elizabeth. *On Death and Dying.* New York: Macmillan Publishing, 1969.

Kunen, James and Greg Walter. "Young Birdie Africa Survives Philly's 'MOVE' Bombing and Is Reborn as Michael Moses Ward." *People Weekly* 2 December 1985: 67–73.

"Last 3 of 'Martinsville 7' Die in Atmosphere of Quiet." *Norfolk Journal and Guide* 10 February 1951: 1.

Leavelle, Charles. "Brick Slayer Is Likened to Jungle Beast." *Chicago Sunday Tribune* 5 June, 1938: 6.

———. "Science Traps Moron in 5 Murders." *Chicago Daily Tribune* 3 June 1938: 1.

Leeming, David. *James Baldwin.* New York: Knopf, 1994.

Lehrer, Jim. "Behind the Numbers." *The NewsHour with Jim Lehrer.* PBS. 6 May 1998. Transcript.

Lemann, Nicholas. *The Promised Land: The Great Migration and How It Changed America.* New York: Vintage Books, 1992.

Lerner, Gerda, ed. *Black Women in White America: A Documentary History.* New York: Vintage Books, 1992.

Lewis, Earl. *In Their Own Interests: Race, Class, and Power in Twentieth-Century Norfolk, Virginia.* Berkeley: U of California P, 1991.

Lincoln, C. Eric. *The Avenue, Clayton City.* New York: William Morrow, 1988.

Locke, Alain. "Enter The New Negro." *Survey Graphic* (March 1925): 631–34.

Love, Spencie. *One Blood: The Death and Resurrection of Charles R. Drew.* Chapel Hill: U of North Carolina P, 1996.

Lovett, Bobby L. *The African-American History of Nashville, Tennessee, 1780–1930: Elites and Dilemmas.* Fayetteville: U of Arkansas P, 1999.

"Macabre Exhibition Canceled on Outburst by Secret Sources." *New York Times* 12 February 1935: 23.

"Man and Monkey Show Disapproved by Clergy." *New York Times* 10 September 1906: 1–2.

Margolick, David. *Strange Fruit: Billie Holiday, Café Society, and an Early Cry for Civil Rights.* Philadelphia: Running Press, 2000.

Marriott, Michele. "Touched by Death: Hip-Hop Turns to Dirges" *New York Times* 10 October 1996.

Mason, Eugene. *Life and Work of Rev. Luke Mason: And a History of the Primitive Baptist Church.* Indianapolis, IN. 1915.

McBride, David. *From TB to AIDS: Epidemics among Urban Blacks since 1900.* Albany: State U of New York P, 1991.

McCray, Carrie Allen. *Freedom's Child: The Life of a Confederate General's Black Daughter*. Chapel Hill, NC; Algonquin Books, 1998.

McElroy, Guy C. *The Black Image in American Art, 1710–1940*. San Francisco: Bedford Arts Publishers, 1990.

McMillen, Neil R. *Dark Journey: Black Mississippians in the Age of Jim Crow*. Urbana: U of Illinois P, 1989.

Metcalf, Peter, and Richard Huntington. *Celebrations of Death: The Anthropology of Mortuary Ritual*. 2nd ed. New York: Cambridge UP, 1991.

Mills, Earl. *Dorothy Dandridge: A Portrait in Black*. Los Angeles: Holloway House, 1970.

Mills, Jeannie. *Six Years with God: Life Inside Reverend Jim Jones's Peoples Temple*. New York: A and W Publishers, 1979.

Mitchell, Broadus. *The Depression Decade from New Era through New Deal, 1929–1941*. Armonk, NY: M. E. Sharpe, 1947.

Mitchell, Henry H. *Black Preaching: The Recovery of a Powerful Art*. Nashville: Abington Press, 1990.

Mitchell, J. Paul. *Race Riots in Black and White*. Englewood Cliffs, NJ: Prentice Hall, 1970.

Mitford, Jessica. "Death, Incorporated." *Vanity Fair* 4.97: 110–31.

Morrison, Toni. *The Bluest Eye*. 1970. New York: Random House, 1993.

———. *Jazz*. New York: Random House, 1987.

———. *Song of Solomon*. New York: Alfred A. Knopf, 1972.

Nalty, Bernard C. *Strength for the Fight: A History of Black Americans in the Military*. New York: Free Press, 1986.

Naylor, Gloria. *Linden Hills*. New York: Ticknor and Fields, 1985.

Nelson, Jill. *Volunteer Slavery: My Authentic Negro Experience*. New York: Penguin, 1993.

Nicholson, Stuart. *Billie Holiday*. London: Indigo, 1995.

"Nightmare in Jonestown." *Time* 4 December 1978: 16–27.

Nuland, Sherwin. *How We Die: Reflections on Life's Final Chapter*. New York: Random House, 1993.

O'Brien, Gail Williams. *The Color of Law: Race, Violence, and Justice in the Post-World War II South*. Chapel Hill: U of North Carolina P, 1999.

Ogletree, Kathryn. "Reflections on the Jonestown Massacre." *Why We Lose: An Anthology for Black People's Cultural Survival*. Ed. Jake P. Beason. WI: Col D'Var Graphics, 1977. 329–32.

O'Meally, Robert. *Lady Day: The Many Faces of Billie Holiday*. New York: Arcade Publishing, 1991.

"One of Doomed 7 Says: 'Meet Me in Heaven. . . .'" *Richmond Afro-American* 10 February 1951: 1.

Osbey, Brenda. "One More Last Chance: Rituals in Jazz Funerals." *Georgia Review* L.1 (spring 1996): 97–107.

"Ota Benga, Pygmy, Tired of America." *New York Times* 16 July 1916: 12.

Ottley, Roi. *Black Odyssey: The Story of the Negro in America.* New York: Charles Scribner's Sons, 1948.

Page, Clarence. *Showing My Color: Impolite Essays on Race and Identity.* New York: Harper Collins, 1996.

Patterson, Orlando. *Rituals of Blood: The Consequences of Slavery in Two American Centuries.* Washington, D.C.: Civitas, 1998.

Patureau, Alan. "Catered Parties Replacing Post-Funeral Potlucks." *Atlanta Journal and Constitution* 20 June 1995: D2.

Polednak, Anthony. *Segregation, Poverty, and Mortality in Urban African Americans.* New York: Oxford UP, 1997.

Powell, Richard J. *Black Art and Culture in the Twentieth Century.* London: Thames and Hudson, 1997.

Powledge, Fred. *Free at Last? The Civil Rights Movement and the People Who Made It.* Boston: Little, Brown, 1991.

Reid, David, ed. *Sex, Death, and God in L.A.* Berkeley: U of California P, 1994.

Roach, Joseph. *Cities of the Dead: Circum-Atlantic Performance.* New York: Columbia UP, 1996.

———. "Culture and Performance in the Circum-Atlantic World." *Performativity and Performance.* Ed. Eve Kosofsky Sedgwick. New York: Routledge, 1995. 45–63.

Roberts, Dorothy. *Killing the Black Body: Race, Reproduction, and the Meaning of Liberty.* New York: Vintage, 1997.

Roberts, Elizabeth. *Drums and Shadows: Survival Studies among the Georgia Coastal Negroes.* Athens, GA: Works Projects Administration, 1940.

Robertson, Gary. "'Martinsville 7' Pain Remains." *Richmond (Virginia) Times-Dispatch* 20 June 1993: D5–7.

Rothenberg, Paula S., ed. *Race, Class, and Gender in the United States: An Integrated Study.* New York: St. Martin's Press, 1998.

Rozsa, Lori. "Massacre in a Small Town." *Atlanta Journal and Constitution* 17 January 1993: M1–4.

Ruby, Jay. *Secure the Shadow: Death and Photography in America.* Cambridge, MA: MIT Press, 1995.

Rudwick, Elliott M. *Race Riot at East St. Louis, July 2, 1917.* Carbondale: Southern Illinois UP, 1964.

Salaam, Yusef. "White Funeral Factories Fight Blacks over Bodies and Burials." *New York Amsterdam News* 27 April 1996: 1.

Sanchez, Rene. "Black Teen Suicide Rate Increases Dramatically." *Washington Post* 20 March 1998.

Sanders, Charles L. "Requiem for Queen Dinah." *Ebony* (February 1964): 146–54.

Schoener, Allon, ed. *Harlem on My Mind: Cultural Capital of Black America 1900–1968*. New York: Random House, 1968.

Shneidman, Edwin. *Voices of Death*. New York: Kodansha, 1995.

Simone, Nina. *I Put a Spell on You*. New York: Da Capo Press, 1992.

SoRelle, James M. *The Darker Side of "Heaven": The Black Community in Houston, Texas, 1917–1945*. Diss. UMI, 1985.

Stolberg, Sheryl Gay. "Experts Question Racial Disparity: Why Black Women More Likely to Die in Childbirth." *Raleigh News and Observer* 8 August 1999: 3A.

Sugrue, Thomas. *The Origins of the Urban Crisis: Race and Inequality in Postwar Detroit*. Princeton, NJ: Princeton University Press, 1996.

Sullivan, Christopher. "Juvenile Suicides Based on Apathy, Impulse, Gaps in Care." *Los Angeles Times* 12 March 1995: A1.

Sullivan, George. *Black Artists in Photography, 1840–1940*. New York: Cobblehill Books, Dutton, 1994.

Taulbert, Clifton. *When We Were Colored*. New York: Penguin Books, 1989.

Terry, Don. "In an 11-Year Old's Funeral, a Grim Lesson." *New York Times* 8 September 1994: A1.

"There's No Justice Here." *Richmond Afro-American* 10 February 1951: 1.

Thielmann, Bonnie. *The Broken God*. Elgin, IL: David C. Cook Publishing, 1979.

Thomas, Jerry. "Emmett's Legacy." *Chicago Tribune* 5 September 1995: 5.

Tilove, Jonathan. "Black Funeral Home Owners Fear for Their Business." *Raleigh News and Observer* 8 March 1997: 3E.

Tolnay, Stewart and E. M. Beck. *A Festival of Violence: An Analysis of Southern Lynchings, 1882–1930*. Urbana: U of Illinois P, 1995.

Touchet, Leo. *Rejoice When You Die: The New Orleans Jazz Funerals*. Baton Rouge: Louisiana State UP, 1998.

Treaster, Joseph B. "Rubble of Commune Yields a Tape of Cultists Dying." *New York Times* 8 December 1978: A1.

Trotter, Joe William. *Black Milwaukee: The Making of an Industrial Proletariat, 1915–45*. Urbana: U of Illinois P, 1985.

Van Der Zee, James, et al. *The Harlem Book of the Dead*. Dobbs Ferry, NY: Morgan and Morgan, 1978.

Waldron, Clarence and Trudy Moore. "Fans and Friends Mourn Tragic Death of Singer Phyllis Hyman." *Jet* 24 July 1995: 53–61.

Walker, Margaret A. *Richard Wright, Daemonic Genius: A Portrait of the Man, A Critical Look at His Work*. New York: Warner Books, 1988.

Walls, Dwayne E. *The Chickenbone Special*. New York: Harcourt Brace Jovanovich, 1971.

Waskow, Arthur. *From Race Riot to Sit-In, 1919 and the 1960s: A Study in the Connections between Conflict and Violence*. New York: Doubleday and Company, 1966.

Webb, Constance. *Richard Wright: A Biography*. New York: Putnam, 1968.

Wedle, Karen and Patrick Mckenry. "Self Destructive Behaviors Among Black Youth: Suicide and Homicide." *African American Youth: Their Social and Economic Status in the United States*. Ed. Ronald Taylor. Westport, CT: Praeger, 1995. 206–219.

Wesley, John Milton. "The Final Days of Emmett Till." *The Washington Post* 27 August 1995: C1.

Whitfield, Stephen J. *A Death in the Delta: The Story of Emmett Till*. Baltimore: Johns Hopkins UP, 1988.

Wideman, John Edgar. "The Killing of Black Boys." *Essence* (November 1997): 123–26.

Wilkinson, Tracy and Stephanie Chavez. "Elaborate Death Rites of Gangs." *Los Angeles Times* 2 March 1992: A15.

Williams, John A. *The Man Who Cried I Am*. Boston: Little, Brown, and Company, 1967.

Wilson, Charles. "The Southern Funeral Director: Managing Death in the New South." *Georgia Historical Quarterly* 67.1 (1983): 24–31.

Winn, Billy. "Under Penalty of Death." *Columbus, Georgia, Ledger Enquirer* 26 May 1991.

Wright, Richard. *Black Boy*. New York: Harper and Brothers Publishers, 1937.

———. *Eight Men*. 1991. New York: Harper Collins, 1996.

———. *The Long Dream*. 1958. New York: Harper and Row, 1987.

———. *Native Son*. 1940. New York: Vintage Library, 1994.

Wright, Roberta and Wilbur Hughes. *Lay Down Body: Living History in African American Cemeteries*. Detroit: Visible Ink Press, 1996.

Zinsser, William. "Time Saver for Busy Mourners." *Life* (10 May 1968): 22.

Index

Karla FC Holloway is

the William R. Kenan Jr. Professor

of English and African American Literature

and Dean of the Humanities and Social

Sciences at Duke University.

*Library of Congress
Cataloging-in-Publication Data*

Holloway, Karla FC
Passed on : African American mourning stories :
a memorial / Karla FC Holloway.
p. cm.
Includes bibliographical references and index.
ISBN 0–8223–2860–7 (alk. paper)
1. African Americans—Funeral customs and rites.
2. African Americans—Death.   I. Title.
GT3203 .H65   2002
393'.089'96073—dc21   2001040717